STUCK HERE

AFRICAN IMMIGRANTS
TELL THEIR STORIES

STUCK HERE

AFRICAN IMMIGRANTS
TELL THEIR STORIES

By

Marvin Opiyo

www.bookstandpublishing.com

Published by
Bookstand Publishing
Morgan Hill, CA 95037
4613_8

Cover Design by Marvin Opiyo

ISBN 978-1-63498-668-7

Library of Congress Control Number: 2018941119

DEDICATION

To my beloved sister, Jennifer, who could not attend school due to paralysis by childhood polio, yet was brilliant enough to educate herself from her chair at home, and teach me and many others how to read.

AUTHOR'S NOTE

C olonial-era, and prolific British novelist George Orwell said that writing was so taxing that one must have "an irresistible demon" inside that compels one to write. For me, that irresistible demon was the fascinating stories of my fellow Africans in America, stories which I have shared herein. I hope that the reader will equally find these stories both informative and intriguing.

I approached the subjects and interviewed them face to face while recording the interviews with their consent. Significant portions of their stories appear herein verbatim. Tito's interview was innovatively conducted by text messaging.

"---many shall run to and fro, and knowledge shall increase."

FOREWORD

By Ngũgĩ wa Thiong'o

The gory and the glory of the experience of African immigrants into the West hide the biggest irony: Western corporations, in colonial and now post-colonial times, control the resources of the richest continent in the world. In cozy alliance with corrupt regimes, they create the hell that makes some citizens seek refuge in the heaven created by the resources stolen from their continent.

They flee the continent, thinking of America, and the West, as their heaven from the hell, real and imagined, of their social conditions. Some find their haven, a good job and a house in the Suburbia, and are able to send remittances back home; others sink into the hell of prostitution, prison, drug use, and homelessness. But all face the racism that is the fate of black people in the Western world.

Stuck Here, is a collection of narratives of grief and relief, tears and laughter, hope and despair, tragedy and triumph, which attend the lives of immigrants from Africa to America.

Ngũgĩ wa Thiongô

Author of *Wizard of the Crow*, and many other acclaimed novels[1]

---

[1] Ngũgĩ wa Thiongô is a prolific novelist and 2010 Nobel Literature Nominee and Finalist. He is a Distinguished Professor of Comparative Literature at UC Irvine.

TABLE OF CONTENTS

x

INTRODUCTION

Our good friend, Sharon, tells the story of her friend who obtained an F-2 visa to join her husband who was then an international student in the United States. She was quite excited as she prepared to leave Malawi and set off for the land of plenty, which some considered to be a mini heaven on earth. She gave away almost all of her personal belongings, including some of her best clothes, to admiring family and friends in anticipation of acquiring better ones when she arrived in the US. Then she rented out their elegant family home in an upscale neighborhood of the capital, Blantyre and left Malawi to go join her husband in the United States.

After the long and tiring journey, she finally landed at the airport in Chicago, where her husband was waiting. The young couple joyfully hugged and kissed as they were finally reunited after nearly two years of separation. When the husband led her to a boneshaker as their transport home, the young lady assumed it was a borrowed car; his real car must have been left at a mechanic's shop for maintenance. This boneshaker was not nearly comparable to the posh car they had been driving in Malawi, which they had sold as they prepared to leave for the Promised Land. So, she did not ask any questions as she continued to bask in the joy of being together after such a long while. Finally, they arrived "home"—a one-bedroom apartment in a run-down neighborhood. The young woman again assumed they had just stopped by a friend's place on their way from the airport. She told her bewildered husband that she was tired after the long flights and now they should go home.

"This is home," responded her husband nervously. The woman broke down in loud ululations, lamenting and wailing that she had donated countless beautiful items in expectation of a new life in America with better everything, only to find that reality and expectation were poles apart.

This young woman's predicament has been the tortured experience of many a young African woman who has come to the United States with high expectations to marry up, get higher education, or generally move up the social and economic ladder, only to be disillusioned.

Similarly, Fred came from an affluent family in Kenya to study in the United States. He found that coming from a rich family in Kenya to being a student in America was like dropping from heaven to earth. Fred complained about the people with whom he lived until they kicked him out of the house. His church pastor helped find him an apartment, but he complained again and two days later moved out. We then helped him find fellow African students who lived close to college to share a room with, but the next night he claimed that they wanted to kill him. Friends offered him temporary accommodation; but at 4:00 AM the following morning, one of them called me in a state of extreme agitation: *"Jamaa ametuitia polisi bwana! Ati tuna taka kumrape!"* ("The fellow has called the police on us, sir! He claims that we want to rape him!")

It was then it occurred to us that Fred, like some before him, was experiencing a nervous breakdown due to stresses associated with his moving to America. While this may not necessarily be the experience of everyone, it is the experience of numerous Africans who came to study in the US but never completed their studies due to the complexities that abound. It was too difficult to complete studies, or they ran out of money or both.

Indeed, as a graduate student in California, I often found myself wondering, "What am I doing here?" Many, like Grandma Wilson[2], would sympathize with "the baby growing up thousands of miles from his grandma."

---

[2] Mother of the late Professor of Chemistry, Lee Wilson.

In 2003, I became the founding chairman of an association we created to help secure the welfare of Kenyan immigrants and students in the region. During a committee meeting, a friend presented to the members "an embarrassing and confidential" request: "I have just discovered that there is a Kenyan who is homeless very nearby here!" We found out that the man had come to the US as a professional athlete—a soccer player. After sustaining an injury and allegedly being abandoned by his sponsors, his life went downhill. He was currently living under a bridge where he reportedly had been beaten and robbed by other homeless individuals who were competing for strategic locations and shelter. My friend wanted us to raise funds to cover the cost of a motel room for the man while we also looked for work prospects he could pursue. We were able to meet these needs and thereby get him off the streets.

Some Africans in America are thriving, albeit certainly not without their own initial challenges and eccentric experiences. Dr. Omobokun, who is from Nigeria, is one such example. With great sense of humor, he tells of his early days in the United States, especially during one summer school break when he "wanted to eat African food." So, he went to a nearby farm auction, bought a goat, and brought it to the animal slaughterhouse but found it closed for the weekend. He therefore took the goat to his apartment. Using a kitchen knife, he slaughtered the goat in his parking lot space at the apartment. But in the process, the goat made a noise that startled Joshua's neighbors. Police officers came shortly, flashing their blue and red lights. "What's going on?" demanded the officers. "Are you making animal sacrifices?"

"No, sir!" he responded calmly, trying to hide his shock and anxiety. "I'm just preparing dinner for my family." The officers left reluctantly after a little more questioning and a stern warning, "Don't kill any more goats here! You're not permitted to slaughter any animals here!"

Now Dr. Omobokun is quite a successful man with a doctorate degree in Administration. We fondly call him "The Mayor of

Riverside" because of his spectacular hilltop home in the best neighborhood in town. Likewise, Sharon adds that her friend completed a master's degree in Public Health, "and now makes good money." Her husband completed a PhD and is a university professor of Mathematics at a State University. "It was worth the sacrifices they made," she concludes.

Dr. Omobokun's House: Remarkable upward mobility, compared to his goat-slaughtering days in an apartment.

Other individuals from Africa come to the US under incredibly dramatic circumstances. One Saturday afternoon we were scheduled to have lunch with my friend Martin and his family, as we often did. Martin called and said they'd be coming with four additional guests—some young ladies. He had helped "rescue them from the airport," but the story was long, and he would tell me more when they arrived. "Rescue them" from whom/what?! I wondered. After church, Martin indeed came with his family and their four guests. The young ladies told us the story of their incredible harrowing experiences.

They had been persuaded by someone in Kenya that they could earn much higher wages by going to work in a kingdom in the Middle East (name of kingdom withheld). They naively obtained passports and left reasonable secretarial jobs in Nairobi to go to the Middle East in quest of better paying ones. According to the young women, once they got to the airport in the kingdom, their eventual employers met them and immediately confiscated their passports. They were then assigned work as nannies in the royal family. From then on, they were the first to wake up before 5:00 a.m., and the last to go to bed after midnight almost daily, cooking, cleaning, and doing all sorts of chores in the palace. It was backbreaking work with no breaks, and they endured significant verbal abuse daily. The young women had no way of reaching anyone for help or escaping the virtual slavery without passports. The only time they left the palace was when the royal family was going to the United States on shopping sprees and brought the ladies along.

On one such trip one of the young women made a desperate effort to possibly get help. She screamed at the top of her voice at a mall in Los Angeles, asking for help — which inevitably caught people's attention. Fortunately for them, one of the people who paid attention was an attorney, and he promptly pursued the matter. The royal family was resisting his demands to free the young women, but the attorney persisted, following them to the Airport. Threatened with exposure of their practices to the press and the international community, the royal family was compelled to release the ladies. As the attorney was searching for a Kenyan family to help, my friend Martin's name was mentioned, and someone called him. He then went and picked up the young women from the airport.

"I'll work and save some money while I'm here," said Njeri (not her real name), the oldest among the four. "And when I go back to Kenya, I will find that man who tricked us into slavery. And what I will do to him, has never been done before," she stated with dreadful determination.

These and other experiences prompted me to research the lives and experiences of Africans in America, many of whom seem to be doing quite well in their various professions—successful doctors, accountants, dentists, and engineers among others whose stories are told herein. Others have not quite made it. These are but a sample of the lives of a much larger African population in the United States. Those who are still on the African continent and are contemplating moving to the US may find this reading not only interesting but informative of the reality that living in the US, as in other places, comes at a cost. The decision to go, or not to go, can then be based on one's readiness and ability to pay the price, which is often exorbitant.

1

IN QUEST FOR THE GOLDEN FLEECE

DR. UCHE

Uche is a Nigerian doctor specializing in pathology. He lives in an elegant house in a quiet suburban Texas neighborhood with his wife, daughter, and two sons. He just turned 70 but looks 50 and daily drives 70 miles one-way to work. He says he first came to the United States in 1958 from Nigeria "in quest for what we then called 'the golden fleece,' that is, education." Education was referred to as *the golden fleece* since it was considered the key to success and better life for young people in the mushrooming independent African states.

Initially, his plans were to pursue a Ph.D. degree in pharmacy. But after obtaining his first degree in pharmacy, Uche switched to medicine "just to show them that it could be done." He states that there were young American doctors who were showing off, and their bragging motivated him to pursue medicine to prove to them that anyone could.

"Did you have any sponsors, the church or the government?"

"I was self-sponsored."

"So, you had some family funds, savings?"

"I was self-sponsored, *self*, not government, not anything. Self!"

Like Waribah whom we will meet later, Dr. Uche's emphasis is on self-sponsorship. Both feel that since they sponsored themselves, they do not owe anyone anything and are therefore under no obligation to return to their home countries to serve in the government or the church institutions.

Uche had earned a certificate in pharmacy in Nigeria and worked as a lab assistant for about a year, then went to neighboring Ghana and worked for two years as a pharmacist assistant while saving money for transport to the United States. After finishing medical school in the United States, Dr. Uche completed a one-year residency in British Guyana, South America. Upon his return to the United States, he completed an additional one-year residency in pathology and then began practicing it, working for a private organization for eight years.

Dr. Uche then "felt a longing to go back to serve my country, and to return to my people. So, we returned in 1982. I was immediately hired as head of the Department of Pathology, Port City Teaching Hospital. Port City is an important state capital city in oil rich southeastern Nigeria. I served in this capacity for nearly seven years. After years of service as head of pathology I left and went to Saudi Arabia, where I worked for nearly two years and raised enough money to transport my family back to the United States."

"You had an important position in a relatively prestigious hospital! What made you leave for Saudi Arabia?"

Suddenly his hitherto calm, dignified face turns tense and angry, showing signs of deep frustration as he searches for the word "frustration." The expression on Dr. Uche's face alone suggests that whatever experiences drove him away from Nigeria to Saudi Arabia then back to the United States in what is now commonly known among his friends as his "second missionary journey" must have been deeply disturbing experiences.

"The system was deteriorating and eventually collapsed."

"How did it collapse? Could you give specific examples?"

"Facilities and equipment were breaking down. There was a breakdown in all the services. *All* the services! It got to a point where I could not provide the service that I was capable of providing."

"Could you give some specific examples?"

"For example, I am a pathologist; I deal with dead bodies. There was no more running water to use during autopsy. Freezing cubicles meant to contain two bodies were stacked with six bodies, which would then be decomposing before I could work on them. There was serious shortage of equipment, such as gloves, to the extent that I had to boil the supposedly disposable gloves to be reused. My assistants had to use their bare hands, a very dangerous and hazardous practice! Combined with the bad odor from decomposing bodies, the system presented a very unhealthy work environment. The conditions were totally unbearable!"

When asked what contributed to or led to the deterioration and collapse of the system, Dr. Uche responds that it was "the mismanagement and embezzlement of funds by government officials who were charged with funding public projects and services."

When he complained to his superiors about the water shortage and the effect it had on his work, Dr. Uche was told, "You are lucky you have a bucket of water; other people do not have any water!" He was told to go ask the Ministry of Water for help.

"So, it was the frustration with such a corrupt system that led you to Saudi Arabia and back to the United States?"

"I had to get my family away and get a break from the impossible situation. I did what was in the best interest of the family. I could survive over there but could not subject my family to all this. The education system was deteriorating, too, and my children were approaching college age."

"So, you went to Saudi Arabia to...?"

"To raise money to bring my family here. All my money was finished. I had savings when I was leaving here, but I kept spending it till it was finished. I had to resort to my savings, and the salary there was not sufficient to transport us to this place. You could be earning good money—US$400 was enough to live like a king. But given the conversion rates, it was not enough for airfare."

"So, you went to Saudi Arabia basically to get airfare to come to the US?"

3

"I went down there not necessarily to get airfare to come here; I went there to get a breather from Nigeria, to get a break from the impossible situation. And going from Nigeria to Saudi Arabia is like from darkness to daylight! But the children could not function there as they were at an age where they form relationships, and that would have been impossible over there."

Dr. Uche says, "In fact, that was *the* key; each time children was the main issue. When we returned to Nigeria, it was mainly because the children were growing; and we figured out if we did not take them home, they would never be able to learn the culture. It was a very important factor. When we returned to the US, it was also mainly because the children were nearing college age. There was no justification at all to let the children stay in a system that had collapsed. It would have been a real disservice to abandon them by leaving them in a system in which *all* aspects of life had broken down."

Surprisingly the subjects so far find it difficult to pinpoint the one most significant reason they are "stuck here." Dr. Uche started out with a clear identification of the "impossible situation"—the corruption and the resulting deterioration and collapse of the system, which made him so frustrated that he had to leave to go get "a breath of fresh air" in Saudi Arabia. But he also clearly admits that children's education was the main issue. At first, children made him return home so they could learn the culture and fit in. Children also caused them to leave a second time to seek better educational opportunities, in an environment with possibilities to form relationships.

It can be argued that the mismanagement of resources and bribery led to the collapse of everything, including educational services, resulting in Dr. Uche removing his children from the mess. He felt that it was his moral obligation to provide his children with the best educational opportunities; staying in Nigeria would not avail such prospects. Had the system not failed, educational services would have been adequate for his children and indeed for other children.

"What would you say is the most important factor influencing your stay?"

"I don't know how to put it, but the whole thing is compounded. Only saving grace would have made it possible to stay. In spite of all this, home is still home, the social, the connection; you can breathe with your own people and have the close ties. I do miss the close family and social ties, but I had to take care of my own family. It is to the best interest of the whole family, not just my interest."

"How does life in Nigeria compare with life in the United States?"

"The difference between Nigeria and here is that while everything works here, virtually nothing works there." Dr. Uche makes this declaration with a tone of profound resignation.

He states that he is currently deputy medical officer for the Office of the County Coroner in one of the major cities of Texas, but he is planning to retire and go back to Nigeria. "My family and friends think it is an unrealistic thing to do, but I'll do it as I'll be of more service there."

"How do you intend to be of service?"

"I can still be an example of honest living to the people. Also, while life in the US has been more predictable in terms of what to expect at work and provision of services and public utilities, there is lack of close family ties, which exists back home."

"Why do your friends and family think it is unrealistic for you to retire at home?"

Dr. Uche looks down the street through the window of the living room of his magnificent home in a very quiet neighborhood of a Texan suburb, laughing. "See this road out here?" he signals with his hand, laughing mockingly. "In Nigeria, there would be a sea of people flocking the road! The traffic condition is impossible," he continues as he paints the picture of a ridiculously hopeless situation.

"Going down the street to buy stamps used to take 15 minutes but now takes two hours. You see, Port City is significant as the capital of oil country. People, therefore, have moved in from all over. Traffic jam is unbelievable. You see," he chuckles as he demonstrates driving, "you're sitting there; the driver is taking you to buy stamps, and it takes two hours!"

"You had a driver at home?"

"This is part of the foolishness we inherited from the British," Dr. Uche replies, his face and tone full of amusement. "Some English guy came to my office, just a very junior agriculture person. But there he was with a driver! Every government person had a driver. You didn't have a driver in your country? Port City is full of people and traffic. But the people seem to go about their business as usual, not minding the heat and the congestion. You know, once you stay there for a while, it just looks normal."

Even though the government system malfunction has caused "everything to collapse," family ties and roots are still strong enough to pull Dr. Uche back to his home country. He can find a rationale for his planned return after retirement although family and friends consider his choice "ridiculous." Life in Nigeria is very frustrating but may look "just normal" if one stays and gets accustomed to it. This confirms that the decision to return to the United States was genuinely for the welfare of the family in the form of providing educational opportunities for his children. Now that this goal has been achieved, Dr. Uche can retire there and endure the inconveniences while being of some service to the community he adores.

"What is your vision for your country?" I ask Dr. Uche, and suddenly, the calm face shows signs of stress again, betraying his remarkably belying youthful appearance.

"I do not want to say that I am a pessimist, but I am not as optimistic as some other people are. I see the situation in Nigeria as a part of what's happening in the world. There are many forces that are working that are beyond the control of the country in and of itself. I do not foresee Nigeria making the progress that it is capable of making, due to many, many factors."

"What are the many factors and forces?"

"Number one is human greed and corruption; and the external forces, driven by greed, capitalizing on the greed of Nigerians. Nigeria has no reason whatsoever to be in the dire condition it is in. Nigeria is endowed with many, many resources—human and material; yet Nigeria has nothing to show for all these resources. You know, that is sad, that is sad. The external forces in collaboration with a few greedy Nigerians in power have virtually raped the country."

"They have raped the country!"

"Yes, for example, Nigeria is quite rich in mineral oil; foreign companies and governments export millions of barrels of oil daily. Yet the devastation they have caused to the environment is immeasurable. There are no more fish in the great ponds, no cassava growing, no crops; and the people can no longer collect rainwater from the roof to drink as before. Oil is a curse! You're lucky you do not have oil in your country. The oil companies have signed contracts with the corrupt Nigerian officials—contracts whose terms are quite unfavorable to the country; yet they are bound by the terms of these unfair contracts."

"What other forces make it hard for Nigeria to develop?"

"Tribalism is another force behind Nigeria's woes. The country is ruled by the majority from the north and west, while the wealth is produced in the south and southeast, whose people have no say in decision making—thus the unfavorable contracts. Now they have decided to give the villagers US$2,000 daily from oil sales. Two thousand dollars is what they make in 0.5 of a second! The few northerners and the foreign oil companies have made themselves billionaires from oil wealth at the expense of the rest of the country. Oil is a curse!"

Dr. Uche asserts that the minority groups that live in the oil rich Niger Delta are not represented in the government where decisions are made. Thus, the decision makers are not affected by the environmental and ecological destruction that plagues the minority groups of the south, whose livelihoods have been devastated by oil mining.

He sketches a map of Nigeria and shows me where he comes from in relation to the oil fields. "This is where oil is produced. This is where I come from. We are sitting on an ocean of oil, but our people are totally impoverished!" he laments, voice choking with rage.

He also points at the northerners' region on his makeshift map. "This is where the rulers come from; this area is dry like a desert but is well-developed, like Saudi Arabia! These people are crazy; they decided to put an oil refinery up here; they decided to pump oil up there so they can have it... you know, in case something happens." He means in case there is a rebellion by the southerners or in case there is a civil war again, like that of the 1960s, which threatened to divide Nigeria into two countries when the southeasterners rebelled and wanted their own country called "Biafra." The deep divide and resentment that caused the Biafra War can still be seen and heard in the faces and voices of Nigerians, especially from the east and south. This tribal conflict is more evidence of problems associated with, if not resulting from, arbitrary colonial boundaries.

"You had said you did not want to be pessimistic, but the picture (of Nigeria) you have painted so far is quite gloomy!"

"I am just being realistic. There are some Nigerians who say that it took this country (the US) more than two hundred years to get where it is; and so, we will make it, too. But I do not see that happening in Nigeria, especially when we have people with Ph.Ds. collaborating with those who are raping the country. Nigeria's case is, therefore, different from that of this country."

CITIZEN WITHOUT A COUNTRY: KEN

Ken lives on the better side of the railroad of his community with his wife and three children. He was 'a primary school teacher' in Uganda before moving to Canada and then to the United Sates. Teachers back in his country of origin are paid according to the level at which they teach. Primary school teachers are paid the least, which is unfortunately usually a manifestation of how high they went in the notorious "education pyramid."

Ken perceives himself as a victim of this unfair system and has been determined to prove that he can exceed the ranks of *primary school teacher*. He has, and quite remarkably so. He states that he earned a doctoral degree in psychotherapy.

Ken moved to Canada in the 1980s, then to the United Sates in the 1990s. "My intentions were to go back home immediately after studies, but now I am a psychotherapist dealing with individuals who are incarcerated for criminal behavior. I do diagnosis, treatment, and referral, medical referrals. I also do crisis intervention."

Asked if he planned to do this kind of work when he first came to North America, Ken answers with an emphatic "no, of course not! Like everyone else who comes here, I came with the idea that I am going to school, and I'm going home immediately when done with school."

"Then, what happened?"

"I didn't go," he states resignedly, feigning a pouting child, and then chuckles. On a more serious note he adds, "Well, I don't know! I didn't go for a few reasons. First, political instability in Africa, you know; I was a 3rd-generation refugee, if I could label myself as refugee; we never went to a refugee camp. When we were in Uganda, we went straight to places where we could find and raise cows in the jungles of Uganda, and, uh—."

Ken laments the problems caused by what he terms "the carving of Africa" by colonial governments. Anyone who arrived in a country after this carving was labeled a refugee. Ken's ancestors were such victims of this practice since they arrived in Uganda after partitioning of Africa into countries.

"I don't want to disclose this, but I attempted to, ah, to apply for a Ugandan passport; but the Ugandan government told me that I was a Rwandan, and Rwanda did not recognize us as Rwandans. So," he adds with bitterness in his tone, "I never held an African passport, unfortunately."

This is another victim of the meaninglessness of colonial boundaries that cut through communities and separated families, making them citizens of different countries. Even though Ken planned to go back to his country, he really does not legally have a country to go back to. Thus, the uneasiness in recounting his futile attempts to obtain a Ugandan passport. The one country in which he was born and raised, Uganda, considers him a refugee; the other country where his family came from, Rwanda, does not consider him a citizen. As a result, he belongs to the United Nations and might as well live in the United States or Canada, which have welcomed him. Ken was able to travel to Canada only because of a United Nations 'refugee' passport.

"You said you did not return home due to political instability. How did this instability affect you personally?"

"I'm referring generally to the political instability of African countries. But when I left Uganda, there was war—a war started in 1981 and continued till 1987. I finished my school in 1990, and of course there was war then in Rwanda. And even today, you cannot say that there is stability in Africa. Maybe war will break out today, maybe Rwanda, maybe somewhere else. Today one community is ruling and tomorrow another community may rule."

"You mean the ethnic communities?"

"Yes, for example now we have people from the west ruling, and they are related to the Tutsi for sure. The Tutsi have enjoyed protection from Museveni's government. But tomorrow another leader may come in who will order all Tutsis in Uganda to go back to Rwanda."

10

In the 1970s, Uganda was ravaged by the brutal rule of Idi Amin, a dictator who grabbed power after overthrowing the government of then-president Milton Obote. Amin's regime targeted educated and businesspeople, such as rich Indians. The educated were eliminated, often by assassination or imprisonment, and tortured since they were considered a threat to his power. Asian merchants were expelled from Uganda with only a 24-hour notice to pack up and leave. Tens of thousands lost their lives under Idi Amin's rule. He was later overthrown in a furious war with neighboring Tanzanian forces. Amin's ouster was followed by a grueling civil war in the 1980s that displaced hundreds of thousands of people, further depleting the already battered Ugandan economy. In the 1990s, a civil war raged in neighboring Rwanda, culminating in the infamous genocide.

Ken estimates that more than 200,000 people of Rwandan Tutsi origins live in Uganda. He fears that if a pro Hutu government took power in Uganda, these people might be expelled from Uganda, triggering a humanitarian crisis "because of all that enmity that has been going on between the groups."

"What would you say is the cause of this enmity?"

"There are several reasons that one can give, but I prefer to refer to the humanistic theories of people like William Glaser and Abraham Maslow that once human needs are not met, there will always be a crisis."

"What are the needs that are not being met?"

"One of the needs that William Glaser mentions is the need for security. And of course, there are other needs, like for love and belonging; Maslow mentions need for food. Once these needs are threatened, people, coming back to our theme, people always run out of their own countries to seek refuge in other countries."

"Are you saying that the existence of one group threatens the satisfaction of these needs in another?"

"Exactly! And this other group also is trying to meet its own needs, but in the process the other group feels threatened."

"How long has this enmity gone on between the Tutsi and the Hutu?"

"It has been there since before the genocide. I would say it started in the 1950s when the Hutu were inspired by the colonial masters, 'Hey you are the majority, and you need to rule!' And so, they have continued to rule; but they don't know that in ruling, they secure more of their needs versus the other group that is left out."

Again, a striking similarity appears between Ken's and Joy's views on causes of strife in Rwanda in particular, and Africa in general: one group satisfying its needs at the expense of other groups. This theme is articulated as well by subjects from Nigeria: Dr. Uche and George, who insist that the northern majority tribes are exploiting the southern minority tribes that are rich in oil but do not benefit from its mining, making them see oil as "a curse."

Ken asserts that they, Tutsis, "had an organized kingdom, an organized parliament, and of course a king. We had organized rulers, called the *Batware*, who were like the chiefs in various parts of the country. That was also the case in Burundi when it was a kingdom, and Ankole also in Uganda." He is indirectly making the case that they were better placed to be the rulers of the two tiny central African countries. Some light is thus shed on the background of the hostilities between the ethnic groups there; one sees itself as the elite and qualified rulers, while the other sees itself as the majority with the right to democratic rule.

"What is your position on going home now?"

"Oh, I want to go home badly; my body is here, but my heart and mind are at home."

"What do you miss the most, making your heart and mind *be* at home?"

"I miss the opportunity to be with the people and see them as they age and die."

Ken would love to go home, for his mind and heart are there. However, the "political instability" he cites makes him reluctant to pack up and leave. He misses the social connections back home but

12

does not want to risk taking his children to an uncertain future. He would also like to be with family and serve his people, but he also sees the opportunities available to his children in the United States. In addition, the countries he considers home would never recognize him and his children as citizens anyway.

"But there are better opportunities here: the opportunity to be what you want to be and take any political position without fear of being targeted."

"What can be done to solve the problems at home so you can go home freely?"

Ken responds that the government must reward professionals adequately, invest in them, and stop threatening successful people. He observes that African leaders have always been afraid of educated and/or successful people. His grandfather, for example, "was killed in Rwanda because he was very successful." He adds that the government needs to strive to promote democracy for this to happen. Besides, rich people and government officials need to invest their money at home to circulate within their economies, not in foreign banks in Geneva.

"I do not blame anyone. I would not blame the colonial governments for the existing problems. We as Africans can learn a lot from Americans, who were also colonized. If they had decided to sit down and criticize their colonial masters, they would still be in the ghettoes. We should follow the examples of others, like the Japanese who take American cars, copy them with some modifications, and call them Japanese. We should follow what Americans themselves did and are still doing—inviting people from all over the world with skills to help them meet their development needs. At least if you cannot do something, you copy from a friend. If we could learn from the Canadians and from the Americans what they did to overcome colonialism and its aftermath, we would realize that the number one objective is to create opportunities for people, you know, opportunities to meet their needs as I was telling you, including the aesthetic needs. But the problem is that we're not willing to learn!"

"If African professionals abroad returned home, would it help our countries?"

"Oh, Africa would probably turn into one of the paradises! However, people cannot return on empty stomachs. People will always say, 'I'm going, I'm going, I'm going,' even me here. There're times actually when I get moved and I just feel I want to go tomorrow! But I would not want to go look for a job. I would like to go and help create jobs. And I get very discouraged every time I see people go, and then they come back."

"What makes them return?"

"Each of the returnees who eventually come back has his own story, but the bottom-line is that remuneration is poor and not commensurate with training and experience. The most you'll get paid is US$500 a month. What can that do for you and your family?"

Ken decries the rampant economic hardship in much of Africa, including the high rate of inflation "that will wipe out whatever saving you may have taken from here." He laments that "African governments do not realize that educated people are a resource, that rich people are a resource and should be treated as such. Instead they are targeted and treated as a threat."

In Ken's view, lack of democracy is another obstacle to African professionals trying to return home. He does not envision an immediate end to the vicious cycle of poverty and dictatorship in Africa. Like George, he believes it will take some revolution from within the continent to bring about change for the better. This may take place but "not in our generation." Ken goes on to recommend the following as needed change:

- Leaders will accept defeat when voted out of office or when two terms expire.

- Governments will adequately reward professionals who return from further studies abroad, following in the American example. He states that America rewarded students who were returning from England; England "was their America" then.

- Governments will entice human resources from anywhere in the world.

- African leaders will stop stashing cash in foreign accounts, like the late Mobutu Sese Seko of Zaire, now Democratic Republic of Congo, who had billions in foreign accounts while his country's economy was ravaged.

"If leaders like Mobutu had their money at home, they would have felt the urge to work hard to keep the economy viable," he concludes.

2

STUCK HERE

TITO AND HIS COUSIN: IMMIGRANT "STATUS" WOES

Tito is a forty-year old man from Uganda. He came to the U.S. sixteen years ago, with plans to drive trucks and "make money quickly and not be stuck with rent, like I am now." But his brother allegedly talked him out of driving trucks and instead convinced him to complete the college education that he had started back home where he had been studying photography. He dropped out of community college and became a machinist with a mid-size transportation company. He had changed his visa from visitor's to F-1 student visa. When he dropped out of school, Tito automatically "went out of status" and thereby joined the ranks of millions of "illegal" immigrants, causing him and his brother to be 'stuck here' in quagmirical circumstances which he often calls "sad issue."

This interview was conducted mainly by text messaging since the subject lives out of state in Oklahoma and prefers to text than speak with the newly acquired "American accent" in which he takes great pride but feels uncomfortable when speaking with a fellow African. He is quite impatient with those Africans who have not tried to erase their African accent and tried to fit in, by speaking *Amerish* or English as it is spoken in America, as is opposed to British English. Tito's cousin lives with him and sleeps on his couch. They are typical *frenemies* and do not see eye-to-eye on much of anything, especially on the issue of his cousin's perceived failure to adapt to the American culture: speech, eye contact, and the like. His cousin views his own mannerisms as being respectful and diplomatic in the African cultural context, but Tito finds it an annoying waste of time and failure to adjust to the new American culture.

"My mother's case makes me sad," writes Tito wistfully "I wish there was something I could do to be available and yet keep living my life as well. Sometimes I feel like I should go home and take care of her. But then I wonder, what happens, what do I do when she is gone?"

Tito cannot change his immigration status yet because he has been out of status for many years after dropping out of school, and the only way to get back on status is to marry an American woman and file for legal status. He would then be able to travel to Uganda and visit his elderly mother. Without this arduous process, he will virtually be unable to return to the U.S., which is where he believes he must live.

"Women have a lot of issues. Many single (women) I've met have kid(s) and get government assistance, so they don't qualify for what I need." He adds that they usually also have criminal history from their younger days. Decent age-appropriate ones have kids and want to settle for marriage.

Finding a suitable woman has therefore been a challenge. "I wasn't planning to get into a ready-made family with ill-disciplined kids running all over that ain't mine to begin with. Young women who want old man like me want me for money and a car they can drive around yet are very immature mind-wise. I can't risk them because they might get me in trouble with what I'm trying to fix to begin with," he states with exasperation.

Later he adds, "I told you I'm getting old. A fifty-two-year-old woman tried to pick me up at the junkyard when I went to pick up a part. Some women are very brave. Has no car, no job. I'm not interested."

"Tried to 'pick you up' meaning? Like ask you out on a date?"

"Yup! That she needs a man like me in her life. I was sooo tickled."

"And how did you know her age?"

"If someone is going to approach me outside a business and do me like that, all conventional rules are broken. She asked me how old I was, so I asked her, too. Even though women should not be asked, I did."

"Sometimes character matters more than age, and she could help you with your status issue."

"Not without a car or a job, man! She's probably getting food stamps like many of them do. That's a disqualifying factor, from papers I've read," he says in reference to the requirement that one marries a U.S. citizen to get legal residency, and that the citizen be able to support the spouse financially so they will not be a burden on society.

"Someone articulated very well on TV yesterday that 'had any of those kids that were shot yesterday been a gun lobbyist's kids, the conversation would be totally different today,' and I totally agree. Shame on all these people who are anti-abortion yet pro-gun in Oklahoma. It is sad that more people will die again in another mass murder just for being somewhere going about their business."

Tito is quite engaged in American politics and social issues. He is a die-hard supporter of President Obama and is quick to add that his support for the president has nothing to do with their common East African ancestry. "A friend's dad once told me that I am a 'lost liberal,' following Obama blindly because he is black. Let's even pretend that assertion is true: so be it! Obama is the type of president we can be proud of; he doesn't make America a laughingstock."

Thus, Tito switches from one topic to another—from politics, to social issues, and then back to his favorite subject: his brother. (It's his cousin, but there is no word for 'cousin' in his mother tongue, thus, his brother.) His brother came to the US a few years after him to attend college in the East Coast. He ran into immigration problems when he could not afford the tuition to register as a full-time student which immigration policy requires of international students. So he moved to the South to live with his brother and possibly find more affordable colleges in Oklahoma. They stayed together for a while, didn't get along, and his brother moved out to an apartment of his own. His savings and investments were wiped out during the economic downturn when one big bank failed and went under.

As job opportunities decrease and finances dwindled, the cousin took a high interest "payday loan" from what Tito calls a "loan shark store." The interest rate was close to 200% and he gave his car title, or *pink slip*, as collateral. He found odd jobs here and there and tried to repay the loans but soon stopped making any more payments. He had repaid the whole amount he had borrowed but stopped when he frustratedly realized that all the payments he had been making barely covered the outrageous interest.

"Life can get better for some," writes Tito, telling of another guy he used to work with at a nationwide transportation company. He was "a moving van body repairman" making the same money as Tito. He got a loan, opened his own body shop in a new building, and now has a second location.

"He has an Audi Account, a big leather office chair, and a big ol' Benz he bought wrecked and fixed. He is hiring body men and painters but wants experienced people only. You know what I wonder?" Tito asks desperately. "How do people who are not rich or have equity or money get a loan to start a business? Or are they just written off poor forever? My brother did it on credit cards. I don't even own one of those!" he writes, exasperated.

I answered him stating that poverty is a vicious and pervasive sociological phenomenon that is difficult to escape. "Now, I know you will not agree, but I'll share only what I have experienced: education and faith have helped. Some have been so lucky as to win the lottery, but they are few. Credit card is a very dangerous thing, even if sometimes helpful. You can start with small department store credit cards which you pay off monthly, but they can build or break you."

"Education, yes, I agree. That church part as you say, I don't agree," he responds characteristically. "For something to be said, shouldn't it be quantitatively measurable? I can't measure faith's rewards since it is based on a belief. I told you of people suffering yet they pray and have faith more than Pastor himself. There're too many excuses in the Bible for things that can't be explained. It's hard for me to believe that your success is due to faith in God. There is no evidence of what part the faith played other than just you saying it is the faith. I'm sorry it is just one of those things that the more I look at it, the more I don't see sense in it. I'll be six feet under and never see that kingdom come. More kids will be born and keep doing the same till they die. Sikhs killed in temple; others shot in Kenyan churches; where was God? If miracles happen, it didn't happen (to the shooting victims)!"

"That may be so, though it can also be measured qualitatively. God has opened many doors for me in ways that I cannot explain, including doors to scholarships, education that you're talking about, and immigration papers. All were possible for me in ways that are humanly incomprehensible. Besides, if I may add to your list of bad things happening while God watches, Jesus was crucified by forces of evil while God watched. So, we must look at the larger picture. By the way, 'has worked for me' doesn't mean I consider myself successful; I'm still a work in progress. But the other side of it was education, hard work, and the self-discipline that goes with it."

"In America if you have a home, a job, and family, you are a successful middleclass. You don't qualify for food stamps (lol)" writes Tito, with laughter.

"I know it may appear so, but I'm struggling, especially now with college tuition and more furlough days. And house is just mortgage payment; it's never yours till you pay it off. But we thank God for life, food, and shelter," I responded.

"Well, that's life. At least it is your money; I have no complaint. Not like some I see here raising kids with food stamps, meaning people's taxes feeding their children. Ridiculous!... I see a missed call here from home; I wonder who died now! Last time I received a call from home it was dominated by conversations about who died and who is deadly ill. I'm not looking forward to!"

"If only we could eliminate the sad realities of life by just dreading or avoiding them! Unfortunately, we can't." Besides, Tito has made it clear he does not want to talk with people from home due to his loss of the Christian faith he was raised in. He fears that they will ask him about church and all that, and he would be hard pressed to answer. He'd either lie about it and have a guilty conscience, or tell the truth that he no longer believes in God, and risk being perceived as rude and disrespectful.

His complaints suddenly switch to his brother and traffic ticket he got in "a city you don't belong in." After obtaining that ticket, his brother decided to go to court to challenge it.

"Once my brother is settled, he is a good book to write as well. He goes to court and starts silly argument with judge in traffic court. I mean, who in America doesn't know when you are in front of a judge, you are at the court's mercy; you humble yourself? If judge has said final word, you leave quietly if mad, or say thank you. You don't keep trying to argue! Judge had bailiff remove him from the courtroom!" A few hours later, Tito says he texted his brother because he "would like to know if there is any news from back home." If someone called or something, because he is "just curious to know." Yet he just said he was not looking forward to such calls and the bad news they bring. Is it that his heart is still "home" with his mother, sister, and others, in spite of himself? Does it mean that when he wants to speak "no *mother tongue*" with his brother, it is just a survival instinct at play, but he still considers Uganda his "home"?

Tito is facing some of the same complex conflicts other subjects have articulated: problems of belonging to two worlds and of adjusting to the new world while being uprooted from the old one. News of power poles and electric cables, including transformers, having finally reached close to his village cheers him up momentarily. All these years, fifty years after independence, his village has never had electricity or running water. And that is probably one of the reasons Tito says that his life in the United States, even with all the employment and immigration issues, is still better than it would be if he had stayed home.

"It's heartbreaking to watch my employer loading off lots of clothes in dumpster out of repos, while people at home walk in rags of clothes. I wish it was simple to help. My neighbor back home used to be a clean, soap-smelling man, yet would have only remnants of a pant, holes all over; but would be clean. Poverty in Africa is so sad. Yet in all that, people still believe there is a God. Where??? And how??? Makes no sense at all!"

This is another one of Tito's favorite subjects: poverty and human suffering as evidence that there is no loving, all-powerful God. His tone sounds very angry with the idea of God.

So, I asked him, "Is it your understanding that if there was God, that there would be no poor people and that there would be no suffering? During the times of Jesus on earth and the miracles you refer to, were there no suffering poor people?"

"Man, let's just leave this alone. We'll never agree on this subject. My brother Ben (his older brother who lives in the UK) is a very good news person; I love his text messages about home. The only problem is, as embarrassing as it is to say, I need to hone my vernacular skills. It's taking me waaay too long to figure out what he is saying."

"Have you forgotten your mother tongue?"

"Not that I have forgotten. I just feel like I am learning to read again when I have to read that many pages. I had to read it over and over to make sure I got it all. It was good. I wish I could go visit home like Ben. It'd be nice to see Mama, my sister, my eldest brother and the rest, or even help with a project like he has done. Ugh!"

The anguish he feels as a result of not being able to travel freely to visit family due to lack of valid travel documents is evident in his voice. It is the same issue that ironically also makes life in the United States quite challenging and less than fulfilling.

"My friend came to visit from Ohio. I'm sure he's wondering if he can move from Ohio and buy a brand-new two-story house, surely what am I doing in this chicken shack?" Tito muses. With no adequate immigration papers and the now rampant e-verify system, he cannot get well-paying jobs that would enable him to live like his peers in a decent home. He must content himself with low-paying hard labor types of jobs that not many Americans want. And Tito and his brother cannot endure the embarrassment they would face if they just returned home without any educational accomplishments, or a lot of money to go invest in something significant.

"These people are killing me, man! Last week I only worked two days; this week I haven't even worked one day. They text me daily A.M.: 'no work!' Said today that business is slow, they haven't sold any cars."

"Sorry to hear. Let's brainstorm what can work. Would you consider trying another employer, moving to a bigger city, or moving out of state to legalize your status?" I asked him.

Tito rejects the idea of moving to a larger city for better employment opportunities, citing his deep roots with much possession in the form of tools acquired over the years. He is not like his brother who had nothing and could easily move. At the same time, his brother is a good example of how difficult it is to make friends, and so he should not move.

"Life is hard enough for me having no family at all, let alone moving somewhere else without any friend. May not make any sense to you, but to me it does matter a little. Not to be stubborn or anything; I just remember all the holidays people enjoy in America, and I know I wouldn't want to be in a strange place alone. You can see even my brother who can live in a car, talks of Kansas City, got maps and this and that, yet still here! I have not totally given up on finding alternative work here; I stopped for a while but will continue to look here," Tito states with finality.

A few days later, he resumed the active search for employment within his familiar environment. But he resisted getting acquainted with technology for too long, and it has come to haunt him. For years, Tito repeatedly refused to open an e-mail account, saying he had no money to buy a computer or subscribe to internet service. Besides, he said, people from home would be sending him too long and too many e-mails, which he did not have time to read.

This resistance to change has finally caught up with Tito, who now says: "I don't even know how to e-mail my resume! This place wants me to e-mail him a very detailed resume. I will go to Oklahoma Workforce, where they provide help with writing resumes. So many places hiring that I can't apply to! New retail company branch is so close to my place. Construction is almost complete; huge property place almost as large as Super Wal-Mart. I just can't go there (due to lack of immigration papers). Indian man calling me now to go start work tomorrow if I want. He wants to fire somebody!"

"What does your instinct tell you? I hope he will not misuse and then fire you!"

"I have no idea. I am desperate for a job. Bills are coming up. I just have to go start tomorrow."

"Let me know how it goes."

Hours later, Tito returns from the job interview with "Indian man." He writes: "A very mean looking man, and he has not learned the (American) culture. He has a business but doesn't know how to be super nice to customers. I saw him serve a woman who came in with a kid for inspection, was so poor; I gave him an "F" grade in customer service. I have learned a lot living here and wish I had a good opportunity to apply what I know in my own business. Guy who was interviewing me now so dumb, any one of us could do a much better job than he is, owning and running that place. He is an Indian man without personality but some money to start a business. He has very poor customer service skills. It is sad that I have to be seeking a job in a rat hole like that. If I had another toolbox, I would leave that one at my other work and not tell them I quit yet."

This is another example of the restrictions that come with life as an illegal immigrant, or as one whose legal status expired but was not renewed. Tito's life is full of regrets of what might have been, if only he had the papers to enable competition in the workplace. As it is now, he can only seek work in "rat holes" like the small business whose owners he feels are less qualified than himself. An even bigger dilemma is that of being unable to travel in and out of the country to go visit his aging and ailing mother, as well as other family members. He used to be very close to his mother, but as it is now, Tito has not seen her for more than fifteen years. She is reportedly increasingly worried that she might die without seeing him.

"My eldest brother is at home with Mama and my sister who want to talk to me."

"It must be a big dilemma for both parties: Mama and sister on the one hand wondering why you are 'lost' (did you read President Obama's book?), and you on the other hand stranded and may be wishing how you could see them!"

"Well, my brothers Peter and Ben are at home and maybe can explain to them what immigration status is. It is very frustrating though, to say the least. The difference between me and my brother here is that I am telling it like it is. I am embarrassed about my situation here and I don't look forward to such phone calls asking me questions I don't have answers for. Last time Peter called he was reminding me as big brother that life is short, asking me about marriage, etc. I would if I was in a position to. And I see his point. I realize I am getting older, so is Mama and everyone. But it is kind of hard for people at home to understand. My brother here is in denial.

His job also is not going well. He gets only twenty-eight to thirty hours a week. He had a buddy from Haiti at work who was let go since March. He can't find a job, speaks limited English. He is so frustrated that he was crying on the phone. Sad issue."

Thus, the conversation with Tito continues to revolve around his work, his family back home, and his annoying brother whom he tolerates in spite of himself.

After his brother stopped paying the payday loan sharks, they hired a repo company that tracked him for a year, caught up with him one day, and forcibly took the car which he had been living in for months after apartment management refused to renew his lease. Tito, who had also kicked him out of his house, is now reluctantly considering taking him back. Tito forwarded the following message a few days later:

"'Repo man got me today!' That's from my brother."

"I am sorry to hear. So, they took his car away, repossessed it? Is it for the pay-day-loans he took on car title?"

"I think so, yes."

"So, your brother will sleep on the city streets?"

"No. I'll talk to him and see if he needs to move back onto my couch. See, he never learns! I told him repo man makes US$300 to US$500 per car they pick up, are very relentless and would find him. He said no; he watches out before he parks. It took them two years, but they got him. Sad issue here!"

"Thanks for your kindness to him."

Later that afternoon he writes, "Yup! They got his car. I have to go pick him up. He needs to borrow mine for a few days. My brother is nuts! He wants to borrow my car to go to (homeless) shelter! Then he is trying to pick which car to borrow. Mind you, I gave him the car I value the most. Apparently, repo company has been tracking him: two trucks blocked him in from front and back, and they forced him out of the car. Sad situation here! This guy my brother calls 'friend' he met at shelter is the one that picked him up while I was at work; picked him up in an old beat-up truck that he uses to haul up junk."

He quickly goes back to the subject of his new job.

"Indian man called me to go to work at 8:30 AM tomorrow, and I hadn't quit my other job yet. Huge dilemma! If I had any choice I wouldn't go there; that is where my brother has got two tickets. And when I took him there long ago, looking for a guy to sell him a car, police showed up claiming suspicious people reported (whereby 'suspicious people' means Blacks.) Today when I went there, police followed me for one mile. When I signaled and turned, he did too but made a U-turn and went back where we came from."

"Maybe you should go register with the police department and tell them 'I'll be working here.' Sounds crazy but may drive the point home."

"LOL! No database to register residents or workers in the neighborhood. A white South-African owns a muffler shop there and says he makes decent money. He is quite friendly; doesn't appear racist... telling me I won't get far working for people, and that I need to start my own business. It takes money to start; rent, equipment, utilities, and I still have to do the same for a roof over my head."

A few weeks later:

"I don't like my new job at all! Looong hours; little pay, in the name of a salary. If I divide hours by pay, I make less than I was making at other job. Then the new manager here is an Iraqi and Afghan veteran, He is doped up on pain pills and is hyper and talks all day long. He's been in IED[3] and is 90% disabled! He acts crazy and is on 600mg synthetic marijuana daily. He asked me if I know anyone selling a handgun. Ugh! I'm sooo frustrated! He sweats so much, his shirt is 90% wet when inspecting a car, yet he is as skinny as me. They all want to smoke around me because it is the habit

---

[3] Improvised explosive device

they've made. Already talking of firing him, yet earlier was telling me how he beat up his sergeant or something and got demoted in rank. 'I knocked him flat out,' he says. He is telling me how he is bad*^#@* sniper; can take people out from far away. He is crazy! PTSD. If that's not enough material from me for your book, I don't know what is!"

"So, you want to try somewhere else before you are too deeply entrenched?"

"Nowhere else to go at this minute."

"Do you think that if you and your brother return home, that your lives might be better; that you might be better off living there than you are here?"

"Man, I am not in the mood to continue with the interview today! Too much stuff on my mind. Another day will work better."

"I'm sorry to hear! I hope you find something meaningful and satisfying."

Several months later, the issue of mother at home has returned with fresh passion after hearing news of siblings' visits with mother.

"Nice to hear from home. Some of it very sad, though. Hope she lives long enough for me to go and see her. I wonder where I'd be if I had stayed home? ...HIV dead? Successful? Or just another villager, like my neighbor? In my heart though, knowing how Mama's situation is now, I wish I had just stayed. She had all these kids, and yes, they have helped her a lot. But no one stayed with her. I think I should have," he states candidly, wistfully.

Then back to his favorite topic of his brother, who seems to be some sort of a pain-killer for Tito—some sort of a distraction from the myriad challenges he is facing as an out-of-status immigrant whose dreams in the land of opportunity have all turned to torturous nightmares.

"My brother eats top-ramen noodles day and night. I confronted him Sunday... He claims that he gets nutritional values when he eats at casino buffet. I asked, 'how often?' He said once a week or two. My brother and I don't agree on anything! He thinks that if I had stayed home, I wouldn't be useful. I would not have the skills I have now to provide technical help, blah blah blah. I think I would be taken for granted if I was there, but they would notice if I'm gone."

"I wonder what you think of where you are now versus where you expected to be when you came to America. Did you imagine you would develop the skills that you now have or even be doing what you're doing now? What were your expectations?"

"I wasn't ignorant of what America is when I came. Remember I got truck driver books but got talked out of it? What I really want is to get papers and have my brother out of my hair."

"So, you wanted to be a truck driver, but someone talked you out of it! Seriously, what did you hope to be?"

"I wanted to be a truck driver. And in my mind, I was upset. This was something I had planned to do almost two years prior to coming to America."

"You were upset for not driving trucks, for being talked out of it?"

"Yup! That was what I had talked to people about when I came here the first time and went back. It was a way to make quick money and do whatever I wanted to do, and not be stuck here with rent like I am now. I really need a solution to my brother. I would like him to move out of here. This thing is just becoming a big headache. I don't want to fight over it. I have told him many times politely and not so politely. Still here with this stupid car he bought; I am sick of it."

So I asked him if he thinks the pending immigration reform bill will pass, and if so, would it help them both?

"I don't know man! I just need my brother gone as soon as possible." Tito goes in a long tirade against his cousin living with him, and how he is tired of their living arrangement and cousin's "stupid car waking me up." He cannot stand it much longer. His cousin, he says, has always relied on temporary jobs obtained through such agencies and is consequently unable to make long-term plans such as apartment lease agreements. Tito is losing his head over it.

"Do you have any suggestions on a new way forward?" I asked.

"No, I don't. My brother living here almost like whether I want or not. American people different. Two close friends telling me to just change locks. He needs his own place especially now when he has a job, or he'll never do it. Too cheap, likes free things." His own job is increasingly more frustrating with both manufacturers and employers adding new technology.

"Work is hard, I don't like it! Too many makes and models. All data insufficient to troubleshoot complex model-specific issues. I looked online where a Ford technician posted procedure of how they diagnose that kind of issue. At the end, if all went as shown, it said to replace PCM[4] computer," states Tito, lamenting how complicated yet ridiculous technology can be.

Several days later, Tito texts, "A girl I know won US$4,000/ gambling. She lost US$3,500 of it the next weekend. 'You can't fix stupid,'" he quotes his favorite Southern saying.

"Is your brother still in the game? Is he gambling?"

"He is. I suspect he has lost a lot of money the last six times he admits he has had 'a losing streak.' He had a lot of money in his account. Last week I noticed very little was left, yet he buys nothing except noodles. I am only speculating. There is too much casino promotional junk mail here. That's my brother for you. Casino owner donates millions, yet ignorant African here eating top-ramen noodles. Sad issue! Every month he gets coupons in mail for free two-day stay in casino hotel, free bed, and buffet. 'Free' food and room: just bait to get your money. Casino is where he lost the US$6,000 he saved for marriage when living in the car and the

---

[4] Pulse-code modulation, a car computer component.

US$2,600 he made from buying and selling used cars. Noodles is all he eats, and he pays no rent or utilities. You can't fix stupid."

And thus, Tito continues to switch back and forth between his own situation and his brother's, which are intertwined by their common predicament of lost immigration status and frustrating, futile efforts to regain it. He pushed his cousin to move out the first time to create room for him to date, marry, and obtain legal status. Cousin stayed at a shelter and later lived in a car for almost a year, yet no marriage happened. Now, cousin has been forced back by strenuous yet dramatic circumstances, and they are both back to square one: no marriage, no money, and no change in immigration status. Thus, the inability to visit his elderly mother at home persists. And the struggle continues.

Several weeks later, he sent the following message: "I am just waking up from a very strange and painful dream, because I never dream much. Very rarely do I ever dream! Last night *Mama* sent a messenger, some woman from home. She explained in great detail why we need to go home. (We can do coffee growing business there, etc.) She was drawing all the details on the ground with a stick. Strange, though, that she had to talk to me and my cousin separately, and we had to meet her at a church."

"A vision!" I responded. "You had more of a vision than a dream," I added, realizing that Tito is not just waking up from a strange and painful dream but maybe finally waking up from what was supposed to be the American Dream, now turned nightmare. A few weeks later, his elderly white neighbor died of a self-inflicted gunshot wound to the head. Later the neighbor's daughters offered to sell Tito the old man's house at a significantly reduced price of US$30,000, but the bank did not approve his loan application, so he gave up on the idea.

A few days later he writes:

"Looks like my neighbor's daughter determined to sell me the house. They're trying to get me financing. They're so nice, so much so that I asked her why. She said I meant so much to her dad. That he always talked about me and just little things I'd help him do here and there. Wish I was able to help my own mother in the same way to where I would mean a lot to her. Yet I'm stuck here. World not very fair--- or is it?"

3

MASSACRE AFTER MASS

JOY'S STORY

(Reader discretion is advised due to the gruesome nature of some of the content.)

Her radiant, smiling face is a true reflection of her name – Joy. Her life experience, though, has been nothing like joy, what could truly be termed as "stranger than fiction."

Joy is a victim and survivor of the infamous1994 Rwanda genocide. She came to the United States in 1995 to seek medical treatment after her cousin, who was then in the U.S., learned that she was the only family member back home to have survived the genocide. Her cousin, in conjunction with fellow African musician friends, organized concerts and raised funds for her visa and airfare to the United States. Joy received medical care and lots of media attention. She has appeared before the United Nations Annual Council in New York, as a living testimony to the disconcerting genocide.

The rest of the story is quite graphic. I interviewed Joy in the lobby of a private university in Atlanta, Georgia.

"Maybe then I need to backtrack and ask you, what happened so that you got injured in the genocide. How did you get caught up in it?"

"I was in the Catholic Church…" Joy tells of how she had lived with her parents and two older sisters in Rwanda. One of her sisters had a two-month old son whom she was nursing. There had been sporadic murder cases directed at members of her Tutsi ethnic group. It was suspected that the majority Hutus were the perpetrators, but there was no evidence. When the country's Hutu president's plane was shot down and the president killed, the killing of Tutsis intensified. It was clear she and her family would soon be targeted.

Joy and her sister ran to the nearby Catholic Church to take shelter. At the time the killings began, her father had been very ill, so their mother stayed behind to take care of him. The other sister decided she would not run to the church and leave their seriously ill father alone with their mother. She would only later learn of the brutal murder of her ill father, mother, and sister.

"We stayed at the church till the next day. That's when the Hutus came to search for the Tutsis, at about 5:00PM."

"Did someone tell them that there were people hiding at the church?"

"Yeah, they knew because lots of people were there, and they were all Tutsi people. So the Hutu came to the church and killed, uh, almost everybody, but uh…"

One can detect the pain and fear in her face as Joy pauses to recollect the appalling incident. She was only eighteen when she witnessed the brutal massacre of family, friends, and neighbors. She herself miraculously escaped being killed with machetes, guns, and grenades.

"They were fellow villagers who had worked as porters carrying travelers' luggage for a fee, most of them, but they were mixed with soldiers. So when I saw them I went to hide in the bathroom, and the bathroom was just a small room this big (demonstrating a 6x6 foot room constructed a few feet from the church building). We stayed there for about three hours, before they left because it was getting dark," she recollects painfully.

The people hiding in the church were not armed at all, so they were slaughtered without any resistance by their attackers who were armed with guns, machetes and grenades.

"Who armed them?"

"The government, the government did. Some of them were trained for four years before this happened. It was like a plan, so, many people who had the money had fled to different countries like Ghana, Kenya, or Burundi. We didn't have enough money, so we didn't flee. My mom had wanted to send us to Uganda, but I was the only one who had a passport, so my sister..." her voice fades.

"What happened at the church?"

"The Hutu killed about a hundred people, in fact more than a hundred! There had been about three hundred of us, but only seventy-five were left, including the priest. When my sister saw that they were going to cut her baby, she threw him down and fell on him to protect him. They cut the back of her head very badly and she was bleeding profusely. And, they left her there, and the baby was..., because the baby was only three or four months old, he was just sucking the blood from his mother's wound.

"When they finished the first (killing) incident, I asked one of the priests to take me back to see if my sister was still alive. I found my sister dying, so I took my nephew. We stayed there for one week with no food. Then the Hutus returned. They ordered all of us to lie down on the grass outside the church building. They then started shooting and killing us one by one, using guns and grenades. I was lying down there with my nephew. When the Red Cross came to take the dead, the priest asked them if they could help my sister, who along with another girl, was badly wounded but still alive. I stayed with my nephew while my sister was taken to the hospital. When I stayed with the baby, the second time when they came, I was too weak to run and hide in the latrine like I did before. We lay down, and they started shooting, one by one. My nephew was killed right here (pointing to her right side.) That's how come I got shot here (showing three bullet scars.) These were made by bullets, but this one was from shrapnel from a grenade. I still have it! It was this big."

"You have it here with you!"

"No, I could not bring it over; it could not go on the airplane, so my friend kept it for me in Rwanda. She still has it. When the killers ran out of bullets and grenades, they started using machetes. As it got darker, they heard that the A.P.I, the Tutsi side, were closer. So they ran away quickly, because most of them were just civilians and not really soldiers."

"The porters, as you said earlier?"

"Yeah. They ran away. One of them said that they would not leave me there because I might tell what happened, I might say who did this and that. They were going to take me to the National Radio to talk about what happened. They told me that I should say that I'm one of their enemies, that I was using a gun. They told me the name of the gun that I should say, that I was on the tree shooting people, and so I said, 'OK,' because I didn't have any choice. And they took me to a car, which had blood all over."

"Is it the same car that they used to transport bodies of the people they killed?"

"No. For people who were with me, they dug a *big* pit, and just buried all of them there together!" states Joy, eyes wide open with lingering horror.

"In a shallow, mass grave!"

"Yes!"

"Did you go to the radio station?"

"No, they, they, they didn't take me there. They took me to a Catholic College which they had turned into their headquarters. There they trained very small children to kill, children as young as six or seven years old! They trained them to kill with guns and machetes. They asked these children to kill me. So I lay down and they started beating me. By this time, I was very weak and bleeding all over, even from this ear," Joy narrates, pointing at her right ear.

"One of the soldiers had brutally kicked me on this side of the head. I had not eaten anything for two weeks, so I was very weak. Anyway, when I did not die, and the kids were called to go eat, I was left lying down there. I was bleeding from my ear, my arm, and my leg. Afterwards, one of the soldiers said they didn't have anywhere to bury me, so I should go outside, and they can use me as a roadblock."

"To use you as a roadblock to whom; who were they trying to block?"

"The Tutsi soldiers' cars. Have you seen the video that showed how they were using dead bodies as roadblocks?"

This is an extreme case of human depravity, just like in apartheid South Africa. The main difference is that the South African one was racially motivated, while the Rwandan one was motivated by ethnocentrism, even though the Hutu and Tutsi of Rwanda speak the same language. To train children to kill, try to annihilate a whole group of people, slaughtering men, women, and children, and burying people alive in mass graves, are incomprehensible, senseless acts of barbarism.

"Yeah, when I talk about it, it is like just talking, but when I see the videotape, it really makes me feel angry for everybody."

"You wonder, 'How could they do such a thing!' You were living together before the nineties, then what happened to make them lose their humanity?"

"Yeah. Tutsi and Hutu, they had issues from a long time ago. But when the Hutu took power, they did not want anyone else from outside their tribal circle to succeed. That's why most of the people who don't know how to read and write in Rwanda, are Tutsis. Tutsis were denied education opportunities back home."

"And why is that so?"

"Because (before the genocide and the war that brought the Tutsis to power) the schools were only for the Hutu, the government was for the Hutu, everything, everything was dominated by the Hutu."

A tone of frustration and anger at the Hutu is apparent for allegedly hanging on to power and selfishly reaping all the benefits that go with it, like educational and economic opportunities, at the expense of her Tutsi community. One begins to understand the source of the conflict between the two groups, though nothing at all to justify the cruelty and brutality. This observation matches what another subject in a later chapter herein, Ken, says about competing for satisfaction of needs amidst limited resources.

Joy explains her perspective on the causes of the genocide: "The Hutu are the majority. So those Tutsi who were outside the country, tried to come back from Uganda and Burundi. But the government said that they could only come like regular people; they're not going to have anything, you can't do anything, you can't work in the government. You can just be home, no school for the kids, nothing. Yet they, just wanted to have equality in everything because Rwanda is their country, too. So, that's when everything started.

"They said, 'If you don't want us to come nicely, we'll come fighting.' So, they got together, and came in fighting. Even then, in 1990, the president said that if they wanted to come fighting, those who were already here would be killed, so the Tutsi coming in would not find anybody in the country. That's when the killings started. Although the killings started in 1990, it was just from house to house, so it wasn't obvious. You'd hear that somebody's house was burned down last night, here and there."

"So, *everybody* else in your family got killed!"

"Yeah. I only have one brother, but he was not home at the time. He left home in 1987 and went to Belgium."

"Your sister who fled to the church with you and her baby, they got killed?"

"Yeah. My nephew, my sister's son, was killed when I had him in my arm. When my sister arrived at the hospital, they were killing people at the hospital, too, if they found out you were still alive. She tried to walk home to my dad's house. They met her there and started asking where I was, where she left me, and she said, 'I don't know, I just came home. Maybe she died.' They came to my dad's house; and they shot, they killed, they cut my dad in pieces; they cut him in pieces! And they shot my mom here," she states, showing left side of head. "And they took my two sisters and buried them alive!"

"They buried your two sisters alive! You were saying that the kids were beating you, and you were bleeding from ear, legs, and arm, and you were to be used as a roadblock. How then did you survive? Do you remember what happened?"

"After the kids had beaten me, they kicked me out of the school, the Catholic Center. I went and sat down where a bomb had made a..." she gestures a hole "in the ground. They call it 'Katusha.' It was said that a *Katusha* bomb will land in the same spot another one landed, and I had heard that it killed you quite painlessly! You knew you were dying anyway. So I crawled into the hole and waited for another *Katusha* to land on me and kill me painlessly. And so, I sat there and prayed. It is like you don't have even any fear of what's going on, because you know you're going to die. And I was sitting there for about five minutes, when I saw a car coming inside the compound. This guy was a captain. He stopped, came outside the car, and asked me what happened. I told him, 'I don't know, I was shot at the Catholic Church.' And he looked at me and said, 'you know what? I know what happened to you even though you don't want to tell me, but because I'm a Christian, I am going to help you!'"

"Was he a Hutu?"

"He was a Hutu. By then I couldn't even walk. I was too weak! So he carried me and put me in the vehicle and sped to the hospital. If the *Kanda* knew he had somebody in the car, he would have been killed too! He was just driving, didn't even stop at the roadblocks. The first hospital did not have enough equipment. They said they didn't have enough medication, we had to go to the Red Cross.

"So, they transferred me to another hospital. When I got there, (clears throat), I was lying down, and one of the nurses who came said, 'You know, they kill people here! And I think I know you. he asked me about my mom. I didn't know if he was Hutu or a Tutsi, I don't know who he was! I didn't say anything because I didn't know if my parents were still alive or not! I said to myself, 'If I say something, he might go back and kill them.' So, I didn't say anything at that time. When he started being nice to me, he said, 'the only thing you have to do, don't talk to anybody, even if it's a doctor, don't talk, they kill people here! Don't say anything.'

"So, the people at the hospital thought I had lost my mind because I kept quiet when they asked me questions. They cleaned my wounds and, and the curious nurse came back and said, 'If I put you in the regular room with other people, they're going to kill you! So he put a bandage around my head, and hid me! He only left an eye, my hands, and my legs uncovered, and took me to the morgue."

"He took you to the morgue!"

"It was not a real morgue with a freezer, and all that; it was just a tent outside where they kept the dead bodies. He left me there and said, 'Don't talk to anybody! It is the Hutu who come here to check for their people, but they don't come here regularly, because they know this is only dead bodies. I stayed there for a week, and..."

"You stayed for a week in the morgue!"

"Yes. I couldn't sleep, I couldn't even smell stuff, I just saw the dead bodies. I didn't know that humans could also have (searching for a word to describe maggot) you know those small, white things, I don't know what they call them..."

"Worms?"

"(Excitedly) Worms! Yes! Worms! Maggots all over their bodies because some of them their heads were opened up!"

"The heads on the dead bodies?"

"Yes. After a week, he found another tent outside, closer to the doctor's room. That's where he was staying. He said, 'This is where you're going to stay, because this is my window. In case something happens, just shout or knock on my window. I stayed there with another lady. That lady was a Hutu, but she was a killer. He told me, 'Don't talk to this lady. She's very dangerous! Don't say anything personal, because she has talked too much of how many people she has killed. She is talking of the houses they still want to go to, so don't pay any attention to her.'

"I stayed in that tent for almost a month, and this guy helped me a lot. Afterwards he gave me his own clothes to wear, my clothes were all blood. He washed my clothes and gave me his clothes to wear and (clearing throat) all that time I was there (emphatically) *I couldn't walk!*" It sounded like the inability to walk, the handicapped condition, was the most frustrating part of the gruesome ordeal.

"I couldn't walk. I couldn't use my hands. I was using bedpans when I needed to use the restroom. They started giving me exercises for my hands, and I was getting better. After I got better, the nurse came and said, 'You know what, it is getting really dark here! I think they're going to bomb this hospital, even though it belongs to the Red Cross, they're going to bomb it! They're beginning to evacuate their own people to another hospital! That hospital was already captured by the Tutsi people, so it was safe; the region was under Tutsi control, so it was safe.

"So the nurse said, 'I'll try and see if you can go with all those people to this other hospital. I wish I could put a blanket on you. He put a bandage all over my face so nobody would recognize me outside. And he put me on a big truck which drove all the wounded people to another hospital. He took me to the other hospital, which was under the *Ngothanyi*."

"That's what the Hutus called them?"

"No, that's the R.P.F., the Rwanda Patriotic Front. They called themselves the *Ngothanyi*; people who are fighting for their rights."

"And so, you went to this other hospital."

"Yes. And, the first surgery I had was here," Joy continues, pointing at a scar on her arm. "They did it with no anesthesia! It was really, really painful, because they just cut the skin with the knife and removed that thing."

"They didn't have any anesthesia!"

"They didn't have anesthesia, so they hired five people to hold me," she recalls, laughing with embarrassment.

"So, I stayed there, started getting better and began working as a nurse, helping other people. I was there for about three or four months when they captured the whole country of Rwanda. So then the *Ngothanyi* were in power."

"Were you able to sleep after that?"

"My friends back home had trauma, and they tried to avoid thinking about what happened. I try to avoid thinking about it too, because when I think about it, I really don't want to talk to anybody. I feel lonely, and I don't like that feeling. So... I don't, sometimes I do, I don't know if I can call it nightmare, but most of the time, like April this year, I have been dreaming about my family all the time, *all the time*! Even last week... I don't think you should use this for the story." (Tape turned off as she tells of more nightmares.)

But the whole story itself is a nightmare to me! I wonder if Joy is in denial of the fact that her stranger-than-fiction ordeal left some long lasting imprints on her life, imprints which she would like to forget yet are not going away. It is a very regrettable and awful tragedy.

"So, you were saying that you worked at the hospital as a nurse helping others?"

"Yes."

"What was your experience like?"

"My experience was like, (tape inaudible) because a lot of people were really injured! We got very close to each other. I met more people than I had before, and those people there are like my family now. I didn't know them before; they didn't know me before, but now it's like..." she pauses, searching for the right word. "It is like they're more than family! If something happens, they call me. If

I need something, I call them. We're great friends, like family now," she says, coughing.

After the war Joy went back to nursing school, and her cousin in the United States heard that she had survived and arranged for her to come for treatment. The cousin and his friend raised funds for Joy's visa, airfare, and related travel expenses. A doctor in California heard of Joy's case and he arranged to see her. He removed some of the shrapnel pieces that were still lodged in Joy's body.

"The bullets were removed at home, but I still have some more here, and this one was the major thing they wanted to do. This one, you see the bone is protruding? Touch it! The time it comes up is when I can't find the doctor; you see it!" she asks, showing her scarred foot.

The shrapnel piece is lodged in a delicate place in her foot, and removal must be carefully timed "because it is between nerves, and so they said they can't take it out when it is inside, otherwise I might never walk again!"

Three large pieces of shrapnel remain lodged in her arm. These can be easily removed, but the doctor wants to wait and do everything at once. The rest of the pieces are too small to be removed and will remain in Joy's arm for the rest of her life–a constant reminder of the tragic tribulation.

"And this one made my arm from here to here numb (indicating wrist to elbow), even right now it is still numb," she states anxiously, pointing at her upper arm. "The doctors hope the numbness will go away once they remove it," she adds with a glimmer of hope.

Joy is planning to graduate from nursing school and later go back and set up a private clinic in Rwanda "if things get better and there is no fighting" or hostility between the Hutus and the Tutsis, Rwanda's rival ethnic communities.

"Do you see things getting better?"

"Not really! Things would get better if there was the rich, poor, and a middleclass. But now there is no middleclass, only rich and poor. My friend who remained back there tells me that those of us who are here should just stay here. 'Just stay there.' No one is telling you to come back home or anything like that. And you go through ups and downs, and personally, sometimes you think it is unsafe, that the situation is not good at home."

"What would happen if you set up a clinic, and a Hutu came to seek treatment?"

Joy lets out a thoughtful, uneasy sigh then states, "I would give them treatment; I would just treat them like anyone else."

Then she adds angrily, "But if they are the people who killed my family then I would not want them anywhere near my clinic. I would not want to see them. It would be very difficult for me. Even though I would treat them, I would not go beyond my call of duty. I would not go out of the way to help them."

Joy does not believe that the international court overseen by the United Nations (ICT) would serve any meaningful justice as the genocide perpetrators would only serve a few years in jail and then be released back into society. But she believes that there is natural justice and it has sufficiently punished those who brutally murdered her parents. Joy's demeanor suddenly relaxes as she calmly adds, "But you know, most of those who killed my family, they died! The person who slashed my dad on the ground, he was running up the hill soon after he left my dad on the ground; he had cholera-like diarrhea there on the hilltop and died there. And the man who shot my mom, he lost his mind and died a lunatic, and one more guy died mysteriously. I don't know why he brutally killed my parents, because my family had helped him a lot!"

Asked to compare life in the United States to life in Rwanda, Joy smiles shyly and says, "Life here makes you more responsible. Back home I was the last-born; I was spoiled! My dad provided everything! But here, you have to be pretty much on your own and you need to know how to manage your money and life!"

4

DARKNESS IN THE DORMS

TABBY

The subject is a 53-year-old single mother from Zimbabwe with two sons who are currently in college. Tabby lives in a large beautiful new home in her suburban neighborhood, a house she recently purchased after moving from one she rented in a nearby town. This is her second stint with buying a house in Florida, having lost her first home in the housing bubble that burst and set off a major economic recession in the US. Tabby commutes about thirty miles to work in her new BMW sedan. I asked her to tell me her story—her background and why and how she came to the US.

"I was born in Matabeleland near the city of Bulawayo. My village, where I lived with my mother and my siblings, was about forty-two kilometers from the city. It was during the war."

"The war! What war?"

"The war of liberation. Zimbabwe was a British colony, so the people of Zimbabwe were fighting for independence."

After completing primary education, Tabby moved to the city to live with her father who worked there. The two parents took turns visiting each other occasionally, like many post-independence African families do. "So, I attended 6th and 7th grades there and learned a new language," she states with laughter.

"What new language?"

"*Shona*. So, When the time came to take exams, they gave me a *Shona* paper. I said, 'I am not Shona!'" she states with intense amusement. The school authorities then looked and found an examination paper in her native *Ndebele*, which she took and passed. But the authorities at the examination council would not release her test result due to her ethnic background. Fortunately, her father had connections with an insider, who helped him secure Tabby's results. Unfortunately, admissions into government high run schools had already taken place, and she was left only with the alternative of enrolling in a private one. Tabby joined a Christian boarding school where she and her friends enjoyed singing hymns.

"Our principal was a great preacher. One day after preaching a powerful sermon, he asked us to sing his favorite song. So, we sang and later went back to the dorm, and we were still singing the song. The liberation war was over, but tribal conflicts continued."

"Who was fighting whom?"

"The *Ndebeles* and the *Shonas*.[5] Things had started to quiet down, and so that night we were taken by surprise. There was full moonlight. During the war, that school had been attacked; and boys and girls had been taken from the school and across the border into Botswana—just like in the Nigerian situation (where many schoolgirls were kidnapped from the dorm) —and were trained to be fighters. So, the school had been closed. but when the liberation war ended, it reopened. That's when I joined. I went to school with veterans!"

"What was that like for them? What did they say of their experiences?"

"Some of them were quiet about it and never talked about it. Others were more open. We knew they had been in the war, but they didn't talk about their experiences. That night we heard gunshots and were shocked to hear them so nearby, coming from the direction of the boys' dorm. Some boys came and knocked on the doors in the

---

[5] The *Ndebeles* and *Shonas* are the two main ethnic groups in Zimbabwe. They had been united in fighting the colonial government; but after gaining independence, they began fighting each other in a power struggle.

girls' section and said, 'Do not open the door no matter who knocks! There is war outside.' They also told us to hide under our beds, and so we did."

Later, Tabby and her fellow girl students were forced from under the beds and out of the dorm and made to line up while men in army camouflage clothes pushed with the butts of their guns and roughed them up.

"I said something in *Shona* and another girl responded. The soldiers were shocked that *Shona* students were at the school. My friend and I then got preferential treatment," she adds, laughing. By the end of the ordeal, the principal's house was a pile of ashy rubble. A few paces away lay his bullet-riddled body in a pool of blood. His wife's body was next to his, in similar condition. "It looks like the principal had a premonition of the incident because that day his sermon had been strange—had been unusually moving."

"Why did they kill him?"

"That school had American sponsors and was thriving in the heart of Matabeleland. The *Shonas* and *Ndebeles* were at war, and *Ndebele* prosperity was targeted to be hurt. Some boys had sneaked out of school to go drink in the bush that day. They came back the following morning and reported that these were soldiers in President Mugabe's government. They had captured the boys and detained them to prevent them from possibly tipping off the principal about the planned attack. They were not dissidents but soldiers with an army truck hidden in tree branches."

After that, the school was closed for the rest of the year. It reopened the following year with half the student population not returning. Tabby returned, determined to complete her studies, which she did. She and other students turned off lights at night to avoid easy detection by any soldiers who might attack them again. This tragic encounter with war and death marked her most memorable high school experience.

Another memorable experience was more on the lighter side. The school had a boys' dormitory built on one side and a girls' dormitory built on the other side "in the middle of nowhere," according to Tabby. A major street ran right through the middle of the school, and they called it "Lovers' Avenue" because boys who had girlfriends would meet on this street and walk towards the gate and back. At dusk, those left behind like Tabby—out of jealousy or sheer malice—would go hide in the woods and throw rocks at the couples. Her malicious adventures ended one day when she and her friend got caught red-handed because Tabby couldn't run fast enough. The boys threatened to beat them up but couldn't because they themselves were not supposed to be there in the first place.

Tabby and her class completed high school. With her particularly high score, she was granted admission into the University of Zimbabwe. "During my stay there, students were demonstrating against corruption in the government, and the university was closed numerous times. Riot police would attack us with tear gas, making our eyes sting. We would respond by covering our cheeks with wet towels. Then the university administration would send us home. I was always a struggling runner, so I went right through the police; but the boys were beaten."

Tabby persevered and completed her university education, then taught high school history. She got married and went back to the university for a master's degree, after which she joined her husband at the school where he was also a teacher.

"So, what made you come to the US?"

"It was an adventure," says Tabby laughing once more. "Everybody was going there, so I wanted to go too and find out what it was like. I called a former workmate who was already in the US. He got me a form I-20 for admission into a community college to go study graphic design," Tabby recalls with more amusement. She arranged to come to the US shortly after her husband, leaving both of their sons at home in the care of her brother. They wanted to prepare accommodation for them first.

"What were expectations versus reality like?"

"Ah, Houston skyline was disheartening," she states, laughing hysterically. I had expected a spectacular skyline with tall buildings, but what I saw was much less than expected; and I thought Zimbabwe's capital Harare was much better." Then she took a connecting flight to Orlando, Florida, which she felt was even worse.

"Fortunately, they came to pick me up in a nice, new car. It was a blue Honda Pilot, a sparkling SUV. So, I thought, 'OK. He's at least driving a nice car.' Only when I got home did I see this huge tail, looking like a plane, in the driveway. That was my husband's car; the Honda belonged to a family friend. You see, he had written to me and said, 'You can't do anything here without a car.' And so I asked how much the car was; and he said, 'US$1,000.' I took a nice picture frame and stashed US$1,000/ cash in it," states Tabby, laughing almost uncontrollably.

"Was it difficult to get foreign exchange in Zimbabwe?"

"No, we were just ignorant." More laughter.

"And so you put it all between the pictures in cash and sent it, and he received it?"

"All in cash, in US dollars, and he received it. So when I came, I expected to find a nice car. I was so disappointed to find this *ground-plane*. When it started off, it looked like it was about to take off like an airplane; but it just went bang, bang, bang. Hahaha! I was *so* disappointed, and I said, 'This is it?' And then I looked at the house and the wooden planks, and I thought, "Even my father's house in the village in Zimbabwe was a mansion."

"So, what was going on in your mind then?"

"Wrong move!" She declares without hesitation. "I thought I made the wrong move. So, I was telling myself, 'I'll wait one month. If I'm still not satisfied, I'll go back home. My ticket is still valid.'"

"So, looking back, where did you get the high expectations of America from?"

"From movies!" she states promptly. "From movies. Beautiful homes . . . I thought everyone lived in homes like the ones they showed in movies, like *Dallas*. But then I said to myself, 'I'm only going to work here for ten years, get my money, then go back home.'"

It has been well over ten years, and no signs of going back home yet. Tabby has completed a second master's degree, started and completed another, and is now a high school teacher who just bought a new five-bedroom home in an upper-scale neighborhood in Miami. The house has a large living room, sparkling hardwood floor, and an elaborate kitchen with numerous cabinets and a spectacular island with polished granite top. Instead of going home, she applied for and obtained a green card—which allows a foreign national to be a US permanent resident. She has also applied for citizenship and it is just a matter of time before she obtains it.

"I applied for a green card because of the same problems I was telling you about. But then again in 2000 things were very bad. My husband had gone out to look for some papers and he never came back. The following morning when we woke up, people were surrounding the house, and we were terrified."

"What kind of people?"

"These were Mugabe's people, *the ex-combatants*, as they were called. These people had fought in the liberation war and were now going around beating or killing white farmers and taking their land. They told us to get out. I saw them carrying sticks and I said, 'We're dead!' When we went outside, they picked up my youngest son by the collar like this," she states, demonstrating a choking hold. They asked for my husband, but I said he was not there; he had gone to the capital, Harare."

"Why were they looking for him?"

"It was a case of mistaken identity. An opposition party member had lived in that house before we did, and they wanted to kill him. They heard me speak Shona with an accent, and my sons weren't speaking Shona at all; so they knew we were *Ndebele*, and the man they were looking for wasn't. They wanted to know how come I spoke *Shona*. I said it was because I had gone to school there. They wanted to know why. One of them spoke *Shona* with the same accent as mine and was kinder to us. Once again, speaking *Shona* saved us. They left and went to the next house, which was just right there. They found a man, an elderly man, in that house and started beating him up."

"So, they just believed in beating people up! And what did they hope to achieve by that?"

"It was election time, so they wanted to intimidate the opposition as well as the voters not to vote for the opposition." Tabby then called her husband and warned him to not come back to the house. She packed their belongings and left in his absence. She emotionally told these stories to US immigration officials who then sympathetically granted her asylum on these grounds.

"What are you doing now and how does it compare with what you did in Zimbabwe?"

Tabby laughs heartily once again and says, "Now I'm babysitting. The only math I did back home was statistics for geography at the university. When I came here, I was worried about my accent, so I said, 'Mmhh, I don't want to teach a subject.' I was told that there are two types of special ed kids: severe, and moderately severe. The one I was assigned to teach was moderately severe, and he bit me."

"The child actually bit you!"

"Yes, the very first day. Sometimes they say that if the administrators don't like you, they'll send you into a difficult classroom. They set you up. So they gave me this kid, a difficult kid; and I didn't know how she was fed. I was feeding her the normal way; and the very first spoon I gave her, she bit me."

"She had a history of biting?"

"Yes! Yes! Later when I became friends with my co-workers, they told me, 'Oh, we wanted one of us to become long-term sub here, so we gave you this kid so you would be intimidated and leave.' I stayed there for one year. I decided I'd not teach this population anymore; instead I'd focus more on math. I also support a language arts person."

"You were going to teach for a season then go back. But now, what happened?"

"It's my children I'm thinking of. I relocated them, and it took a while for them to adjust (to the American system.) Now they have adjusted; and if I uproot them and take them home, it's really going to take them time to get rooted into something they really like. I can't keep moving them from here to here; I think that would be a mistake. That's what they say. Honestly, I do not want to take them back to the environment that is prone to such erratic violence as we experienced."

Tabby does not live with her husband anymore, a phenomenon that plagues many African women in America. But she chooses not to talk about the divorce "out of respect for him," she states. She argues that the migration of African professionals to the US and other Western countries is a serious brain drain to the sending countries, like Zimbabwe, because it leaves them with fewer trained workers than what is needed to adequately run the economies, schools, and hospitals. For the few that remain, morale is at its lowest level, which in turn has a negative impact on productivity.

"If you think of how many doctors have left, how many teachers have left, it is a serious brain drain. Not many graduates are entering the workplace in Zimbabwe. The pay is low and living standards have drastically dropped. People are just doing their job without commitment," Tabby observes.

"What was your first job when you came here? How did it compare to your job back in Zimbabwe?"

"Oh no, sometimes coming here is like shooting yourself in the foot."

"Do you think you are better off here than you were there?"

"No, professionally (and spiritually) I don't think I'm better off; I was better off at home. I had advanced a lot. Here I am stuck; I'm stuck in the classroom. I can't break through because of my accent. I can't advance."

"You feel like you're stuck because of your accent?"

"Yes. Because sometimes [when] they call me for an interview, I can tell they don't understand me; and some are asking, 'You think you can do this job with your accent?'"

"Like what type of job?"

"I went for a special education coordinator job interview one time. And another time I went for an administrative job, and I turned it down. It was in a neighboring city. They said they'd give me five hundred dollars for every person I referred. But everyone I tried to refer said, 'Oh my goodness, those kids are tough!' And I have not been able to get anything else."

Thus, Tabby joins the ranks of many African professionals who are under-employed in jobs they are overqualified for due to problems with accent, whether perceived or real. Real because of what an interviewer actually asked her; perceived because many other African professionals do teach and thrive in spite of their accents.

"OK. Now, going back to what we were discussing earlier, what was your first job?"

Tabby laughs heartily before composing herself and narrating how a friend came to give her a ride to a job interview in a nearby town. It was a Halloween day. When they arrived at the workplace-to-be, she saw a man dressed in Halloween costume and she ran away from the job interview.

"You actually ran!?"

"Actually, *ran* is an understatement; I flew!"

"And why did you fly?"

"I flew because I thought I was seeing *tikoloch*! The man I saw looked like the people who practice witchcraft back home. We call them *tikoloch*. And so, I went and stayed home for a month, babysitting," She recalls, laughing more heartily. "We never celebrated Halloween in Zimbabwe." Tabby then sought a job caring for the severely handicapped in another group home. Nobody could give her a ride, so she walked along the freeway in the middle of summer heat, wondering, 'Why are there no other people walking along the freeway?'

At the job interview, she was asked about her experience working with handicapped children. She laughs at herself as she remembers how she was "too honest" and "very polite" in answering the interviewer's questions. She let them know of her background as a high-school teacher. They did not hire her due to 'lack of experience in dealing with this kind of population,' (meaning she was overqualified for that position.)

Tabby remembers walking back home along the same freeway and eventually ending up dejectedly sitting on the stairs of a church, crying. "I wanted to go back home but couldn't. I was penniless." After buying air tickets and sending her husband US$1,000 for the *airplane car*, her mother had died. The funeral arrangements and service, in addition to everything else, depleted her financial resources. When she arrived in the United States, Tabby did not have any money left except for a US$20 bill.

Tabby lived in a three-bedroom house with several other people. On her second day, one of the residents asked her to go with her to shop for groceries. At the checkout, the other lady said, "We take turns buying food, and now it is your turn to pay." Tabby was very embarrassed because the relationship with her husband was already shaky, which her friends did not yet know. They thought her husband was supporting her financially, but he wasn't. He had started a relationship with another woman. Thus, she spent her last penny on buying grocery. The relationship with her husband deteriorated and ended in a divorce. As she sat on the stairs of the church crying, the wind blew a dollar bill toward her. She picked it up and put it in her purse, "a treasure, a sign that God would look upon my misery with mercy."

When Tabby was still home in Zimbabwe, she had had a premonition of her mother's death. She saw her mother asking her to sing her favorite songs and giving her specific instructions on how the funeral service should be conducted. She woke up with a start, sweating. Next day, word came that her mother was dead. At the funeral service, church members and friends were singing the exact same hymns that Tabby had heard in her disturbing dream, or rather nightmare.

Such revelations through dreams and visions were common with Tabby when she was home but have since died down. She attributes this to the fact that she was more spiritual back then than now. "Spiritually, I was much stronger at home. Politically, it is much more stable and secure here," Tabby states wistfully. "I'm staying here mainly because of my children. It would be unconscionable to return them to the political instability and insecurity in Zimbabwe."

And so, like thousands of other Africans in the West, Tabby is "stuck here" due to the myriad socioeconomic and political phenomena that push professionals from Africa while conversely attracting them to the West. She feels stranded, unable to advance in her career as much as she would like to. On the other hand, she cannot relocate her children back to Zimbabwe's politically and economically harsh and uncertain environment.

5

IMMIGRANTS IN LITERATURE

Over the past five decades, a significant number of African professionals and non-professionals have relocated to Europe and the United States. Most of the relocation starts with a student going to study in these countries, but then finding work and settling there. Some students are fully or partially sponsored by the institutions that matriculated them; by their home church, employer, government; or by individual donors or other nongovernmental agencies. In many cases, they are self-sponsored or are supported by parents or family. Others have gone to the United States intending to settle and work or to escape from an oppressive government. The perceived result of all the migration, regardless of the cause, is the loss by African countries of much-needed skilled human resources—often referred to as "brain drain," a term that was coined by the British Royal Society in the 1950s and 1960s to describe the outflow of scientists and technologists to the United States and Canada (Cervantes and Guellec, 2002.)

This study focuses on migration to the United States by Africans who start out as students seeking further studies and by individuals who come to this country for other previously stated reasons. An attempt is made to determine the reasons behind such migrations, the advantages and disadvantages of migration, and the impact migration has on African communities and economies.

In most cases, the unstated mutual understanding between the sponsor and the sponsored is that the latter will return to the home country to use the acquired skills in fostering the country's development. His or her failure to return home results in the continued shortage of skilled manpower, a form of brain drain. The sponsored individual's settlement in the United States may therefore be seen as a betrayal of this common original understanding.

It is important to emphasize at this point that skilled migrants are not always in search of educational, economic, or intellectual opportunities but are sometimes forced to leave their homes as a result of social unrest, such as war; or political, ethnic, and religious persecution (Cervantes and Guellec, 2002). The UN Commission on Human Security "recognized that... while the developed world was focused on military issues, Third World security was threatened by poverty, deprivation and economic inequality. They understood that the developed world (in particular) must deal more intentionally with these non-military threats to security" (Vietti, 2013). Ortega and Peri (2013) echo the same sentiments by stating that "the existing large income per capita differences between rich and poor countries will continue to generate large international worker mobility." But those who come for the purpose of higher education comprise a significant percentage of African migrants to the United States. Cervantes and Guellec state that higher education is a major channel used by US firms recruiting professional migrants. As many as 25 percent of H1B visa holders in 1999 were previously students enrolled in American universities.

According to Gordon (1998, p. 1), "a growing number of Africans are entering the stream of international migration from the continent." Gordon calls this "an exodus" and refers to it as the "new Diaspora." She cites five main reasons behind the mass emigration from Africa to the United States: globalization of the world economies, economic and political development failures in Africa, immigration and refugee policies in Europe and the United States, Anglophone background of the sending countries, and historical ties of sending countries with the United States. Economic disparity between the rich and poorer nations is alarming. Gordon reports that in 1960, the poorest 20 percent of the world's people received 2.3 percent of global income; in 1991, they received only 1.4 percent. In sharp contrast to this, the richest increased their share of world income from 70 percent to 85 percent—60 times more income than that received by the poor. To make it worse, she states, most jobs, trade, and production are in rich countries. "Unfortunately, most job seekers are in the world's poor countries, as will be the one billion new workers in the next twenty years" (Gordon 1998, p. 2).

With the reality of inadequate educational resources and institutions of developing countries, most African states cannot provide adequate educational opportunities for all citizens who need and desire it. This is especially true at the higher education level. The average population growth rate of 3 percent is much higher than that of the economic growth rate as measured by the countries' GDPs. As a result, learning institutions are overwhelmed by the number of applicants for the few student vacancies at the universities and colleges. Even secondary schools cannot cope with the number of prospective student applicants.

The problem of lack of educational opportunity for all is one that is partially inherited from colonial education systems that favored the privileged few. The result is an "educational pyramid" whereby almost everyone gets basic elementary education, but only a few proceed to secondary school due to rigorous examination systems. The secondary school examination also eliminates most of its takers, leaving only a few to enter two-year colleges and fewer still to matriculate to university. In the event of an illness or adversity on testing day, a student's future is in great jeopardy since those eliminated are left with the option to drop out and face a bleak future in which even the educated are unemployed. The alternative is to try to seek educational and/or employment opportunities abroad where better facilities and higher wages are possible. Others return to school and wait another year to retake the fateful exams, hoping for better results. Many victims of the system have sought visas to study in the United States, visas which only the fortunate few obtain.

Others have gone to India which offers numerous college opportunities.; However, hardly anyone stays in India after completing an academic program because unemployment and poverty are equally, if not more, rampant than one's home country.

Strife and civil wars are other factors contributing to the mass exodus of Africans. According to Gordon, more armed conflicts have occurred in the late twentieth century than before. The conflicts last longer and cause greater devastation. Many African countries have been affected by such civil wars and strife. In addition, countries of the Western world have increased their industrial and other production, leading to increased demand for cheap labor. Political instability and economic crises in Africa form a vicious circle; one leads to another, which in turn makes the first one more severe. Two-thirds of all war victims during the 1980s were Africans. In 1991 alone, military conflict affected one-third of Africa's 54 countries. By 1994, Africa had surpassed Asia as the continent with the most refugees (Gordon, 1998). The United Nations Human Rights Commission estimates that the 1994 genocide in Rwanda claimed as many as 800,000 lives.

Migrants from war-torn countries, however, usually come to the United States as asylum seekers rather than as students. Ogbu (1998) classifies minorities into two categories: voluntary and involuntary. The voluntary ones are in the United States by choice as an attempt to improve their quality of life and get opportunities for educational and economic success. They therefore strive to adapt to the ways of the mainstream culture and value education for themselves and for their children. The involuntary minority, on the other hand, are in the United States as descendants of slaves who were brought here by force. They resent the mainstream culture and distrust all its institutions, including educational ones. Africans in the United States belong in the voluntary category, which values education highly. They may, therefore, stay in the United States to ensure that their children get the educational opportunities that they themselves received here. Such opportunities may not be available at home.

Gordon *et al.* (1998) states that the new diaspora of Black Africans to the United States began in the 1950s, after many African countries obtained independence. Although most came for an education and returned to Africa, a few remained and provided a nucleus for those who began arriving and staying in greater numbers in the 1970s. During this era of what is known in Kenya as "airlifts," Barack Obama, Sr., attended the University of Hawaii, married an American woman, and became the father of the forty-fourth president of the United States. The airlifts were the brainchild of Kenya's then minister for economic planning and development, Thomas Joseph Mboya. After Kenya gained independence from Britain, the popular and charismatic minister realized that a shortage of manpower existed to fill key positions in both the fledgling government and the private sector. He therefore launched a scholarship fund for promising young Kenyan scholars to study in the United States. Many of them, like Barack Obama, Sr., returned to serve in Kenya, while many others stayed in the U.S. The international Organization for Migration estimates that some 300,000 professionals from Africa live and work in Europe and North America. The number is significantly higher now. Recent studies show that the early 2000s have "witnessed growing international mobility, especially towards OECD countries" largely due to economic factors, especially "the large income differentials between countries" (Ortega and Peri, 2013).

The original purpose of this study was to research the phenomenon of immigration and brain drain as it applies to Africans studying and remaining in the United States rather than returning to their respective countries to join in the development efforts there. The researcher obtained from several individuals verbal descriptions of their experiences back in Africa and here in the US, as well as their plans and aspirations. If there were comparable educational opportunities in their home countries, would they still come to and stay in the United States?

The researcher approached and verbally interviewed several Africans then living in the US. All information gathered was tape recorded, typed verbatim, and then analyzed and interpreted using the categorical aggregation approach. The researcher sought a collection of instances from the data, hoping that issue-relevant meanings would emerge (Stake 1995). Such meanings did emerge and have been discussed in chapter thirteen of this book.

The subjects in the study were African men and women born and reared in Africa but now living and working in the United States. They represent a large segment of the continent, ranging from East, West, Central, and Southern Africa. The absence of subjects from Northern Africa makes this more a study of sub-Saharan Africans in America.

CHURCHES AND SOCIAL INSTITUTIONS

In the past decade or two, a few African churches have been established across the United States. These churches cater to the spiritual needs of the growing number of African immigrants whose unique cultural backgrounds make their worship styles significantly different from that of Black, White, and other Americans. These churches also aim to act as a channel through which development funds and ideas can be passed back to Africa. In addition to these African churches, several welfare and social organizations emerged with goals that include sending funds and developmental aid to Africa.

Some African church leaders have observed that while Africans were underemployed in America, positions they could fill at home were left vacant or were occupied by under-qualified personnel. This view is supported by Brandi (2001) who did a qualitative study of immigrants in Rome, Italy. She found that many foreign residents held managerial and/or intellectual positions.;

However, many more were underemployed or were in "unqualified jobs," and most of them possessed higher qualifications than were required for the jobs they did.

On the other hand, some African immigrant church members state that the church administration back in Africa is part of the reason they have opted to stay in the United States rather than return home to serve. Are church and state leadership problems making it difficult for Africans who return from studying in America to serve meaningfully in their home countries, whether in the church or in the government? Are African governments run in a way that leaves little room for returning students to participate meaningfully in the development of their countries? In addition to frustrating governmental and other organizational policy, what other issues discourage African professionals from returning home to serve? Is it the view of these individuals that sociopolitical issues also affect their decisions not to return to Africa? This study attempted to learn if participants perceive other issues and if these issues are largely socioeconomic and political.

Apparently, most Africans in America came with the intention to study and to subsequently return to Africa. However, many social, economic, and political issues cause them to remain in the United States. In addition, several students in the United States have difficulty studying and working to support themselves and therefore take longer than intended to complete their academic programs. When they are eventually done, they often want to work in the United States to earn decent wages that will help compensate for the years of toiling.

BRAIN DRAIN

According to Cervantes and Guellec (2002), competition for talented workers in industrialized and developed countries is increasing. They state that the British Royal Society first coined the term "brain drain" to describe the outflow of scientists and technologists to the United States and Canada in the 1950s and early 1960s.

The problem was initially thought to affect only developing and transition economies. A case in point is the dilemma that faces the South African Ministry of Health, which reportedly has 29,000 vacancies. Joan Collinge, spokeswoman for the ministry, states that preventing people from traveling and working outside the country would be unconstitutional. But given the reality—that much-needed skills are being lost—measures must be taken to reverse that pattern. Iravani (2011) states that the "objective economic factors of brain drain are also stimulated by the actually realized intention of the developed countries to acquire intellectual capital free, and [as] quick as possible" (p.285).

The South African Medical Association (SAMA) estimates that 5,000 doctors have left the country. The health minister is alarmed and is working on an incentive program to keep physicians in the country (Nevin, 2003.) The 2002 South African Health Review found that 43 percent of doctors plan to work overseas after completing their community service—an increase of 9 percent since a 1999 survey. The review concludes that the government must prepare for the prospect of a nonfunctioning health system if public health workers are not compensated sufficiently, prepared, supported, and uniformly disseminated.

Odunsi (1996) defines "brain drain" as the depletion of intellectual or professional resources of a country or region through emigration, a definition which he attributes to *Webster's New World Dictionary*. He argues that through this process, the technologically underdeveloped and poorer countries pass on a significant part of their expert possessions every year to richer countries, which already have greater technical competence. Odunsi therefore clearly views the brain drain as a negative phenomenon, representing substantial loss of much-needed skilled human resource by developing countries.

Carrington and Detragiache (1999) conducted a study in which they examined the extent of the brain drain. Revisiting the old economic question of why some countries are rich while others are poor, they concluded that differences in the educational levels of the population form a major part of the answer, pointing out that improved educational opportunities should result in higher incomes in developing countries. They assert that while highly educated workers are obviously in short supply in many developing countries, it is also evident that many scientists, engineers, physicians, and other professionals from developing countries work in Canada, the United States, and Western Europe. This phenomenon is often referred to as "brain drain."

As a result, the implication is that investment in education by a developing country does not always result in the desired faster economic development if a large number of its highly educated population leaves the country. Iravani (2011, p.285) adds, "It is a fact that human capital as strategic resource is flowing out of economies where it can make the greatest contribution to human welfare, into economies already well developed and having large numbers of trained, capable, scientific and administrative personnel." If steps are not taken to counteract present enticements for highly trained people to emigrate, attempts to reduce certain skills deficiencies through improved educational opportunities may be unproductive.

Immigrants to the United States, Carrington *et al* also noted, are among the more highly educated populations of their sending countries, although they acknowledged that immigrants with lower education levels may be undercounted. This is especially true of Africa, where immigrant numbers are less than from Asia, South America, and Central America. The largest migratory streams from Africa are from Egypt, Ghana, and South Africa, with more than 60 percent of immigrants from those three countries having a tertiary education. Almost no Africans with only a primary education migrate to the United States. Thus, African migrants to the United States tend to be better educated than the average person in their home or sending country. In addition, many of the very highly educated people migrate to the United States. For South Africa, this proportion is as high as 26 percent of the very highly educated, while for most of the smaller African countries, the Caribbean, and Central America, it is as high as 30 percent. It is a devastating phenomenon for a developing country to lose as much as 30 percent of its highest educated population. It strikes a heavy blow to economic development efforts. Regarding emigration from these Caribbean countries, Johnson (2008, p.2) asserts, "Smaller, less developed and poorer countries are most likely to experience this flight of human capital." Essentially, these poor countries are subsidizing the bigger, richer ones.

CAUSES OF BRAIN DRAIN

As stated before, some skilled immigrants are not necessarily in search of educational or economic opportunities. They may have been driven out of Africa by some unfavorable social conditions, such as war and strife or political persecution. The Health Commission was ordered by a group of doctors concerned by South Africa's mounting brain drain to probe government impropriety. The investigation highlighted such problems as a lack of respect and appreciation, criminal syndicates and gangs in hospitals, the AIDS epidemic, a lack of uniform legislation, staff shortages, and heavy workloads. Nevin et al. (2003, p. 2) adds that "ninety-five percent of doctors, nurses, and medical technologists consulted said they would rather remain in South Africa but have decided to leave or are considering emigrating because of conditions prevailing in the South African medical environment." As of the time of this writing, doctors in Kenya are and have been on strike for nearly one month, citing the same reasons: poor and dangerous working conditions in addition to inadequate remuneration.

Odunsi (1996, p. 194) attributes brain drain to one of two factors. On the one hand is the "push factor," the adverse socioeconomic conditions driving professionals away from the sending countries. On the other hand, are the "pull factors," the favorable and attractive conditions in the host countries. While this is a concise explanation, he argues that it oversimplifies the otherwise complicated migration process, which often has psychological and sociological issues attached. He states that the "brain drain is a direct result of several factors often fueled by negative pressures imposed by the socio-political and economic climate, coupled with questionable government policies operative in the migrant's home country."

Aka (2001, p. 21) laments Nigeria's fall from glory as a middle-class country with the potential for educational and economic world power status to that of one of the world's poorest countries. He attributes this demise to one brutal military regime after another—a trend that led to massive brain drain. Under Generals Abacha and Babangida, "Nigerians left the country in droves... rather than in trickles as was the case before, due to a combination of difficult factors, including growing economic hardship, poor environment of work and living conditions, and the brutal repressive nature of military rule."

He further states that funding for universities almost dried up during these military regimes when economic sanctions due to human rights violations took their toll. The brain drain under these repressive rules was so severe that it robbed Nigeria of, among other notable professionals, the continent's first Nobel Laureate, Wole Soyinka.

Other professionals, mainly doctors, nurses, engineers, and scientists, left in large numbers. Aka (op cit, p. 22) decries the fact that Nigerian doctors staff hospitals in Middle Eastern countries, such as Saudi Arabia, while many hospitals in Nigeria desperately lack physicians. According to Aka, military personnel noticed the gravity of the situation and commissioned a report on the future of higher education in Nigeria. The report described the educational problems as "legion" and said that the system "had almost sunk to a state of emergency"

Aka concludes that "the dilapidation that the educational system Nigeria confronts today is blamable on, and is among the dubious legacies of military rule in the country" (Aka 2001, p. 38).

These views are supported by Leiman (2004) who states that skilled emigrants do not just leave to earn more money. Oppressive dictatorial governments often threaten them, a phenomenon that prompted a UN official to encourage African governments not to view highly educated people as opponents. She suggests that solving problems of the brain drain should include efforts to train Africans within Africa, and to create a political climate that is welcoming to professionals.

Corruption and misappropriation of funds has affected development and education in other African countries, such as Mozambique, where Sweden suspended financial aid to Eduardo Mondlane University based on alleged corruption. The move is said to have "dealt a severe blow to Mozambique's higher education reform program, with fears that other key donors in the program may follow Sweden's example (Kigotho, 2003, p. 1.)

SCOPE OF BRAIN DRAIN

The fact that the British government in the year 2000 launched a 20-million-pound scheme aimed at attracting the return of Britain's leading expatriate scientists and the migration of top young researchers to the United Kingdom (UK), negates the notion that brain drain affects only developing countries. It is a universal phenomenon. In addition, "sources confirm an increase in migration flows during the 1990s from Asia to the United States, Canada, Australia, and the UK. The increase comes from strong demands in Organization for Economic Cooperation and Development (OECD) countries for Information Technology (IT) and other skills in science and technology as well as the selective immigration policies that favor skilled workers" (Cervantes and Guellec 2002, p. 41). The United States and Canada attract the most talent, but they are not alone. France and Germany have recently implemented immigration policies that are aimed at attracting foreign students, researchers, and skilled IT workers.

Sarah Dunkin (1996, p. 430), a British specialist in planetary science research, makes an impassioned call to the British government to increase and sustain funding for their space programs and research as a means of ensuring their success and of keeping the top brains within the UK. "Each year, a number of our scientists and engineers leave the UK to work abroad. Some of them never come back."

She says that even though such mobility of engineers and scientists is healthy in that it stimulates and exposes scientists to new working practices and contacts, it is important to increase funding and be competitive in the UK to get such skilled workers to return. "To maintain UK's leadership in the field, we must ensure that we keep hold of our best people, and not lose them at the point where they are able to contribute most."

Werlin (2000) decries the fact that Canada is losing its top scientists and IT workers, mainly to the United States. The Canadian government is taking measures to curb this trend, such as lowering taxes, improving salaries, and altering immigration policies to make them more attractive to scientists and IT workers. Sheppard (2001, p. 50) reports on a forum for discussion called in Georgia "to discuss the brain drain from the point of view of the *drainees*—to determine how Canada can be the Northern Magnet." The concern was that Canada was losing some of its top brains in science and business to the United States.

One of the young participants said: "Professional salaries are better in the United States, venture capital is more plentiful, and universities push their students to carry their ideas into the real world. The Canadians that go down to the States, they thrive. I mean, look at us." The perception is that US universities provide better opportunities to satisfy intellectual curiosity; and these universities, as well as corporations, are deliberately wooing Canadian talent at an increasingly younger age.

Canada has taken significant steps to reverse the damaging brain drain. The Canadian Research Chairs Program (CRC) has spent US$585 million to help meet this goal. The result is that 35 percent of the recent hires under the CRC program were lured from abroad (Kondro, 2002.) Developing countries, such as most sub-Saharan Africa, may not be in a position to spend that kind of money to reverse the brain drain.

Thus, African countries are not the only ones affected by brain drain. After years of communist rule, many Eastern European (EU) countries are feeling the pinch of the socioeconomic phenomenon. "All of the former communist party states are confronted by the same problem—the emigration of the more talented of their young people—a process which has been called the brain drain. This loss of intellectual resources represents one of the greatest threats to post-communist society . . . throughout the region" (Tascu, 2002, p. 204).

The main reason cited for young specialists and the best graduates of higher education deciding to study abroad is that employment opportunities in their native countries are extremely low. In 1994, researchers surveyed students of the University of Bucharest. Only 9 percent said they would like to study abroad. Six years later in 2000, 66 percent of respondents said they wanted to emigrate. (Tascu, *op cit.)*

Australia and New Zealand are no exception. Kerr (2001, p. 1) notes that the fact that New Zealanders are "voting with their feet"— that is, moving overseas for better opportunities and better earnings—attests to the fact that their public policy at home has failed. Australia, too, has seen an increase in its emigration patterns over the past decade.

Khadria (2001, p. 46) notes shifts in migration patterns in India. While in the past it was doctors and engineers leaving in large numbers, now it involves mostly IT workers and students. They migrate to the traditional host countries (i.e., the UK, the United States, and Canada) and to newly emerging destinations (i.e., Germany, France, Australia, Korea, Denmark, and Japan).

A developed country, like Russia, is not an exception. It is estimated that "in the last ten years, Russia has lost 2.2 million workers in a massive exodus that reflects the 'low level of wages and salaries, the low standard of living, the present low and further declining level of prestige and science in society, the climate of uncertainty, and lack of protection surrounding the field of science, the uncertain prospect for careers and the paucity of demand for scientists' professional knowledge and creative ability" (Khadria, 2001, p. 83).

The brain drain has weakened Russia's scientific and technical potential and wastes the resources Russia has spent on educating those emigrating. The country does not reap the contributions such emigrants would have made to its economic and social development (Ushkalov and Malakha, 2000).

Brain drain from the former Soviet Union is of major concern to the international community, especially the West. It is feared that the prevailing low wages in Russia and former Soviet republics makes their nuclear scientists vulnerable to lucrative offers from the so called "rogue nations." Stone (2003) states that then Georgian president Eduard Shevardnadze claimed that several such scientists from a break-away province were already working in Iran. Docquier and Rapopot (2012) examined the case studies of African medical brain drain, the mass migration of European scientists to the United States, and the role that returning Indian professionals have played in the expansion of the IT sector in India. They concluded that the emigration of high skilled professionals should not necessarily have a negative impact on the sending countries' human resources. In fact, it can benefit those countries in the long run when these professionals return and invest money and skills in these economies.

Iraq is another country that has been hit by a unique form of brain drain. Years of political oppression, economic sanctions, and a brutal invasion by the United States left most Iraqi universities suffering from severe brain drain. The universities were plundered, looted, and burned during the invasion, further depleting their already dwindling material and human resources (Lawler, 2003.)

IMPACT ON AFRICA

Even though both developed and developing countries are affected by brain drain, the latter bear the greater burden. African countries are probably the worst hit. They are often at an economic disadvantage and thus do not offer equal intellectually stimulating opportunities to their skilled people. Remuneration for skilled workers in most African countries does not match that of their developed counterparts, which often also offer higher standards of living.

Cervantes *et al.* (2002) state that migrants from developing countries are generally more likely to stay in the host country than migrants from developed countries. As noted earlier, the International Organization for Migration estimates that there are 300,000 professionals from the African continent living and working in Europe and North America. These most likely are the highest educated Africans. Sierra Leone, for example, has a literacy rate of only 15 percent; yet, it has almost no educated people left in the country (Leiman, 2004.) Other estimates are that about 20,000 African professionals leave the country annually for Western destinations.

According to Tullio (1998, p. 118), South Africa's impressive relative development is threatened by a number of factors that result in related brain drain. Rising crime is identified as a push factor driving professionals away. Tullio states: "Johannesburg, the country's economic center, has earned a reputation as one of the most dangerous cities in the world."

Crush (2002, p. 120-121) adds that "globalization and skills migration profoundly damage national economies, increase poverty rates, reduce access to essential services, and challenge the ability of states to govern." He adds that South Africa is a vulnerable "hot spot for skills raiders from Europe, North America, and Australia." He states that Canada saves millions of dollars by deliberately making government-sponsored efforts to recruit South African doctors. It costs South Africa an estimated US$6,000,000 to train forty doctors; it costs Canada only US$1.2 million to recruit these doctors. Another group of forty-four South African doctors followed on their own. This skill-raiding practice has crippled the South African health system and its developing economy. Similarly, Ojo et al (2011) lament the escalation of the brain drain from Nigeria. They identify the causes as "poor leadership of the country, poor salaries of workers and conditions of service," and point out that "the effects of brain drain on the economy of the country are: underdevelopment of Nigeria in the comity of nations, shortage of manpower resources, loss of tax to the country…" (p. 450). The latter leads to loss of social services, which leads to more brain drain, creating a vicious circle. Raji, Akowe, et al (2018) support this view, saying, "…the effects of brain drain include dropping in the quality of service due to the absence of skilled personnel in the home countries... One of the palpable consequences of brain drain is the shortage of qualified manpower in the critical sectors like education, health, science, technology, and business (p.69).

Mahroum (2001) suggests that skills-raiding practices are not limited to Canada; it also occurs in the EU, whose members compete for skilled labor both from within the union and from developing countries. Many EU countries are facing the challenge of an increasingly older workforce population ages 49 to 64, with a decreasing younger workforce population, ages 29-40. As a result, numerous positions remain unfilled, especially in the IT, medical, and engineering sectors. EU countries such as France, Germany, and Ireland have taken measures to create new immigration laws aimed at attracting skilled workers from other countries to fill these positions. Such laws range from issuing "green cards" in Germany to easing tax laws for immigrants in Britain and Ireland. These laws primarily target immigrants from EU and Africa, thereby exposing these developing economies to the dangers inherent in losing much of their skilled labor, which they train at exorbitant costs.

Leiman (2004) asserts that the loss of skilled workers by a developing country creates a hard-to-break chain reaction with considerable negative effect on the developing country. It makes foreign investment more complex and inhibits technological advancement. In addition, the departure of a skilled professional will affect the morale of other professionals left behind, as well as the less skilled ones. It leads to more departures, thus compounding the problems of the brain drain. Srivastava (2014) states that "brain drain causes developing countries to lose the ability to progress. Talented people are born, raised, and educated in their country, and when it comes time to work and give back what they were provided, they leave and seek employment elsewhere" (p.4).

The Economist (June 1998) observes that numerous South African professionals, especially white ones, have left the country— with 96 percent of them citing fear of criminal violence as a reason for their departure. It was feared that the transition of power to majority blacks would unleash violence on whites. The violence did not materialize as anticipated, but poor blacks who are now freer to move to previously white neighborhoods now do so and some of them frequently rob the residents. The government sees the drain of talent as hurting the economy. Given that under the apartheid system, a large population of South Africa was denied adequate education, the country now cannot afford to lose any of its few college-educated individuals. And unfortunately, these are the ones who often leave. The deprivation of education to a larger part of its population by the apartheid government prompted a government official to call the criminal violence "apartheid's gift to South Africa."

Pillay and Kramers (2003) conducted a study on race, gender, and the brain drain in the Midlands Hospital between 1981 and 2000 where 60 percent of the clinical psychology interns were female and about 75 percent were white. At the end of the twenty-year period, about a quarter of the interns were working outside South Africa, mostly in Europe. Thus, South Africa was not reaping the full benefit of its investment in the training.

Similarly, educational services in Nigeria and in other African countries are hard hit by the brain drain. Aka (2001) further succinctly states:

> An important function of education . . . is the growth of human resource for economic development. The brain drain neutralizes and negates this function because it denies to the country whose brain is being drained and puts at the disposal of the draining countries precious skilled manpower the drained country "produced" for its own development needs.

This view is supported by Odunsi (1996, p. 196), who states that "the increasing outflow of Nigerian professionals to foreign countries . . . if left unchecked might endanger development programs, particularly in the areas of, training, research, technical and human resource development." He decries the fact that Nigeria has failed to receive the total profit of its skilled human resource, which is reflected in the existence of grave deficiencies of administrative, specialized, and qualified manpower; the large number of vacancies, and by the extent of use of expatriate personnel, both in the government and private sectors.

Perhaps the most insightful look at the impact of brain drain on Africa is a report by *New York Times* correspondent Celia Dugger (July 2004, p. 1) She embedded herself with nurses in the South-Eastern African country of Malawi and did an in-depth report of their overwhelming work, frustrations, poor pay, and subsequent departure for work in England. Dugger followed them to England and witnessed their improved work conditions and vastly increased pay—fifteen times more than they earned in Malawi. The 36-year-old midwife nurse she shadowed at Lilongwe Central Hospital was planning to soon leave for Britain "where she would make in a day's overtime what she earns in a month in Malawi" , and where she would not be among the ten nurses delivering 10,000 babies in a year.

Her report (2004, p. 1.) suggests *that* numerous problems face the "grossly insufficient" African countries' health systems. "But none are creating [more] anxiety in Africa than the flight of nurses discouraged by low pay and grueling conditions." As a result, the sick are often neglected to the extent that one nurse is assigned to take care of fifty patients, a stark contrast to the less strenuous work in Britain, where the former Lilongwe nurses will now "minister to the elderly in the carpeted lounges of nursing homes, and to patients in hushed private hospital rooms.". She laments that it is a case of "the poor subsidizing the rich, since African governments paid to educate many of the health care workers who are leaving.".

Many affected African countries have recently asked for compensation by developed countries now recruiting nurses and health care workers from the continent. Dugger (op cit, p. 2) reports that Lilongwe Central Hospital, with its 830 beds, requires 532 nurses. but only 183 are left, of which only 30 are registered nurses. These highly skilled nurses are in great demand in the developed countries. "More registered nurses have left to work abroad in the past four years than the 336 who remain in the public hospitals and clinics that serve most of the country's 11.6 million people, according to Malawi's Nurses and Midwives Council.". She adds that the British trend of recruiting nurses from Africa could be an indication of where the United States is headed, given that it too is faced with a shortage of nurses. In fact, recruitment programs are already underway, and green card visas are more readily issued to registered nurses seeking entry or residency in this country than to other types of professionals.

But the desperation left behind by the emigrating nurses is devastating. Dugger continues, "To spend a few weeks roaming the wards of Lilongwe Central is to see the human cost of the nursing shortage." (p. 3.) On one night, only one nurse was on duty at the nursery for sick and premature babies. She stepped aside for a moment, leaving behind 26 on their own. One baby lay dead in a crib. The nurse tried to keep other babies alive but ran out of the tiny tubes for draining miniature throats, and wearily sighed, "Today, I'm stranded!"

On another night in the delivery ward, a woman's uterus ruptured and then became infected. The nurse ran out of stronger antibiotics, so she continued giving the same ineffective, weaker one. On another night, the midwife nurse on duty had to attend to 20 patients. Several patients went into labor at once, and four ended up having babies on their own. The result was miserable human suffering. Dugger (p.4) observes that "in Malawi as a whole, the rate at which women die of causes related to pregnancy almost doubled from 1992 to 2000. One in 89 births results in the death of the mother, among the worst such rates in the world."

Whereas the human cost of the flight of health workers is colossal, the financial cost is equally phenomenal. When Nelson Mandela was South Africa's president, he criticized Britain for recruiting South Africa's healthcare workers, saying his country had spent US$1 billion educating such workers who then migrated abroad. According to a report of the Organization for Economic Cooperation and Development (2002), this is "the equivalent of a third of all development aid it received from 1994 to 2000."

In an ensuing editorial, the *New York Times'* editorial board wrote about the consequences of America and Britain recruiting nurses from developing countries instead of paying salaries that would attract homegrown nurses. One of the problems "is that the world's poorest countries are providing enormous quantities of medical aid to the richest. The United Nations estimates that every time Malawi educates a doctor who practices in Britain, it saves Britain US$184,000" (*NYT: Africa's Health-Care Brain Drain,* August 13, 2004, p. 1).

BENEFITS AND RISKS OF BRAIN DRAIN

Cervantes *et al.* 2002 (p. 41) state that migration between the developed countries has also been on the rise, though it appears dominated by temporary flows of advanced students, researchers, managers, and IT specialists. This suggests more a pattern of "brain circulation" than a brain drain, a drain of skills from one place to another. The authors concede that it is challenging for sending developing countries to offer incentives and programs that will lure back their drained human resources. But in the long run, "return flows of people and capital may not only offset some potential negative effects of international migration but also constitute an economic development strategy in itself," especially when such professionals help establish businesses and companies in their home countries. Srivastava (2014) suggests that, despite the negative effects of brain drain, it has some benefits. "Talented people should not be burdened by a country's limitations or boundaries. Brain drain brings talented people into a growing atmosphere and it promotes globalization, ... This raises the average level of human capital and the productivity levels of the economy" (p. 3).

Nyikilu (1999) warily supports this view, saying: "African nationals abroad can contribute to the development of the continent through capital transfers and ideas. But these contributions lack the wider benefits of deploying the manpower in their respective countries" (p. 634). He cites International Finance Corporation studies showing that companies are more attracted by a readily available, educated, and skilled workforce when determining where to invest. Ironically, it is this readily available, skilled workforce that reportedly encourages immigrant professionals to establish businesses in their home countries. Decrying doctor brain drain from Nigeria to western countries, Egbejule (2019) affirms the idea that "the brain drain is costing the country more than it benefits it in remittances."

An example of immigrants returning to establish businesses in their home countries is reported by Patel (2002, p. 52), who defines brain drain as "highly skilled professionals moving to North America and Europe for jobs," attributing this to increased labor mobility and globalization.

He cites the study Local and Global Networks of Immigrant Professionals in Silicon Valley by Public Policy Institute of California (P.P.I.C., 2000), which found that engineers and scientists from India, China, and Taiwan are maintaining and fostering extensive ties to their native countries.

> Chinese and Indian professionals working in the United States advise companies and arrange business contracts in their home countries as well as meet with government officials and invest their own money in business ventures in those countries. About every three of four survey participants said they would consider starting businesses in their own countries (Patel, 2002).

Reports from the BBC show patterns of African professionals abroad beginning to make efforts to return. Professionals in the UK recently gathered at a job fair that was organized to help them return home in order to stimulate African economies. The perceptions are that opportunities are possible back home if the legal and political system is reformed, and these professionals reportedly are looking for jobs that will allow them to return home and move away from growing "anti-Nigerian sentiments" in the UK.

Patel argues that this process of foreign-born US workers investing in their native countries stimulates economic activities both in those countries and in the United States. This trend provides tremendous opportunities for economic growth in the developing countries but may also pose policy problems for the United States and other receiving countries.

For example, companies that allow their foreign-born employees to establish businesses abroad may benefit by gaining access to markets in those countries. But on the other hand, they may have problems with intellectual property rights. In addition, as skilled workers in these countries find employment at home, the United States risks facing a serious shortage of high-tech workers. Patel states that as many as 30 percent of hi-tech workers in the US are from India, and Chinese software engineers are not too far behind. If more of these professionals got involved in their countries, labor shortages in the technology industry in the US could worsen.

Brown and Kirkpatrick (2002, p. 39) portray a gloomier side of the problem of losing foreign-born workers. They foresee the risk of the United States ceding its overall dominance in the technology world. They quote Intel CEO Pat Gelsinger as having "fretted that 'perhaps the current downsizing of the U.S. IT industry is not a temporary thing. Maybe we are headed for becoming a second-class citizen in the world of IT.'"

Microsoft's Craig Mundie later mused in apparent agreement: "If the U.S. cedes its leadership in IT to countries such as India and China, there will not be a second chance" Brown and Kirkpatrick (2002, p. 39). An example of what they call "the reverse brain drain" is an Indian-born US engineer who quit working for Oracle and started his own company in India, where the monthly cost of running his business is US$30,000; and his mortgage is US$1,000 a month for a five-bedroom house in the best part of town. Such low costs of living and operation are a likely incentive for professionals living in industrialized countries to return and start businesses in their own countries. Thus, the risk is greater for the host countries than for the sending countries.

The view that brain drain benefits both sending and receiving countries is supported by Cervantes et al., who assert that even though it may be challenging, sending countries may in fact benefit from the brain drain, at least in the long run and with the right policies in place: "Return flows of people and capital may not only offset some potential negative effects of international migration but also constitute an economic development strategy in its own right."

They cite, as an example of receiving country benefits, the number of foreign-born US Nobel Prize winners or founders of giant high-tech companies like Intel or eBay, among others. Such dual benefits of brain drain have prompted the use of phrases like "brain circulation," "reverse brain drain," or "round trip brain drain." It shows that the brain drain, though primarily a problem, may have some advantages to both sending and receiving countries, sometimes only in the long run.

Nica (2013) argues that the brain gain, as it is sometimes called, is only possible in countries where emigration rates are very low. In the most part, emigration of skilled professionals damages the economies of sending countries while benefitting those of the receiving ones.

Some Africans regard themselves as missionaries to the United States because "the church in Africa is on fire, while the church in America is, for the most part, losing its zeal" (Pastor Ivey Williams of the Nigerian-based Redeemed Christian Church of God, Tallahassee, Florida).

For generations, Christian missionaries from the U.S. journeyed to Africa to teach their religion. Now, however, amid burgeoning of Christianity in Africa, churches there are sending thousands of missionaries overseas to preach the Christian message in their own unique style. And many of those missionaries are coming to the U. S. (*The Christian Century*, 1997).

This view concurs with that of Dr. Poindexter, whom we meet later chapter, and says that Christianity is increasingly becoming a "southern, more than a northern, phenomenon." As Africa surpasses Europe and America in those who profess the Christian faith, the missionary pattern has begun to shift, too, so that there are more African missionaries to the Western world.

There is a general feeling that Africans were blessed with the gospel by early American missionaries, and now they are returning the favor by being missionaries to Americans. These missionary concerns are clearly expressed by Dr. Malekha and Dr. Poindexter, two subjects who appear in a later chapter, consider themselves missionaries from Africa to the United States. This is not to downplay the devastating effects of the brain drain, as exemplified in cases such as the exodus of Malawian nurses to Britain, and Nigerian doctors to the west, a massive problem that needs to be addressed. These thoughts demonstrate possible ways to at least get something out of the worst situation.

6

BROTHER'S KEEPER

BARACK MBAJAH: THE COST OF SEEKING JUSTICE

At the time of our interview, Barack Mbajah, 69, lives in Tacoma, Washington. The children are grown and gone, and he and his wife are evidently empty nesters in their beautiful home that overlooks the sea at Tacoma. This, his second stint living in the United States, has lasted 20 years. It can hardly be called his second missionary journey, like Dr. Uche's, although he jokingly boasts of belonging to two different church organizations.

"I have two baptismal certificates," States Mbajah with great amusement. "I have a Seventh-day Adventist certificate from here and an AIC certificate from back home. You see, my late mother raised us in AIC (African Inland Church) and was not happy when I got baptized into Adventism," he says reflectively.

"But I speak with her in my dreams and I tell her: 'When I got here, the Adventists were the only ones who welcomed me and took me to church. I arrived here with the clothes of a shepherd and only this as my ticket, passport, and visa,'" he narrates excitedly as he displays a bunch of papers from the US embassy in Kenya.

The document states in part: "To airline officials and immigration authorities: this letter serves as valid travel document for Mr. Barack Mbajah. Please accept him as a passenger on your airplane and grant him entry into the United States. Signed, Smith Hempston, US Ambassador in Nairobi."

Barack Mbajah at a lake-front church service in Tacoma, Washington. (Face obscured to protect minor.) Photo courtesy of Rehema.

Mr. Mbajah proceeds to relate how he had attended college in this very state of Washington, studying to be a pilot before his mother heard of it and stopped him. "I flew a plane from here to California and back as a student pilot," he states elatedly. "But my mother would have none of it; she ordered me to stop as she did not want her son dead in a plane crash," he adds, laughing heartily. He then changed majors and graduated with a bachelor's degree in public administration.

"The moment I graduated, the same day I graduated, I returned home! Immediately after they called my name and I got my diploma in my hand, I had someone drive me to the airport when the graduation ceremony was still going on. I went to the airport with my gown on. Everyone was cheering and clapping at the airport," he continues with intense amusement.

He was then 24-years old, and the juvenile government of Kenya immediately offered him an administrative job as a District Officer (DO). "I was 24, and I had a government Land Rover with a driver and a policeman as bodyguard," he recounts, laughing and amused that he had that much responsibility at such a youthful age.

"I looked at my son when he turned 24 and laughed: Did I really become a DO at this age? It was when I observed my children growing up that I realized that I started to serve in the government at a very young age."

Mr. Mbajah had had a successful career as a civil servant, rising to the ranks of DO 1 and district commissioner. He was almost promoted to provincial commissioner when things took a dramatic negative turn.

His older brother, Dr. Robert Ouko, was a high-profile member of the cabinet and was simply referred to as "the minister." Family members and friends respectfully called him *Japuonj*, or the teacher. One day the nation was stunned when the minister was declared "missing." Everywhere an eerie feeling was in the air as people had their ears glued to the radio news or read the newspapers with bold headlines about the minister's "missing" status. How could a high-profile minister of foreign affairs, with government security detail at home and at work, go missing? Everyone feared for the worst while praying for the best.

A few days later, the minister's body was found by the riverbank near his home, badly broken and charred. Commenting on the matter, the president of the country said the condition in which the body was found "suggested foul play," and that "no stones would be left unturned" in finding and punishing those responsible.

As they kept vigil at the minister's house in Runda, Mr. Mbajah's sister Dorothy and her friend spontaneously composed a song satirizing the government statement that Dr. Ouko had been "missing." She sang the solo and her friend responded in chorus:

Soloist: Ouko'lal manade! (How can Ouko disappear/be lost!)

Chorus: Askar'ochungo (Guards standing at attention)

Soloist: Ouko, kane wadhi Arusha (Ouko, when we went to Arusha)

Chorus: Askar'ochungo (Guards standing at attention)

Soloist: Ouko, mane wadhi Kisumu (Ouko, when we went to Kisumu)

Chorus: Askar'ochungo (Guards standing at attention)

Soloist: To bange nee wadhi Narobi (And later we went to Nairobi)

Chorus: Askar'ochungo! (Guards standing at attention)

Soloist: Kata kane wadhi Amerka (Even when we went to America)

Chorus: Askar'ochungo (Guards standing at attention)

And they thrust their chests and sang their hearts out with loud, clear voices that needed no microphones, their eyes sparkling with fresh tears of sorrow and pain. Both were big, black *Luo* women with a no-nonsense air around them. They did not seem to care what the feared government could do to harm them. Or maybe they did not think the government through their special branch would understand their subtle criticism in their *Luo* language. Next to them, Mrs. Mbajah and Mrs. Ouko sat side by side diplomatically on the family room sofa, receiving visitors who came to express sympathy and support for the family.

Shortly after, the nation was shocked again when Mr. Mbajah was suddenly arrested and accused of killing his own brother. A few days later, his wife was also arrested. The matter was scandalous! He states that, while in police custody, he was tortured, beaten, and humiliated in an attempt to have him surrender a handwritten document he had obtained from his brother's house servant. This document contained the names of the individuals who had lured the minister away from the house to his grisly death. The interrogators took Mr. Mbajah at night to a dark room filled with cold water in the infamous *Nyati House* in Nairobi. He was effectively in the government torture chambers. If he slept, sat down, or lay down, he would drown.

"What we went through, nobody knows; nobody will understand," Mbajah states grimly. "But God is great. After I came here, my head was split open from here," he narrates, showing lines on both sides of his head. "They had hit me several times on the head, and my skull was knocked in here and there," he says, touching his head.

"The surgeons here said I may not wake up from my surgery; but even if I did, I would never even recognize my family. But God is great! I'm 69 and turning 70 soon. I've been very strong, you know. I used to be a soccer player. But now the beatings I was subjected to are catching up with me. It is more difficult to walk now, so I use this walking stick. But I don't take it to church," he quickly adds, laughing. "I can go to church without a walking stick!"

Eventually Mr. Mbajah gave in and revealed where he had hidden the wanted crucial document, but he maintains that he had made copies and hidden them in various places. Only then was he and his wife released and returned to their house, his clothes torn and ripped.

It became increasingly apparent that government elements at the highest places were involved in the "foul play" that eliminated the minister because he was viewed as a potential rival in ascending to the presidency. Widespread riots in the country were accompanied by unprecedented chants of antigovernment slogans. Some officials tried to downplay the turmoil by saying the minister's death "was a passing cloud."

Mbajah angrily spoke out saying his brother's death was not a passing cloud, as one cabinet member had suggested. He was immediately ordered to appear before the commission of inquiry that had been set up to investigate the cause of the minister's death. He would be required to respond to charges of "contempt of court."

Individuals or the press were prohibited from making comments on legal matters before a court of law or a commission of inquiry.

Knowing what he had experienced at the hands of the police, Mbajah went underground, and with the help of the American embassy, he obtained the travel document mentioned earlier. With the assistance of contacts whom he knew as a provincial administrator, he walked to a neighboring country and eventually flew to the United States disguised in a shepherd's attire, and nothing else except the document.

"When I got here, my story was all over the newspapers. Since I had gone to school here, newspapers had my name and picture on front pages. So this lady saw me one morning and asked, 'Are you not the one in the newspapers?' and I said I was. So, she invited me to church. She took me to a Seventh-day Adventist church. That's why I tell my mother that the Adventists were good to me and [that] is why I joined them," he states, lost in deep reflection.

Asked about his experiences in provincial administration, Mr. Mbajah laughs nostalgically and says there are some secrets he cannot disclose because he had sworn to keep government secrets, especially when they pertained to national security:

"Every day we received and sent memos to statehouse; and they contained secrets I cannot tell you, even right now!" he states excitedly. "As DCs, we had to meet with the president once a month—sometimes twice. Sometimes he was very harsh on us; but Nyachae, uh, Nyachae had his way with Moi. He would say, *'We'e Mzee cheka kidogo! Cheka kidogo hawa waone vizuri!'* (You old Man, laugh a little bit! Laugh a little and let these people feel happy.)' And Moi would laugh! Moi would laugh! Nyachae was my mentor, and he really helped me get going," Mr. Mbajah states, referring to Simon Nyachae, former Kenya government official and later a politician.

One day a woman came to see Mr. Mbajah with a letter supposedly from the president, directing him to allocate (Nobel Lauriat) Professor Wangare Maathai's land to this woman. Professor

Maathai had already planted trees on it. "I told her I could not do that because the land had already been allocated to someone else and it would not be fair or legal to reallocate it to another person. In the office we had several phone lines and one was red. We had it in the office and at home. If the phone rang and the red light was on, you knew it was the president calling, and you had to stand up and say, 'Yes, sir' or 'No, sir. You couldn't say anything else. The people sitting in the office with you would never know what you talked about. And so, that afternoon the phone rang, and it was the red line, and I stood up and it was the president on the other end asking:

'Did you get a letter from me this morning?'

'Yes, sir!'

'Did you do as I said in the letter?'

'No, sir!'

'Uh huh! Mhm! Go do as I said.'

'Yes, sir!'

"And there was the woman again that afternoon saying, 'Now, did I not tell you so? Why did you waste so much time? You could have had this done much earlier!'" he continues, laughing with embarrassment.

"Great humiliation! *Ori,* I was very humiliated! That's how public land was allocated. But my late brother had advised me to never take or allocate myself any land. And that's what has helped me, because they looked for excuses to have me extradited. But they couldn't find anything. If they had found that I did anything like illegally acquire land, I would have been extradited."

Mr. Mbajah says he allocated the woman a piece of land but changed a number so that she did not get Professor Maathai's plot. By the time she discovered it was the wrong plot, it was too late to go back to the president.

Months after Mr. Mbajah fled the country, his family followed in an equally dramatic flight. By the time of this interview, the government leadership in Kenya had changed, and he had returned home a few times, only to find that he has lost most of his property he had before the said ordeal. His property was presumably allocated to other people in the same manner as described above. Now he is trying to work with people in the current government to get his property back. He cannot wait for his wife to retire so they can both return to Kenya, where his heart is and has been since his college graduation day.

7

INDISPENSABLE PROFESSIONAL SKILLS

GEORGE

George is a 47-year-old civil engineer who first came to the United States in 1981, with plans to complete a bachelor's degree and return to Nigeria within four years. He currently lives in one of the most affluent suburban areas of Corona, California with his wife and five children. He commutes daily to and from San Diego. As the children and their mother drove off in their brand-new minivan—a reflection of their middle-class social status—he started the CD player to provide some background music from Eastern Nigeria, his ancestral homeland.

He politely offered to turn down the CD player's volume when I asked for permission to record our conversation. "My mother did not go to school; she practiced shifting cultivation, moving from one plot to another, different farm areas or locations. You rotate from one location to another; we had six locations. I had counted where my mom would be planting by the end of my four-year studies. I told my mom, 'By the time you are planting here, I'll be back.'

"I finished my bachelor's in 1986. Unfortunately, my mother died just shortly after I was done and was trying to decide, should I stay, or should I return?" He states that he was not able to return due to the economic situation in Nigeria. Instead of returning to Nigeria, he started another degree in civil engineering and then got a job in Southern California, moving through the ranks of Caltrans (California Transport Authority) to the position of project manager.

His responsibilities include designing, supervising, and implementing highway and freeway building or widening, and sound-walling.

"Back then, obtaining a bachelor's degree was a sure ticket to the middle class in Nigeria. You were guaranteed a job, sometimes even hired, before you finished college. But by the time I got mine, the country had switched hands back and forth from democracy to military dictatorship and things had considerably deteriorated. Jobs were no longer assured by virtue of having a B.Sc. degree, and the economy was mired in a recession. Nigeria has been alternating between dictatorship and democracy since independence in 1960. 1979 is when we had elections; we had a civil war, which started in 1966 and ended in 1970."

George asserts that life in Nigeria was reasonably good in the 1970s, with a thriving middle class. If one obtained a bachelor's degree or any kind of degree, it would improve his or her economic situation because it guaranteed housing allowance, car allowance, and scholarship allowance for dependents, no matter how many.

George was motivated to improve his economic situation by earning a degree, which would then lead to a better job and increased income. Unfortunately, things changed so rapidly that by the time he earned his degree, the degree was not an automatic means to a better life. Corruption was rampant at all levels and sectors of the government and was worsened by a ruthless military dictatorship that had usurped power in a military *coup d'etat*.

He continues despondently, "Things were great in the seventies. But in the early eighties, I think it was in '84, a military junta took overpower in a coup. They ruined the economy, there was corruption, and the economy was really bad. This October we will celebrate 44 years of independence, and most of those years we have been under military rule."

"So, what you're saying is that military rule had a direct impact on your not going home, due to the bad economy that resulted from the military's reign?"

"Oh yeah! Oh, yeah. Oh, well, they didn't bring the bad economy; it worsened the situation. Not that civilian governments are not corrupt; but at least people can speak up and change things under civilian rule. Under military rule, you're not free to speak your mind and affect government policy. If you speak your mind, it may mean death."

George would like to return to Nigeria and contribute to the development of his country but is himself trapped in the labyrinths of American life, as well as discouraged by the stark realities of life in Nigeria. The state of insecurity in his country initially tops George's list as the number one reason he has not returned to work in Nigeria or do business there, as he would prefer to. However, he also expresses the fear that he might not find comparable jobs. Years of corrupt military rule have bungled the economy so badly that social services like education are inadequately funded. George thus worries about educational opportunities for his children if he were to go home.

The poor economy has also led to widespread unemployment and desperation among the population. Crime rates have soared, making him feel vulnerable if he were to return. "They would think you have lots of money since you're coming from the US where dollars grow on trees," he states with a chuckle as he refers to the misconception among some in his home country that people in America have a lot of money.

"Right now, if I went to Nigeria to stay, I would not get a comparable job, and my security could not be guaranteed. In fact, that weighs more than anything else. If I could feel secure, I wouldn't mind going home because I could survive anywhere with my profession. In fact, I would like to go home and start my own business and have a way of giving back to my country," he affirms.

He also cites educational opportunities for the children as another reason for staying in the United States. He can adjust to life in Nigeria, but the children may not.

"Do you think they may end up living here?"

"I'm scared that *that* could end up happening; I don't like it, but you have to be realistic. It is likely going to happen because right now Nigeria is not doing great. If Nigeria could get its house in order and have a good government, minimize corruption, ensure safety, improve the country, provide essential services like water, electricity, road system—you know, government services—*then they would feel comfortable and live there. Otherwise it would be next to impossible;* they'll feel frustrated. I can go there as an adult and live there. I'm ready to go home! But they will be frustrated. I don't think they can handle it."

While decrying the problems of life in Nigeria, George also acknowledges the difficulties of living in the United States, despite the availability of relatively better job opportunities, security, and plenty of everything. He narrates a story forwarded to him by his friend, which tells of the harrowing experiences of bus travelers in Nigeria. Thugs stopped a bus and robbed and sexually assaulted passengers.

"To think of such a thing happening to anyone just traveling and you run into something like this. And with AIDS nowadays, you don't know what one has! Can you imagine! Things like this should not happen in a civilized country. And the government should be able to stop it. So, insecurity is the major factor," he asserts.

On the other hand, George states that people are still returning home despite the insecurity because "even though there is a lot of good things, plenty of food, plenty of everything, things are not that great in the US, either.

"What makes life in the US 'not that great?' What are the challenges?"

"Well, you probably know this saying that 'North, south, east, or west, home is best,' I am patriotic. I have my country at heart. Besides," he says chuckling, "here in America, you can't deny it, my brother, you have to deal with racism, discrimination; and you have to deal with lack of respect. Many of us do in our daily lives. For example, I did not get the promotion that I deserved in my first job as civil engineer, even though I was well qualified and experienced. I had to go work in San Diego, which is a larger city and, therefore, provides more room for (smiles and gestures) you know, diversity. But I have to drive long distance to get something close to equal treatment stipulated in American law."

Another problem for Africans living in the United States is lack of a family support system, which has led to many Nigerian families in America breaking up. George points out this concern: "At home we value family; if you have a problem with your wife, relatives on both sides will put pressure on both of you to solve it and save the marriage. Whenever a family is destroyed, a nation is lost. American life is money-driven—which puts too much strain on family life, causing many marriages to break. Many Nigerian families in America have broken down—especially these women in nursing. All they do is work, work, and make more money while ignoring their families. They end up being divorced."

The Luo of East Africa have a proverb: "*Ogwang chamo to thoo rome*" (meaning, the wild cat eats, but must endure the dew.) This is true of the life of an African in America, as portrayed by George. In spite of all these nice cars, houses, and plenty of everything; life is still "not that great" because one has to endure the lack of family ties, lack of respect, and discrimination; as well as risk the possibility of a broken family. In short, Africans who live in America make substantial sacrifices to do so.

Asked what his vision for Nigeria is, George spells it out readily: "My vision for Nigeria is to have a state of security, improved government services, and improved road networks."

"Do you see this happening?"

"It may happen; but it may take a catastrophic revolution— something that will change the mindset of the people to not think that one good way to make big money is to get into government. You could award people contracts and get 10 *percent*; you could award contracts and share the money between yourselves. They've been doing that for years. The higher you go in government, the more money you make. Nigerians want to get as much as they can from the government; that's why we can't develop. It is a shame! It is a shame that a country as resourceful as Nigeria cannot get it right, can't develop," he reiterates in deep frustration.

Nigerians protest corruption in high places of government while food and oil subsidies are being eliminated. Stock Photo.

Asked if Nigerians are greedier than people of other nationalities? George is quick to say, "No! People here are greedy, too; there is corruption everywhere, even in America; but the American government has a way of controlling it," he answers, alluding to the checks and balances system in the United States constitution. George states in anger and frustration:

"If they could prosecute corrupt officials and imprison those who are found guilty, corruption would stop. But as it is now, corruption in Nigeria has reached epidemic levels. One of the

Nigerian dictators was overthrown in a *coup d'état;* and US$700 *million* in cash was found in his residence! US dollars, Japanese yen, German *marks*! All in hard currency! Meanwhile, he also stashed billions in foreign accounts! How long would it take a family of, say, ten to spend one million dollars? It is madness! It is madness, my brother! Once you are the leader, you have a gun, you have no challenger; anybody who opens his mouth, you kill him. It is madness!"

George laments the fact that Nigeria's cultural diversity "is a curse" instead of being a blessing. This is mainly due to the differences in belief systems between the religious fundamentalists in the north and the Ibos and Yoruba in the south and west. He goes on to give a detailed description of the problems arising from these differences. Some of his statements are too graphic to safely put in print. "That's why we had riots during the Miss World contest last year."

A journalist reportedly made remarks that were considered insensitive and offensive to one religious segment of the population. The contest had to be postponed, and eventually its venue was moved from Nigeria. George decries the bad publicity this incident gave Nigeria. He cites another example of extremism in the case of a woman called Aminah who was sentenced to death by stoning for getting pregnant after her divorce. The case prompted an international uproar, and Aminah's life was spared at the last minute.

Religious and cultural differences play an evident role in the Nigerian sticky situation, as narrated by George. To him, the religious beliefs and practices of the northerners have direct influence on the social and political problems in Nigeria.

Like Uche, George sounds utterly frustrated by the corruption in the Nigerian system of government. He seems resigned to the "madness" and to the brutality that spells the fate of those who may oppose the dictatorial leaders. In contrast, he mentions the "Asian tigers," such as Taiwan, Singapore, and South Korea, that have recently sprung up as highly developed countries, while Nigeria, which has much more human and natural resources, has been trying to do the same without success.

"It is shameful that a country with resources like Nigeria cannot develop. Greed is in America, but it is nowhere near what it is in Nigeria. We need a change of direction. For Nigeria to get anywhere, corruption must go. Corruption in Nigeria is what is most frustrating to those of us living here. We have to have a change in direction; in the way we do things. If everyone could understand our goals, our needs, what we need to focus on, Nigeria could become a great country!"

This assessment agrees with the way another Nigerian man put it when I asked him what the main problem with life in Nigeria was. He replied, "It is the bribe!" And *the bribe* in Nigeria has soared to tragic echelons, despite newly elected President having sworn to declare war on corruption. A recent NPR report carried a heart-breaking story of a taxi operator who was stopped by a policeman; the policeman demanded a bribe that was nearly half the man's day's earning of US$25. He refused to give the bribe and the policeman promptly shot him twice on the shoulder. A stray bullet shot his wife on the head, killing her instantly. She was sitting in the back seat. Schifrin, 2016.[6]

My conversation with George over, I realized the CD player was still softly on and asked George to turn it back up. The music was in a kind of pidgin, a mixture of his native Igbo language and English.

"What is the song about?" I asked inquisitively.

"The same thing!"

"The same thing?"

---

[6] The story may be found on this link:
http://www.npr.org/2016/01/03/461818452/in-nigeria-a-culture-of-bribery-turns-deadly.)

"Yes! The same thing we're talking about: corruption in Nigeria. The words of the song, which are partly in English and are sung to a reggae tune, go something like this:

> *Can we keep on living this way (this corrupt way)?*
> *Oh, my Lord, we do not like it*
> *We practice it every day,*
> *Oh, my Lord, we do not like it*
> *Bribery, we make it hard for the poor.*
> *Oh, my Lord, we do not like it.*

Maybe it will take more of this type of song to inspire the type of revolution that George suggests is needed to bring about change of direction in Nigeria. "I do not know if we Nigerians can do it; but we need a people's revolution, like the one they did in the Philippines. There are more than 100 million of us; how many people can they kill? Maybe 20 million. The rest of us will jump on them! Maybe that's what will change Nigeria."

Maybe.

DR. KANUMA

The subject is a 53-year-old professional with a doctoral degree in science. His wife is a teacher, and they have three teenage children. Their beautiful new house is well furnished and quite decent, but very quiet, to the point of being lonely, the symbol of their "empty nester" status. Two of the children are now in college in the United States. Dr. Kanuma was hot and sweaty from mowing the lawn, an occupation that he reckons would be too mean for a man of his academic and social status back in his home country of Rwanda. He beckoned me to sit down and offered me a cold, refreshing soft drink, a welcome contrast to the oppressive heat outside. Our interview began shortly after.

Dr. Kanuma first came to the United States in the 1980s and completed a master's program in science at a prominent university in the Midwest. He went back to teach at a private university in Rwanda, then returned to the United States a few years later for his PhD.

"The main reason for coming the second time was to satisfy my intellectual curiosity and to be able to teach science at a higher level. The original intention was to go back and teach at the university in my country," he states.

But he is still here 15 years later. What made him stay? Did he get a better job here, or could he not find work at the intended university, which was badly affected by the genocide and civil war in Rwanda? Or was it something else? If so, what? He works in the Human Resource Department at a university in Southern Virginia while also teaching science on a part-time basis.

"As a science PhD holder, is human resource a satisfying job for you?"

"As I said, I wanted to go teach chemistry at the private university in Rwanda, and I could get a teaching position anywhere in the US, too, but I chose to stay in this area."

"What prevented you from going to teach at the private university in Rwanda as you had intended to?"

"I do not like to use the war as an excuse for not returning, but the private university in Rwanda was closed in 1995 shortly after the war."

The church-operated university where he had intended to return and teach was closed shortly after the infamous Rwanda Genocide of the mid 1990s in which nearly 800,000 people were reportedly killed. Victims were mostly the minority ethnic Tutsi, while the perpetrators were the majority Hutu. The two ethnic groups speak the same language, Kinyarwanda, but are reportedly different in physical features and origins. While the Hutus are local Bantus, the Tutsis are believed to have come from the north, specifically of Ethiopian origin. The two groups have been involved in protracted deadly power struggle since the days of colonial rule by European powers. In the genocide, the Hutu purportedly attempted to wipe out the Tutsi population when they suspected that the Tutsi might have been responsible for the shooting down of a Hutu president's airplane, killing him instantly, and were planning to take over political power in Rwanda.

"Did the genocide affect the university where you wanted to go and teach?"

"As I said I'm not using the war as an excuse for not returning. But the university was destroyed."

Dr. Kanuma insists that the genocide is not the excuse he is still here. Rather, he sees it as a sacrifice he has made for his family. His wife needed to complete a college program; this would not have been possible if they had gone back immediately after he graduated. In the meantime, the children became rooted in the education system in the United States. Taking them back to Rwanda would have meant that they start over in a system that uses French as the medium of instruction.

This illustrates the impact of colonialism playing a remote but significant role. Africa was colonized primarily by European powers such as Britain, France, and Portugal, as well as Germany. The imprints of their languages remain all over the continent. The continent now has two major common languages, namely English and French, while Portuguese is spoken in at least three African countries. The continent is divided into Commonwealth countries that mainly use English and Francophone ones that use French. Dr. Kanuma comes from a Francophone country, thus his dilemma. Now that the children are in college, Dr. Kanuma says that he is contemplating returning home.

"In your opinion, how would you be of better service to your country; by staying here or going back?"

"Economically, it helps more to be here; politically, it probably would help more by being there. By staying here, we can send money home to support the people back there, or to invest. Politically, we can probably help better by being there and advocating democracy."

I asked Dr. Kanuma if he sees this change to democracy happening in Rwanda, for example if professionals abroad returned and encouraged reform. He states that he sees little if any hope for Rwanda, or any other African countries for that matter, to make progress politically, and subsequently economically.

"No, we can't. We'll still be a minority. It is very, very difficult to operate in a corrupt system. You'll be crushed or converted to join in the corruption. The people are neither ready nor capable of instituting and handling political change, mainly because they do not trust one another. And it is for some things that happened so long ago that no one in today's society has an idea what it was or why they dislike each other. In Rwanda, the Tutsi dominated the Hutu in the past, so when things changed, it was difficult to accept."

"So, the Tutsi now find it difficult to be dominated by the Hutu whom they used to rule over?"

"Yes."

"So, what would you say caused the genocide? Is it the mistrust, or is the mistrust a result of the genocide?"

"The genocide was a product of the mistrust. I have sometimes asked my work colleagues from Rwanda, those we can freely talk with, if they have stopped on the way to Los Angeles to give someone a ride, and they almost always say no. I ask them why, and the answer is usually that they do not know if the person is really desperate, or if he is just faking it and might turn out to be a robber."

"So, it is the fear of the unknown?"

"It is the fear of the unknown. Anytime you do not know somebody, there is an element of mistrust."

"Is there any religious role in the mistrust?"

"No! I don't believe so."

A few weeks later news reports from the International Tribunal for Rwanda in Arusha, Tanzania, stated that a pastor from his church had been indeed convicted of participating in the genocide. The elderly pastor was subsequently sent to several years in prison. The tribunal was established by the United Nations to try and bring to justice the perpetrators of the Rwanda genocide.

"So, everything happened just because these people were of different ethnic background?"

"Yes, but also because of fear; they were told to kill or be killed. Even those who were married to Tutsis were told to kill their spouses or they'd be killed. The genocide mainly resulted from ethnic hostilities."

Dr. Kanuma's elderly neighbor and family friend was killed in the genocide or its aftermath. The genocide was indeed a tragic phenomenon that pervaded all sectors of society, including the religious realm. The conviction of the said pastor in the Arusha trials under the United Nations was widely publicized; the church was tainted and stunned.

"How does living here compare to living at home?"

"Well, you are one paycheck away from being homeless here. At home I am at least assured of a home, plus I had help for the house and at the farm."

Dr. Kanuma has a nostalgic smile on his face as he tells of the workers he could afford at home. He could have at least a helper in the house to cook and keep the house and others in the farm. He would not have to mow his own lawn or clean up his house, chores which he must do by himself now. Asked what advice he would give to someone in Rwanda who was trying to come to the United States; whether he would encourage or discourage him/her, Dr Kanuma responds that he would not give a blanket advice; it would depend on the individual and his/her needs. "For someone who is looking forward to getting married and having a family, I would say this is not the right place for them. This is because finding a suitable partner with similar background and interests would be difficult, especially for ladies. Men have a little bit more leeway."

"Does this concern you as a parent of college students who may soon be seeking partners?"

"Not really. You see, my children grew up here. They went to elementary and high school here and are now in college. So they're familiar with the system of dating here."

Dr. Kanuma declares that there was no dating in Rwanda; it was a family affair. "You know this family, they know you. Your family has married from their family for a long time, and they have married from your family for a long time. So you marry from them again." It would therefore be very difficult for someone from Rwanda to come and start dating here and get married.

MR. CHIBANDA

Mr. Chibanda is a Malawian in his late forties. The whole family was in the garage of their magnificent suburban home, cleaning up when I arrived for the interview. He ushered me into his office on the backside of the house and offered soft drinks to share as we talked. A strikingly neatly kept house contained splendid furniture.

Mr. Chibanda had come to the United States in the early 1980s with his wife, who was then a model, to visit his sister-in-law who was living in the United States at that time. Before returning to Malawi, he learned of the educational opportunities in the United States and so he later returned to pursue a bachelor's degree in finance, something he says he had always wanted to do in Malawi but could not due to lack of such a program in Malawi at that time. The public university was the only one in Malawi, which made matriculation quite competitive; and even after one got in, the school did not offer many courses. "I could only get a diploma in accounting (the equivalent of an associate degree in the United States) but not the bachelor's that I wanted."

Mr. Chibanda obtained a bachelor's degree in finance and then decided to stay and work in the United States "for the sake of the children so that they could get similar educational opportunities here. If I took the children back to Malawi, they would have slim chances of making it to the university due to limited opportunities, which results in stiff competition."

Mr. Chibanda is another product of limited educational opportunities in his country in Africa. He has benefited from the abundant educational prospects in the United States and would willingly do what it takes to extend similar opportunities to his children to avoid "stiff competition" for the few spots available in the education system at home.

Mr. Chibanda now works for a business marketing firm as an auditor in Seattle, Washington. Prior to that, he was an accountant with an auditing firm in the same city. In his home country of Malawi, he had been an accountant with the government; then he worked for a private firm and briefly for the World Bank.

"How would you compare your work experience here versus your work in Malawi in terms of remuneration, working conditions, and job satisfaction?"

"The pay is better here than it is in Malawi, though there are more benefits back in Malawi: fringe benefits such as free housing, car, and gasoline expenses for individuals with similar rank and profession. But there were also unfavorable working conditions, such as expatriate employees who got more benefits, such as children's tuition paid by employer and got paid nearly twice as much as local Malawians with comparable qualifications."

Faint but noticeable anger marks his tone as Mr. Chibanda describes the preferential treatment expatriates received over himself and his fellow Malawians. He would be very reluctant to quit his present job and go back to this perceived unfair discrimination in his own country. How such bias could still be prevalent several years after independence from colonialism is difficult to imagine.

Mr. Chibanda states that the main advantage of living in the United States is that "it offers educational opportunities for the children and for anyone who wants it. There is opportunity to be anything you want to be and achieve anything you want to achieve."

Besides, better health facilities exist in the United States. "Back in Malawi, if one gets seriously ill but does not have money to go to South Africa, there is little hope for survival," he says pensively. "The hospitals do not have enough equipment, like the machines that 'jumpstart' the heart."

Those who are well off, like government ministers, go to South Africa for treatment. Not enough personnel are available either: doctors or nurses. The nurses would rather migrate to England for better pay and working conditions than stay in Malawi. "I was talking with a friend at work, and she asked, 'Are you from Malawi?' and I said, 'Yes!' She then said she read in the papers that there are only 356 nurses left in Malawi. The whole country has only 356 nurses left! One hospital reportedly had one nurse to thirty women in labor! One nurse to thirty women in labor!" he exclaims.

"The other main problem is lack of political freedom. Malawi was a dictatorship under Kamuzu Banda. There was only one party and Kamuzu was its president." Kamuzu Banda declared himself "president for life." Mr. Chibanda says that everyone had to join the Malawi National Congress Party by buying a membership card, without which one could not travel on buses, buy from the markets, and the like. "It was forced membership."

"What would happen if one refused to buy the card? How would they enforce that requirement?"

"Kamuzu ruled with an iron fist. He had a bunch of youth all over the country, called 'the Young Pioneers.' They would harass and even beat up anyone who resisted buying party membership. They would also force people to attend Kamuzu's political rallies, and you could get killed if you resisted! Since it was a one-party dictatorship, we had no say. No opposition was tolerated. In fact, Kamuzu's political opponents were either killed or they fled the country. If Kamuzu was going to, say, Sacramento for a state function, children would have no school that day; they would instead line up the side of the road and cheer him and wait till he came back at the end of the day, and cheer him again! Anyone who dared oppose him was imprisoned or killed or roughed up by 'the Young Pioneers.'"

Mr. Chibanda is definitely in shock at the way health services have deteriorated in his country. It seems to confirm his pessimism about things not getting better soon. Limited educational opportunities, political freedom, or lack of it, seem to have either directly or indirectly influenced his decision to not return: directly by being oppressive, making it unappealing to live in Malawi; indirectly by promoting poor governance, which in turn has resulted in inadequate educational opportunities, leaving children with little prospect for academic attainment. Limited access to quality education is detrimental to success in life.

On the other hand, one faces challenges living in the United States. The greatest nightmare is that of raising children in a different culture where they do not easily learn to speak their native language, a key link with their people at home. "There is also the fear of kids getting into drugs or gangs. Immigration policies are tough, making it difficult to work and keep one's status legal. One also experiences some covert (racial) discrimination, which exists but is hard to prove as they are quite subtle in nature." This resembles George's experiences with "lack of respect" and racism.

Mr. Chibanda states that the main advantages of living in Malawi is the close family ties. "Right now, this is my community; but this house is all that's mine. Nobody knows me, and I don't know anybody that well in the neighborhood. If this were home, I would know everyone on this block by name, and they would know me," he states wistfully.

In spite of the said benefits of living in Malawi, the preceding problems are compounded by the frustrations of lack of political freedom in a dictatorial government. Malawi's first postcolonial president has long since been out of power, but Mr. Chibanda and his fellow Malawians who left for the West are deeply rooted in their newfound homes. They cannot easily just pack up and return without pondering several issues, chief among them being educational opportunities for children and the likelihood that the children will live and work here in the United States.

"What are your plans for the future? Are you likely to go work at home?"

"Maybe I'll retire there because with children now in college here..." he pauses uneasily.

"It would be difficult to leave them."

"Yeah, and they are likely to stay. And if grandchildren come... it is something to ponder!"

Even though Kamuzu had declared himself "president for life," he did not die a president. International pressure forced him to allow opposition parties, followed by an election that he lost. So, have things changed for the better? "Only a little bit," says Mr. Chibanda, adding that "there is still corruption; and the opposition is easily bribed and weakened. There is corruption here, too, but they're rich first. And because they are rich, the effects of corruption are not felt as much as it is felt at home. The poverty there increases corruption."

"What can be done to solve Malawi's problems; can you help best from here or by being there?"

"The situation can't change overnight! If you go back with new ideas for change, there will be resistance; and you could get killed," he states candidly.

"So, what will help, what is your vision for Malawi?"

"It would be better to train children, the younger generation, to become better statesmen and women."

"Do you see this happening?"

"It is possible but will take time; it will take time."

Even though Kamuzu Banda is long gone and a new government is in place, corruption and poverty still exist —such poverty that Mr. Chibanda would feel uncomfortable living decently with so many people suffering around him. Therefore, he, thinks of home as a place of retirement although he foresees himself getting tied down here while his three daughters, now in college, "are likely to marry and settle down here; and if they have grandchildren, then…" he winces in uncertainty. His belief that going back to Africa to try to change things could get one killed is quite in agreement with Dr. Kanuma's statement that the system "will crash you" or change you to be like them.

8

REFORM WARRIOR

DR. OMARI

Dr. Onyango Omari speaking at a youth-mentoring conference at the All Nations African Church of Seventh-Day Adventists, San Bernardino, California. Seated next to him is Dr. Larry Rutebuka, and far right is President Obama's Senior Advisor Wale Adeyemo Photo by the author, August 2015.

D r. Onyango Omari is a dental surgeon from Kenya. He has had vast experience teaching health related subjects at the public university's school of medicine, while also being actively involved in the country's volatile political process. He is a warrior in the war of reforms, and like most warriors, Dr. Omari is not without his wounds. His story focuses on a time when the country was trying to rewrite its constitution to better serve the needs of Kenyans while making the government more accountable to the people. This is something that the government reluctantly and grudgingly allowed.

Before allowing such reforms, government agents roughed up people like Dr. Omari who were involved in pushing for change. Eventually, some change was realized, and Daniel Moi, Kenya's second president in 40 years of independence, was removed from power after 24 years as president and 12 years prior to that as vice-president. He was replaced, however, by his one-time vice president Mwai Kibaki, who is one of the old guards and perceived by many as a representation of the status quo.

Dr. Omari was addressing a group of his fellow Kenyans, lamenting the pathetic political situation in their country. He said he had gone beyond the stage of lamentations. He now was in a new phase and had rewritten the book of *Lamentations.* He wanted to know what others thought about the problems and how to solve them.

One person said what would help was to have Moi's defeated party K.A.N.U. reorganized as a strong opposition party and hold the party that was then in power accountable. One lady said that the only thing that would save Kenya was a revolution, which would serve as a purging wake-up call to the leaders that people are tired of their wicked ways. Another companion said he had despaired reading about the problems in Kenya and it appeared there was "no visible way out as corruption and tribalism were deeply embedded in the leaders' bone marrows."

It was then Dr. Omari disclosed his new vision for Kenya, a vision of moral leadership whereby leaders would be held accountable to some preset moral standards and would be automatically disqualified from leadership if they violated these moral values. This dialogue provided a fitting backdrop to my interview with Dr. Omari, which started soon after the others' departure.

"I was involved in improving terms of service for university lecturers, and when that did not go down well with the government, the government dismissed all the leadership."

"You mean you were involved in a labor union type of organization?" I asked curiously.

"A labor union, formation of a union to agitate for better terms for the lecturers, and the government refused to register the union, then went ahead and dismissed the union leadership," he states reflectively.

"The government dismissed them from university employment?"

"From university employment! So, we were actually rendered jobless."

"Was that for a specific university, or all of the public universities?"

"All the public universities in Kenya: Nairobi, Kenyatta, Moi, and Egerton Universities."

Dr. Omari and his colleagues found themselves jobless in Kenya and were forced to move outside the country beginning with the fateful union's leadership, followed by sympathizing lectures who sought greener pastures elsewhere "because they felt that their efforts were not well remunerated," he states somberly. "We lost very key members, highly trained and experienced professors leaving Kenya to various universities inside and outside of Africa. To the best of my knowledge, not many have gone back since then."

Dr. Omari taught Health Services Management and Health Administration Services to both undergraduate and post-graduate medical students studying public health. He was also trained as a Dental Surgeon and practiced this for a few years before starting his teaching career. Asked what he is doing now, Dr. Omari replies, "I'm in the process of going back to my profession. There are several examinations to do. I've done a number, and I'm left with a number to do so I can go back to practice. But while waiting, I am involved in research in my first area of training, which is dentistry, and on dental materials."

Dr. Omari is back to a stage he had passed in his previous life, the stage of being a student before he can practice dentistry or teach public health in the United States, mainly due to intolerance of contrary political views.

"You were saying a number of factors are responsible for brain drain. Could you address these factors?"

"One major factor is that the government is insensitive to people who have been highly trained in terms of putting together an attractive package to them. Secondly, the government is intolerant to their views. They find it very difficult to welcome those people's views, which of course are born out of their training! Through their training, they have come across theories, practices, and procedures that they think can make things better, but the government is not ready to follow these procedures. These people have not been trained in the abstract but in their various disciplines. A medical person is trained in medicine; a teacher has been trained in teaching; a lawyer, the same. So, these professionals are saying, 'OK let's offer practical advice to the government, based on our training.' But the government is not ready for it. Another thing is that many people find that there is no room to further their careers in research; there's a lot of demand for an academician to continue doing research so they can expand their knowledge in their area. Opportunities for research are very limited in the country," he states, sounding much like the intellectual he is.

"And why is that so? Why the limitation?"

"Well, the universities have not been geared toward operational research, applied research, where research is taken to the industry to help improve various aspects of production. So, one feels frustrated: 'I didn't go to school just to have book knowledge. I want to put it into practice.' And that seems not catered for; if it is catered for, it is to a very small extent."

"I'd like to hear more about this!"

"Any developed country, any country that has had industrial take-off, relies very heavily on institutions of higher learning for ideas, experiment, innovation, and discovery. And the academia feels challenged and useful when they're given problems to solve, ideas to develop, and programs to come up with. So, when that is missing, they sort of feel that they have been reduced to a very narrow aspect of their discipline."

"What happens when the professors in Kenya say they want to engage in this kind of research?"

"Well, one has to go through a lot of bureaucracy. If you want to write a proposal for funding, you must first go through a lot of red tape and get approved even before you can apply for funding. Secondly, when you get funding approved, there's even much more red tape to go through to get the money released to you, to continue with the funding. Thirdly, the government does not feel obliged to even support your application for funding, such that you can strengthen the case by saying, 'Hey look! This research is going to help the country in this and that manner,' in order to be fully funded. Thus, people feel that they're left on their own to fight for this money. Even if they get it, too many hands now want to control the money. This becomes very, very difficult. We have not developed the culture of encouraging research."

"Now, going back to number two--government intolerance to professors' views; could you elaborate with a few examples?"

"This owes to the fact that Kenya has not developed a strong democratic culture. Any views opposing the government are considered very negatively. The government becomes very agitated when a contrary view is expressed, like a proposed change in curriculum. Such a change would not be viewed as an academic exercise but as a political statement and therefore twisted out of context. Very soon you may find that you're being attacked for giving your views on a subject instead of being encouraged or instead of your views being considered and you being asked to elaborate so that people can understand what you mean. That's one. Number two, the university being an institution of higher learning, you would expect the students to be better informed than the general public and see more than the general public. But such views on procedures and paractices are not considered as contributing to the pool of good governance but as destructive ones from people opposed to the government for their own self-interest. And the government normally says, 'these individuals are being told by somebody to do this,'" Dr. Omari states regretfully.

Repressive government, poor funding for research, and poor remuneration for professors and lecturers appear here again as major causes of brain drain. Professors do not work in a free academic environment that offers professional satisfaction. Rather, they lack freedom of speech, are poorly paid, and their programs under-funded. This deadly combination of factors is sure to ruin the morale of any professional. By fighting rather than supporting its academia, the said government has hurt the country's development efforts, thereby reducing its own ability to offer better pay which in turn leads to a vicious cycle of brain drain.

"Now, a little while ago you were talking about your lamentations; could you tell me more about it; what're you lamenting?"

"First of all, I said I've gone out of lamentation, but I can tell you what I was lamenting before I went out of it." We both laughed as I encouraged him to proceed and tell.

"My greatest lamentation is that Kenya is endowed with a lot of resources. I believe Kenya can easily be a superpower in Africa, considering what it has been endowed with. My lamentation is that after almost 50 years of being given the chance to chart our own course as a country, we have very little to show for it! Very little that is positive, that is sustainable. All we have is failed projects, stalled projects, and numerous cases of misappropriation. All sorts of examples of how you should not do things. And that has caused me a lot of pain."

One can indeed hear the pain in his voice. Dr. Omari sounds like he was quoting Dr. Uche, another subject who lamented how "Nigeria is endowed with numerous resources, human and otherwise, yet we have nothing to show for it."

The similarity of their statements is incredible, suggesting the truthfulness of their content. Both countries are truly rich in agricultural and mineral resources as well as highly educated human resources. Yet, largely due to poor management of these resources, tribalism, and nepotism, both countries are languishing near the foot of the development ladder. This surely does cause pain to many professionals and nonprofessionals from said countries and other African countries similarly afflicted. No wonder Dr. Omari is "going into and out of lamentations."

"The other thing that has caused pain to me is that I have spent a good part of my productive life trying to bring about meaningful change in Kenya, in my own small way. And up to this point, I still feel that I can't show a lot for my efforts."

"You see no tangible results!"

"There's nothing I can pinpoint and say, 'Yes! This has changed because I stuck out my neck for it.' That has been the basis of most of my lamentations. But what makes me lament the most is that for a long time I've not been seeing light at the end of the tunnel. It has been like one dark journey, with no end in sight...

"I spent quite a bit of time thinking about that and enumerating the many reasons why I feel sad that things have not changed. I have now turned another leaf. I have started asking, 'What are some things that have happened that are positive?' One positive thing is that we have demonstrated that we can bring about positive change. That's extremely significant because a few years back, it looked impossible. Kenyans lived in hopelessness that these things could not be changed, that these people were too powerful. We have demonstrated that things can change."

Dr. Omari says that his current preoccupation is to ensure that we do not remove one bad government from power and replace it with an equally bad one. "This would be very disheartening to most Kenyans. They would lose faith in the election system. They'll say it's a futile exercise. We need to be very careful who will replace the current president, because we do not want Kenyans to tell us, 'This thing doesn't work; leave us alone!'"

Unfortunately, his fears just came true since the government that succeeded Kibaki's has been plagued with one corruption scandal after another, to the point that the economy is sagging, and the shilling has lost much of its value against major international currencies. Many individuals now do not want to participate in the political process, stating that the election process is always rigged anyway and their voting or not voting will not make a difference when the result is predetermined.

"Right! Could you mention some of the things you've done? You said you've spent a lot of time trying to bring about positive change. Can you give an example what you have done?"

"Right now, at a personal level, I've gone back to the drawing board, to address various tangible ways of bringing about meaningful change in Kenya. I'm trying to solicit ideas from people in a manner that enables me to fine tune those ideas that I think can work. I'm hoping that, at the end of the day a few of us of like-minds can put together some protocol that can be used to bring about meaningful, sustainable change in Kenya."

"OK, that's what you're doing now, but in the past what did you do that you felt was not successful?"

"After the government refused to register our union in 1993, a number of us who remained in Kenya resolved to join other groups of like-minds and formed several pressure groups, if I may call them, to push forward the agenda for change. Many of those pressure groups, called SEES called for constitutional change. We formed National Convention Executive Committee (NCEC), and through those bodies we put together groups of people who were interested in seeing change in Kenya." He narrates almost nostalgically how he and his like-minded team pressured the Kenyan government to change the constitution "because our constitution had been revised so many times that it had lost meaning. So, we forced the government to implement what we called minimum constitutional reforms before the 1997 general elections. The major breakthrough was that we prevailed upon the government to institute a constitution-writing body which put together a draft constitution by the end of March this year. In a way I feel that, though the changes have not been where I wanted them to be, we have made progress by moving to a point where we have a draft constitution."

Dr. Omari served as the chairman for mass action for N.C.E.C. His duties were to organize Kenyans for mass action demonstrations to force the government to agree to constitutional change. "We held very successful meetings in Nairobi and around the country that were fruitful, and it is actually out of one of those meetings that, uh, the government decided to arrest me, and that's how I decided to leave the country."

Dr. Omari narrates how an arrest warrant was issued for him because of his role in organizing such a meeting and so he escaped. "Uh…, I escaped from the country," he narrates haltingly. "It was in the newspapers; it was not a rumor! I'll give you a copy if you want. They went to the offices of N. C. E. C. looking for me; I was not there. They went to my house; I was not there. They left a report that I should report to the police headquarters in Nairobi. Knowing the police department as I did, I did not think I would achieve much by going there."

Why Dr. Omari chose to flee the country rather than report to police headquarters is easy to understand: avoid torture in police detention. Yet the changes for which Dr. Omari and his like-minded colleagues are fighting would make Kenya a better place for everyone, including the police and their families. It is noteworthy that many of them do serve with honor.

"So, you fled the country?"

"Yeah! I escaped the country, came to this country, sought political asylum, and I believe I'm among the very first few Kenyans to be awarded political asylum in the United States."

"How did you escape?"

"Ah, it's a long story. The short of it is that I escaped to a neighboring country. From there I got assistance from one of the human rights organizations, which processed my travel documents, and I came here."

Dr. Omari admits that this was indeed a very challenging experience: "I stayed for two years without my family, and with a young family that was tough. My wife had lost her job because of my involvement in the constitutional change process."

His wife had been a manager in one of the private organizations and was victimized because of his political activism. "If you understand how the system worked at that time, if you were on the 'wrong' side of the government, you were not safe anywhere, whether private or public sector. The private sector somehow interfaced with the government and did not want to attain any label as the rebel. So, one day she lost her job with no explanation! She could not be hired by anybody who wanted to keep his or her job also. While some of us decided to stay in the country, if I may mention, we were not only unemployed, but we actually became unemployable. No sane employer would hire some like us, no matter our qualifications. The government had a very elaborate machinery, to beat anybody to submission."

"But eventually you succeeded in bringing about change!"

"We succeeded! Out of sheer determination. Because given the facilities at our disposal, it is amazing what a determined will can do! Quite amazing, because all those people who participated in bringing about change were not a threat to the government, beyond their mere words and determination."

"What was the government doing that you wanted to be changed?"

"Many things! One, the governance was definitely wrong; it was too heavy. All decisions were centralized in one person, so whatever he said weighs. The president was everything: he was chief executive, planning officer, finance minister, minister of education, legal adviser to himself," he states, laughing heartily.

"He did everything, and I mean everything. He honored no institution. The separation of powers between the executive, the legislature, and the judiciary was completely eroded in the country. And I'm afraid this is coming back under the current government, too. Employment was not based on merit but on whom you knew and what tribe you belonged. Government projects were not based on who is competent but on who knows whom. And I can go down the line. And the government had infiltrated human life up to the village level, under the provincial administration system, which was controlled by the Office of the President. So, whatever you did, even at your own house, was monitored through the local sub-chief, all the way from local up to the central government.

"The government permeated everything that happened in the country. Even freedom of speech and association were controlled: a meeting could not be held without a permit from the government! And if the government agents said the meeting did not meet its criteria, they cancelled it! To top it off, the government became excessively corrupt, too much corruption to even think about.

"Resources were wasted, to the extent that the common man did not receive basic services! There are no roads; if they are there, they're in tatters. No hospital facilities; a patient might go to the wards but could not get treatment! All the doctor could do was diagnose and prescribe; beyond that they could do nothing. Schools existed but were empty. Everything service delivered by the government existed in form but not in substance. In other words, the government was operating way below expectations of the electorate!"

The similarities between this case and that of Dr. Uche are quite striking. Dr. Omari makes a direct link between a failed system and a despotic government. Dr. Uche, who appears elsewhere in this book, implies such a link. But the result is the same: a total collapse of infrastructure and social and health services, to an extent that the situation is "impossible" to live and thrive in. One is forced to either stay and function below potential or leave the country to seek opportunities abroad. Many African professionals have opted for the latter, compounding the brain drain. Even more pathetic is the fact that those who have seen the need for positive change and reform are seen as a threat to the government and therefore brutally victimized. The situation is literally out of control, to the point doctors, teachers, and other professionals have repeatedly gone on strike, sometimes for several weeks, leaving behind the ordinary Kenyans in pathetic lack of healthcare and other crucial services while the overpaid politicians go to England for medical care and send their children abroad for education.

"So, those were your lamentations!"

"Yeah. Before I got involved in bringing about change, I lamented a lot. And then I said, 'No, this is not going to work. I need to get involved in bringing about change no matter at what level. We started to move people to act. From 1992 when the opposition lost elections, it took us three years to move people to action. The first successful meeting we had about the constitution was in 1995! That's when we produced the first draft ever of the constitution."

"It took time and sacrifice!"

"Yeah. Three years! And from 1995 to 97 we were basically challenging people to join. But they were too afraid! Some were afraid; others felt hopeless that these things could not be done. So, by 97 we were at the climax! If we had continued at that level, we would have brought about a lot of changes in the country.

Unfortunately, it didn't happen yet, we got what we call minimum reforms, and that's what has remained up to now."

For several months, Kenya was engulfed in an extended political wrangle over the constitutional review process. The Kenyan people asked for the constitution to be rewritten and adapted, but the government was playing delaying tactics because it might include major changes which would erode much of the president's powers. The president could not stand the idea. In 2003, the chairman of this constitution review committee, a law professor at one of the public universities, was gunned down in cold blood by what is largely believed to be government agents trying to slow down or stall the process. He was a very close friend to Dr. Omari, who went for several days without food after learning of the tragic incident, part of his lamentations. The professor's assassination left his department scrambling to find replacement, and his young wife and children without a husband and father.

"So, now you're in the second phase of action."

"Yes, after moving out of the country and lamenting all these years, I've now decided I want to start acting again. I want to start putting ideas together for another plan for a meaningful change of the country. Dr. Omari states that the government is still underperforming and is engaged "in doing the wrong thing for the country, in corruption, in resurrecting tribalism and nepotism...all these things that are not positive."

"So, where do you see us going in the next few years?"

"We need to go back to the drawing board. We need to look at this thing from a completely different perspective. Personally, I don't believe we can expect much out of the current crop of leaders in the country because, unfortunately, they've all been socialized through the same system. Those who are in opposition now are the same people who were in K.A.N.U. under the previous president. If the current leadership is removed, K.A.N.U. will come back in another form. I do not think that K.A.N.U. has gone through any change that will bring about meaningful reforms in the country. The same story will be repeated, even in worse dimensions. My current thinking is that we need to convince ourselves to chart a different course, completely different, one that has not been tried before, something innovative. I have not put my finger on it yet, but..."

"You talked about moral leadership. How can we achieve that?"

"That's my current thinking! I have not fully collated my ideas into a form that I can present to people, but I do feel the only way to go now is to enforce a moral code on our leaders and hold them to it! What we need to work on is the mechanism of enforcing that moral code, so that leaders know, 'If I cross this line, I have said bye-bye to leadership.' That's what I think can work. But it is not for me alone: it is for everyone to think about, so we can come up with a workable idea."

"How doable do you think this is?"

"I strongly believe it is doable because, as a person, I operate on one maxim: if it can be done, it has to be done."

"Is there anything else you want to say on brain drain? What is its impact on Kenyan society and economy, for example?"

"It is very saddening to think about the effects of brain drain in our country!" Dr. Omari says insightfully. "As I said earlier, no country can have an economic take off, an industrial take off, unless it has a critical mass of trained manpower. At present Kenya does not have the luxury of losing even the little trained resources it has to any other country, because it needs more. A certain critical mass must exist before individuals can become effective. Besides, it takes a lot to train one person until that person becomes an authority in his field. It takes a long, long, time! Normally the people who leave the country, any country, because of brain drain, are the top cream! You know! The professors, assistant professors, and associate professors-- those are the first ones to go. These people have almost reached the top and are at a position to deliver in their fields of training. When their skills are lost, miles are lost, and we are several steps behind! This is a cycle that feeds on itself; it spirals. People can't be trained because trainers are not available. Development cannot happen without trained people, but professional trainers cannot be retained without development. So, we go back to square one, and we cannot develop. The country doesn't have all that time. The problems in Kenya cannot wait for people to be trained to solve them; the problems keep increasing!"

Thus Dr. Omari sums up Kenya's dire situation quite succinctly.

9

AN IMMIGRANT'S DILEMMA

WARIBAH'S TALE OF LIVING ON TWO CONTINENTS

Waribah is from Cameroon, West Africa, where he attended school and college and graduated with a B.A. degree in business administration. I asked Mr. Waribah to tell me the story of his journey to the United States.

His home church organization recruited him and a few others and sent them abroad to train as business and finance managers for the church system. Prior to his selection, he had been selling books in the Scandinavians in order to raise money for further studies. He remitted the money thus earned to his sister who was then living in the US. His sister helped him gain admission to a midwestern university in the mid-1980s. The private university proved to be too expensive, so Waribah transferred to a public university, where he earned an M.B.A. degree two years later.

"I was always curious to find out what was on the West Coast, so I moved to Oregon in 1987 and got stuck here," Waribah adds with an exasperated sigh.

"You got stuck here! There is a connotation of one part of you wanting to leave, and another part wanting to stay."

"Yes! Yes, I've always wanted to go back—"

"You've always wanted to go back to Cameroon?"

"Yes, I've always wanted to go. Number one, what I studied would have been very good for Cameroon. But when you are here, the tradition is discrimination." Waribah recounts how he had wanted to work for a major multinational retail corporation which was then hiring managers for various newly opened branches. He is confident he had excellent qualification, references, and everything, "but these people would not hire me! And they would hire people much less qualified than me, but they wouldn't hire me! I said, 'wait a minute, what is this?' Later someone told me, 'They don't want to hire you with your qualifications because after you stay there for ten years and a bigger post opens, they would have to give it to you. Yet they don't want you at the top where key decisions are made."

Waribah tried several places but received similar reception. Many other businesses were family-owned, and family members held management positions. He found the experience quite frustrating. The only job he was offered was as an auditor in a big city that was sixty miles from his residence. The long daily commute was stressful. His blood pressure rose, and he became quite irritable. Friends and family advised him to quit the job, which he did. Later he was offered a job as a counselor in a group home, which was convenient for family life, with children coming into the picture. Waribah adds that he wants to move from Oregon to the East Coast because he feels it would be easier for him as an African man to get a job in the East.

"It seems like the people on the East Coast are much more used to foreigners, or Africans, or something. Even the Africans in the East Coast are quite different from the Africans in the West Coast, because most of them came to work and earn money, then go home and invest; but the people on the West Coast are living normally, if you watch. And maybe it's because East coast is closer to Africa, so that's the first point they get to. Some people get to New York or Baltimore, and they don't get further. We even went there to check it out, but when you have lived on the West Coast, most of the other states are not very appealing," Waribah states confidently.

Frustration drove Mr. Waribah to find a job well below and outside his qualifications in a totally unrelated field. Besides, it provided a convenient schedule for family life. Waribah is an epitome of phenomenon referenced by one pastor; that Africans are under-employed in the US while they could be serving in more useful positions in their home countries.

A few years later, Waribah made a drastic decision to move back to Cameroon with his children. He states that this move was an experiment to test the waters. To find out how well the children could tolerate "the inconveniences back home. I mean the inconsistent supply of services such as electricity, water, etc. Nothing is guaranteed. Power can go out anytime without any warning and can stay out for several hours!"

"How are the children taking it, so far?"

"The children have adjusted well and like it there; they do not want to come back."

"I know you are at a transition point whereby you're deciding whether to relocate to Cameroon or not. If you were to return to stay, what would you do?"

"Right now, where I am, I would start my own business."

"Do you have an idea what business?"

"Umm, uh, we have not pinned down what we want to do, but our options are wide. I was talking to a friend, and we were looking at computers and retail and transportation. The opportunities are there. Some people are doing businesses there and are able to pay their children's fees here!"

"So, if you did that, would you go with the whole family or would you be there by yourself?"

"Well, initially no, but very soon, yes. We still want to see how the children adjust."

Mr. Waribah is seriously contemplating returning to stay, but he still has one foot stuck here and another foot in Cameroon, which he fondly regards as home. He wants to sell the house and either buy a bigger one or move to Cameroon. On one hand, Waribah has had quite a frustrating experience living in America, as shown in his experiences when searching for employment. On the other hand, he feels that the system here works better and "a lot can be learned," which could be used to help bring about development at home. The problem, however, is that the system back home is rooted in what he calls "the old order," of corruption, bribery, and inefficiency—making it even more frustrating because leadership does not want change.

At the government level, deeply rooted corruption and inefficiency exist. Having to bribe one's way through the system in order to establish a business causes frustration. The infrastructure is inefficient, with an unreliable utility supplies that can mean the extended interruption of water or power at any time without warning. These realities hurt business and make life difficult for Waribah and individuals like him who are aspiring to do business in Cameroon.

Another disturbing factor is political instability. Many African countries have experienced *coup d'états*, followed by civil unrest. This creates an environment of fear and uncertainty, making many potential returnees indefinitely postpone their return home. They fear the money they have spent so much time and effort to earn could easily disappear in such unstable political atmospheres. This applies to potential investors, too.

"Other than inadequate utilities, what concerns would you have when returning home?"

"Another major concern is the number of youths with education but no prospective job opportunities to absorb them. They may resort to crime, as is already happening in other parts of Africa. Part of what I was telling you of the people in the East Coast is that you could find them working and sleeping even six people in a room while they are saving. When they go home, they have money. They are showing off money left and right [in] their dressing, cars, and everything! But we in the West Coast are buying houses here in the US; they invest at home and buy houses there. When you go home people will be asking, 'Where is the money? You came from the American money tree?'" he states, laughing.

"How do they invest the money there?"

"They buy houses."

"Who lives in their houses back home?"

"Some of them nobody lives in, except the watchman; some of them their relatives live in; some of them, they call 'funeral homes,'" states Waribah, laughing, "because you don't come home frequently; and when you die in the US is when they ship your body home and perform a funeral service there."

"Do you think building and investing at home are helping develop the country better than those who are buying homes here?"

"Yes, because they are sending money home. Think of a university like *Vue de Montagne* in Cameroon, where the tuition is now almost US$1,000 a quarter. But student enrolment is up, and the reason is that almost every family has someone over here in the US who is sending tuition to their relatives. I don't know about other African countries' nationals, but we have Cameroonian associations, like those of us from Yaoundé; we have an association, and we support projects back home. Last time we contributed money and decided we were going to put lights, poles, and electricity on the streets," Waribah declares with understandable satisfaction.

"How much did that take?"

"About ten thousand dollars! And I understand the people in England are helping in a similar way. I understand Nigerians and Ghanaians are doing the same. Right now, my family and I, my brothers and sisters, we are building a school right now in my dad's hometown."

The community back home receives undisputed benefits. Students with relatives abroad can afford to pay high tuition in a private university, an opportunity they would be denied were it not for the support of relatives who went and remained abroad. Those living and working abroad also fund such projects as streetlight installations and school building. It is doubtful that they would be able to support these projects if they were living in their home country limited by reduced wages and income and choked by the vice of corruption.

"Is working for the church something that you would still consider?"

"Oh yes, oh yes..." Waribah is momentarily lost in thought, then adds, "Many pastors have come to study in the US. They go through the schools but never go back. I personally do not have a problem with those who do not return; the only people I have a problem with are those who get sponsored by the church and fail to honor their obligation to return and serve, finding all sorts of excuses to not return. That's wrong, you see. I am on my own, I sponsored myself through school, and I decided to stay here. I'm not bothering with anybody!"

Possible feelings of culpability are revealed here, too. Waribah appears to feel that he has run away from the call to serve God, like Jonah of the Bible. This feeling is dealt with by acknowledging the need to work for the church, then uneasily but quickly shifting the blame onto those who stay in the West after being sponsored by the church back home. The fact that he did not receive sponsorship is therefore a comfortable exoneration. He states that the church organization in Cameroon has now stopped sponsoring students to study in the United States due to the high default rate.

"Right now, what they do is to reimburse you, and some people still abuse that," he observes.

"Do you think the mass exodus of Cameroonian pastors to the West is a problem to the church there?"

"Oh yes! The church is exploding but the workers are running away."

"What is your vision for Cameroon? Which direction would you like to see Cameroon go, and how?"

"My vision for Cameroon is to see that the Cameroon government facilitates the return of those who came here, even if they don't want to return, but to make it easier to establish businesses for the development of the country," Waribah states reflectively.

"Do you think that this development will happen if they return?"

"Yes, oh yes. It will help to even create jobs. So many people who have money and want to go, but then most of Africa is unstable. Tomorrow there's a coup here, a coup there; there's this there's that. You can't guarantee anything. You invest your money there; you may lose it! Unemployed people become armed robbers! People finish university but they can't find jobs. I was telling a friend of mine when I went to the Statehouse that if I could find a minute with the president, I would tell him, 'You need to establish a very serious dynamic department that will lobby Western companies to bring jobs, to bring manufacturing, to bring business into Cameroon. Give them tax breaks, give them everything because from New York to West Africa are direct flights! If China and Korea and India make things and sell to the US, we can do it too. We now have skilled labor everywhere you go, computers everywhere. People have been trained. So, they need to send investors here, and we can tell them, 'We'll cut your labor costs by 80 percent, so bring your business here and employ the people,'" he concludes.

Mr. Waribah asserts that his role in this vision for Cameroon is to be a success story as a businessman whom people will look up to and emulate. If his business picks up and he is able to live in Cameroon and pay tuition for his kids in America, then he will have realized the dream. But for now, he is still 'stuck here.'

10

WOMEN

LAURA

S he is a single mother of five, from Nigeria. At the time of our interview, her first-born son had just completed medical school, while the last-born girl is still in high school. The medical school graduate welcomed me warmly to their nice new house, with drinks and articulate conversation while we awaited the arrival of his mother, who is a nurse practitioner, holding several other degrees. They are evidently holding on to their African cultural values, including a strong belief in pursuing higher education. Presently the mother enters the room, and the son quietly retreats to the living room. Laura talks with her children in their native Nigerian language of Yoruba, which they understand more than speak.

Laura came to the United States in the 1970s to join her fiancé. They had had a traditional marriage in Nigeria two years earlier, and then he left to pursue further education in North Carolina. She states that the traditional marriage is performed between the family of the bride and that of the groom: "if the families agree that the marriage take place, there are celebrations." They then legalized their marriage in a court of law, and after Laura completed nursing school, she joined her husband in Charlotte. "I came here with a green card," she asserts proudly.

Laura is one of the few cases that did not come to the United States to pursue education, yet she has had more education than most. She came to the United States as an RN but now has a doctoral degree as a health professional. She has gone probably as high as one can go in her career, to a managerial position, quite a remarkable achievement for one who has been raising five children as a single mother. She credits a strong family foundation and the support she had back in Nigeria as what enabled her to accomplish this much. Ironically, Laura came specifically to get married to her fiancé but now is a single mother raising her children alone, having divorced the man she came to marry.

Now Laura is the Director of Health Services of suburban community hospital where she works. Despite evidently having worked hard and climbing to the top rank in her profession, she is very humble about it. "It's been about 30 years! And in my case, I attribute it to luck. The reason I say that is because there are many people in my category who did not have the same opportunities as I did. So, I say, it's luck! Purely."

"And how was the way up?"

"Well, ups and downs, but I consider myself one of the lucky ones. Opportunities will come and go, but I take risks. That's why I consider myself lucky."

"What are some of the risks you took on your way up?"

"First, as a black person, I knew you have to know more, you have to do more to be given half the credit. So, I became seriously more educated, more, you know, go to school, get a Bachelors, get a Masters, even go ahead and get my second Masters, make sure you can maintain the job. In this country as a black person, if you're well educated, it is difficult to push you aside. The people will respect you for what you know."

"You said 'you need to know more to be given half the credit'?"

"Yes! You need to know twice as much to get half the credit!"

"Do you have any specific examples of experiences you have had to illustrate this maxim?"

"For example, in my field, you only require a Bachelor's degree to be a Director of Public Health Services, some even have only Associate, but they're white people. But as a black person, you have to get more and more (education), for them to even trust you with that position!"

"Have you experienced directly or indirectly cases of mistrust or discrimination as a black person?"

"Oh, definitely! Definitely, all along. It's out there. It's out there. Only a person, who wants to be naive, will say there is no whatever. It's out there in a subtle way. For example, whatever position you're entitled to, you don't get it. Even my position! You know, sometimes some doctors will come, they would prefer to talk to the nurse's aide, because they're white and that's whom they're comfortable with and looks to them like should be in charge. And the aide would tell them, 'Go talk to my manager.' And then they come to me; they're shocked! In their mind, you're not even expected to be there!"

"How about in relations to your clients—the patients; have you had any experiences with discrimination?"

"A typical example is when I was working three to eleven. I went in there and the patient said, 'Sorry! No offence to you, but last night I had a Filipino nurse, and this morning I had an Indian nurse, and now a black nurse!' She said, 'I've had it! Are there no white nurses here?'"

"So, it is not just the organization but also the patients!"

"Oh! The patients are worse! Now, the organization is the area I'd say I've been lucky. I've really, really been lucky! When I was getting ready to move up, I did my homework, the education, the enthusiasm, volunteered to do a lot more projects in the hospital research to show that I can excel. So, when I was ready to move up and applied for management position, I had already done the groundwork. I did not experience 'now being given the position.' No!"

"How about your juniors taking orders from you; have you had a problem with that? Are they comfortable with you being their boss?"

Laura states that some of her juniors sometimes have difficulty following her orders and will turn around and talk behind her back. When that happens, she just follows the established policy in dealing with non-compliant employees. She observes, however, that "you don't get as much support as you should," meaning support from the top leadership of the organization.

She also points out the cultural differences that make her work experience less satisfying; "For example, I was telling one of my two white assistants: in this kind of position, if I were in Nigeria, working among my people, I would invite them to my house, and I would know their houses. But as it is now, the extent of our relationship is limited to the job. That takes away something."

Laura agrees with Waribah, Ken, and George about discrimination against blacks and Africans in the American society. But she seems to have had a lot of experience in how to work one's way up despite the discriminative experiences, doing her groundwork carefully as she positioned herself for the upward mobility. She was very careful to not appear like a product of affirmative action that may be seen by some as being incompetent.

"How does healthcare at home compare with healthcare here?"

"You know, Nigeria is a so-called third-world country. From the time we trained, things have deteriorated a lot, instead of getting better! When we were training, we had equipment, we had linen, and we had excellent supplies. And so, when I came here, you know, you feel good about your training, you feel you can compete! And so, that's how I found it. In fact, when I came from Nigeria, I passed my RN board exams right away, fortunately. There are some things you learn along the way, but it wasn't much different. But the gap has really expanded now, looking at those who are just coming."

"How has the situation deteriorated in Nigeria?"

"The economy has substantially declined! When you visit the hospitals, you feel really sad because there is no money! The care they're given is substandard. The physical environment of the hospitals is rundown, there are no bedsheets, and no basic supplies. We used to pride ourselves that even as nurses in the hostel they gave us linen and there were housekeepers who changed our beddings every morning! Now, patients' families must bring their own bedsheets from home! Now if you go to the teaching hospital, the linens are different lower quality print, instead of the beautiful one that the government used to supply."

"Now, Nigeria is one of the leading oil-producing countries in the world. How do you explain the decline in the economy, the lack of money to run institutions like hospitals?"

Laura laughs derisively and then responds, "That's kind of interesting! When you're inside the country, it is different from when you're outside. From the point of view of an insider, the economy is never clear to the common man. You don't know why gasoline prices in Nigeria are higher than they are in America; yet we produce oil."

"You're saying that there is no government transparency."

"I cannot tell you what goes on with the economy of my country. Does the (oil) money come to the general public? The roads are awful; *everything* is in disrepair. How do you explain that? And nobody knows; you don't even know whom to go complain to. There is no transparency."

The frustration and anger in Laura's voice is unambiguous as she laments the disgraceful fall of her country from the once enviable position as a potential economic superpower in Africa, to one of the most ridiculed for its corruption, bribery, and military coups. It is hard to explain how one of the world's leading oil producing and exporting countries is also one of its poorest, with many of its population literally fleeing the country for better life elsewhere. This mysterious gross mismanagement of resources is keeping Laura and her likes away from returning, to stay and build their beloved country.

"What has been your life experience in America, especially as a parent raising children in America?"

"My life… has been a challenge. Life has really, really been a challenge! There is the opportunity to work and get money, have a house, and have transportation, but it's a challenge having a family. Raising children is different. There is lack of family involvement."

"You mean the extended family, the larger family?"

"Yes, the larger family. We're lonely. We're very lonely!"

"What impact does that have on the children?"

"The children fail to experience the things we grew up with, like just being able to walk around the neighborhood freely. No! Here, you raise the kids inside the four corners of your home, and there is a lot that they're missing out, just being raised under your roof. They'll not be able to run around freely, play, walk in the neighborhood, and that kind of thing."

It is quite ironic that Laura came to the United States to get married, but now is divorced and raising children as a single mother, which she finds very challenging. She states that the divorce might have been avoided if they had stayed in Nigeria, where there is a strong family support system.

"So, life as a single parent has been challenging!"

"Life as a single parent, that has been the most difficult and most challenging, because life in America, even between husband and wife, is difficult. You just don't have that little extension that makes life a little easier for you, like taking the kids to the grandparents, and not having to worry about baby-sitters. Here you're taking your children to soccer games. That's fun, but it would be more fun if your other nephews and nieces were there. That's why it is challenging, and it is tough! Really, really tough! Because all these things that two parents are supposed to do, you're still supposed to do them alone."

"Given what they are missing versus what they are gaining by being here, suppose you took the kids back to Nigeria, would that be more beneficial?"

"I have taken all my children to Nigeria. And they went to school there."

"Oh, they did!"

"All of them did, including the last one!"

"How long did she stay?"

"She stayed for 10 months only because my brother died."

"I'm sorry to hear that!"

"Yes, that was the only 'father' whom she was staying with and so it did not work out as I had planned for her to stay for two years. And so, it was my turn to take my brother's children here instead of him taking mine there. It is close family ties we have there. The family ties, the impact of family, is way undermined here."

Laura provides a practical example of the significance of the extended family concept in Africa that Ken and Dr. Uche alluded to. She lives in the United States but prefers that her children learn the Nigerian culture and establish ties with her family back there. Her brother's death reversed the plan, so that she ended up caring for his children. Laura's experience quite illustrates the African proverb, "It takes the whole village to raise a child."

"You said that there was a void in children raised here that you couldn't fill or fathom."

"It is the impact of family. That's what makes us survive here in spite of the pressures we're going through. Even when they are no longer in that environment, the foundation that was laid when we were young makes us. Our children's generation cannot cope the way we do!"

"Now, our children are missing all this! Is it worth it?"

"You lose and gain! Our children are raised with these fancy things, but they lose the touch and the strength that they should get from family and community. They don't have it! Because if my children were put under my conditions, they cannot come out excelling the way you and I do. They're very delicate. They can't! It's not possible. That's why you see the second and subsequent generations of Africans in Americans in jail and all that. If we are not careful, and I'm already seeing this out there!"

"In the African community?"

"In the African community! Our next generation and the one after, they're going to be exactly like the African American! Because they are going to school here, and I have been there, following closely what the kids go through. You just have to be there for them and watch what they are being told and taught. They tell them, 'You're an African, you have a funny name, you are too black, you are too this and that!' How are they coping with that? How much is that destroying them emotionally? They will tell you by high school that they can handle it, but you have to watch! They may easily yield to the peer pressure in order to be accepted. So, we have to watch out."

"We have to watch out because there is danger ahead. What do we do to watch out?"

"We have to have a network in our community, where our children are going to see other Africans and know and feel that they are part of family life. Everybody is an auntie; every man is an uncle in our community, either church, or social, so that my son can see you and come to you and jump on you as an uncle. So that you can just drop off your daughter here any weekend without any question and you just say, 'Go spend the week-end over there with Grandma,' and there's no question. That we open the door for our children.

"We haven't done that. And this women's organization that we have established, we need to bring the children, we need to have functions; we have events, that's why I brought these two kids yesterday. I have not seen these children for I don't know how long! And I just went there and said, 'Let's go with Grandma.' We've got to do that, because our children are growing up not caring about next-door neighbor's children!"

Laura proceeds to narrate how her daughter met someone from our African community in Washington DC, someone from her church. Her daughter excitedly went all out to greet the young woman, only to be shunned and embarrassed by the lady who said, "I don't really know them; it's my mom who is her mom's friend!" Her daughter said, "Mom, I was about to pass out! I said, 'You do not know me, yet we go to the same church!'"

"That's where we've failed. Every parent needs to take that challenge on to raise their kids to be open minded because that neighbor there is your sister, is your brother. I know how busy everybody is, to make time for the little things. But it would help us to do so, in our church and in our community. Organizing a little basketball game for our kids is going to take time, but it's going to be worth it. I'm serious! I'm serious!"

Laura is quite passionate about the issue of raising children in America. Her tone has changed from calm and deliberate to quite excited and serious as she addresses this subject. That she is talking from personal life experience is evident when she says raising children "has been really, really challenging." No wonder she believed so strongly on the positive impact of the extended family on child-raising that she sent each of her children home to live with her brother's family. This issue of raising children is an area of concern to almost every African parent in America and is one that provides a yet an unanswered challenge. It is quite tragic that Laura's brother died, striking a deadly blow to her efforts to instill a sense of community in her children, as now she has no one in Nigeria to send them to.

"If I may take you back to what we discussed earlier, you said you took your children home for two years. What was their response, what was the outcome? How did they take it?"

"They liked it! Of course, they didn't like it at first, but later on, they loved it because they were able to establish relationships with friends, cousins, family, and the education, too. It is nice they were exposed to work."

"What are your plans for the future? Is there any likelihood that you might go and work in Nigeria, or this is it?"

"You know, that would be my dream, because I've gone to Nigeria at least twice, trying to relocate, but it hasn't worked out. It hasn't worked out because people there constantly want to come here! And you go home, and people are wondering, 'What's wrong with you?'" she narrates, laughing with a mixture of amusement and embarrassment. "'Why would you want to come home?' So, it is beginning to appear more and more that this is it."

"And what reasons do they give for not expecting you to want to return to Nigeria, or for them wanting to come here?"

"The continuing poor economy, instability, war, no water, no electricity, I mean, no stable supply of these. Poor roads, poor healthcare, I mean every part of life is a lot poorer. And everybody is wondering, 'Why do you want to do that, and everybody is trying to get out?'"

"It looks to me though that you have the resources there, and if we wanted to make these things work, it could be done."

Laura nods in agreement.

"What do you think it will take to get this done? Suppose you and I and other professionals here went back there with the experience we have, could we make it better?"

"Ah, everyone thinks you can make it better, but it is very complex because people out there who have not had the opportunities that you and I have had have set up a system of government that is very complex, that is very tight and nobody can get through. You cannot penetrate that to begin to want to make changes. I'll give you an example; in Nigeria if you come home, which I have tried, I have tried to work at the university there…"

"You have tried to work at the university there in what capacity?"

"Many things. As a lecturer, I started working in the school of nursing. The system is 'take your turn.' It doesn't matter what you have; you start at the bottom of the salary scale. And so, when you're at the bottom, you have no voice," She utters with frustration.

"And so, they tell you, 'This is how we do things here; it won't work, don't even try it.' And so, you're frustrated, and they're frustrated. There is no forum to bridge the gap, so it is difficult! Nobody is going home. We have wanted to go home even before I divorced; we went home, tried to re-establish. It didn't work. It is very tough in my country!"

Laura is torn between the love for close social ties in her country and the stalled system where "every part of life is a lot poorer," or as Dr. Uche puts it, "over there, nothing works." She would prefer to return to Nigeria and work there and raise her children among cousins, uncles, and other relatives, and get old there, but is deterred by the failures of the society to make things run smoothly in the predictable ways she has grown accustomed to in the western world. The bureaucratic way of conducting business in Nigeria is clearly a major stumbling block in the development process, as new ideas are discarded with no chance to be tested and proven. In turn, this bureaucracy contributes significantly to her being stuck here.

"What do you see as the future of Nigeria, and other African countries, that have lost intellectuals to the western world?"

Laura speaks very deliberately and carefully selects her words in response. "Well, seeing the future, I'd like to think that as more and more Africans are here, and we continue to collaborate with each other (because I know in the Nigerian community we do that) we will begin to take our skills back home, this time around not trying to work for the government as we were brought up to do! But to establish something in the private sector, and I think privatization will come back to Africa, and that's what's going to change it. It's going to be slow. But it is going to be coming to Nigeria, for example, in the area of communication, there're cell phone companies all over the country, and that's good!"

"So, the cell phone companies are competing with the government-operated telephone system, what they call landline?"

"Oh yes! They've already rendered the landlines obsolete."

"And so, when they realize they're losing business, they'll be forced to change!"

"Yes. They may be forced to change or just give up! They'll give up in many areas; technology, I know many people who have gone back and have started projects and businesses back home. Many, many people are doing that. And they came back home from overseas."

"Is there anything else that you want to say about brain drain? What is causing it, and what can be done to prevent it?"

"I want to say that I wish the African countries would adjust and make education free, because many people are coming here to study, then they stay on. And the main reason is that there are no educational opportunities there. So, make education free, so you cannot bribe them. Otherwise people find another way, which is to go abroad."

"So, to get to the university there one might need to bribe one's way?"

"Mhm!"

"Whom do you bribe?"

"Everybody!" she asserts. And then adds resignedly, "Everybody from the vice chancellor, down to the clerk."

"How much is the bribe?"

"Oh, I don't know! Because, you come in, you want to discuss your child's results, the clerk that you go to talk to can delay you, until you say, 'Oh, here is five hundred *Nira*, I want to check the results.' It's *so bad!*" she stresses with exasperation.

"Is this part of the traditional life there or when did the bribery start?"

"I want to say, it's part of life!"

"Even before the British left?"

"Even before they left, but it became worse after. Traditionally I grew up knowing that it was expected to go back and say thank you and give something, after; not before. In the airport after you carry my luggage. But now things have changed! In the airport, to even get to the line where you're going to buy your ticket, you have to give people money! And it's not official. It's so bad in my country! Worse than any other place."

"So, is it like a tip here that you give in a restaurant...?"

148

"But you tip after! You tip after the service!"

"There, you tip before the service!"

"Yes, that's why it is called bribery," she states with a chuckle.

Different Ministries and Departments are now struggling to eliminate "the bribe" and anticorruption posters like this can be found in several places. But it is an uphill task as the cancer has spread. Photo by Teewee.

"Thank you. Is there anything else you want to say?

Laura pauses in deep thought, then speaks quite articulately, "I see a brighter future, though, for Africa in general. I really do, because as much as we are able to identify the sins of our continent, many people don't want to grow old here. If I'm going to be productive in Nigeria I should be planning. I'm over 50 years old now. I should be planning on going home! In the next five years when I'm still strong and able to do something. But if I'll be here, I'll retire in ten years' time."

"What's the reason people don't want to grow old here?"

"For the same reason you don't want to raise your kids here, really. Because in your old age it's hard to be lonely! So, it's always nice to go home."

"So, if you retired home, you'll have some family there, but then you'll have to leave your children here!"

"Mhm!" she agrees, then follows it with a long silence, after which she adds, "Many people are doing both!"

That is the best compromise for a complex situation: people's hearts are at home in Africa, like Ken puts it; "my body is here but my heart is at home." Yet persistent socioeconomic and political issues make it difficult to return, work, and live there. A middle ground is to live in both worlds, like Laura sums it, "People, like me now, will make provision to have a nice home in Nigeria, so that when you retire and go home, you have a nice, comfortable place; at the same time make provision to be back here and see your children and grandchildren."

ROSA

Rosa is a mother of three children who is in her late forties. A heart-warming solo rendition of "His Eye Is on the Sparrow" by their second daughter, who is in high school, fills their finely furnished house. Having been a high school teacher back in her home country of Zimbabwe for 23 years, Rosa is now enrolled in the G. E. D. (General Education Diploma - the high school diploma equivalent) program in an Arizona school district.

I asked her what prompted her to make such a dramatic move from a respectable high school teacher to G.E.D. candidate, and got an honest response loaded with three reasons: educational opportunities for children, adverse economic situation in her home country, and a corrupt and dictatorial and oppressive government. "Well, mainly we came for two things: one, the first one, was for our children to get a better education. This is a land of opportunities!

Two, the situation in our country is not good right now, so we wanted to (emphatically) *get away from it all.*"

"The political, or economic situation, or both?"

"Both, both! The economy is affected by the political situation. So, we had to leave home and come. And I wanted to further my studies also."

"You wanted to further your studies; what are you doing now?"

Rosa hesitates, then chuckles in embarrassment. "Right now, I'm doing the longer way; I'm doing the G.E.D."

"You're doing the G.E.D!"

"Yes, for two reasons. One, it is easier for me to help my kids with homework. Before, I could help them with math and come up with the right answer, but the method I used was different from the one they use here. So, I had to do the G. E. D. so that I know what they do here. So, it's like (tape inaudible), because I really don't need it. But when I'm done, I'm going to enroll myself... I'm going back to school, because I had stopped, because I needed fees for my daughter, who is now in her second year of college."

She states that the "situation in Zimbabwe wasn't that good, with so many children after finishing 'A' levels, they can't get to the university. So that was the most important thing why we came. It is *so bad!*" Seeking educational opportunities for herself and for her children is thus the main reason for migrating to the United States, in Rosa's case. Even though she hopes to return to Zimbabwe, the conditions she has set for her return are a long shot. Time will tell if Rosa will actually return home.

"What are some of the ways the bad situation manifests itself?"

"For example, a loaf of bread is now selling at 5,000 Zimbabwean dollars!"

Just recently, the Zimbabwean dollar was very powerful compared to other African countries' currencies, but now it is the weakest in Southern Africa. "We used to say Zambia was poor, but now Zimbabwe is poorer. All the white farmers have migrated to Zambia and that has boosted the Zambian economy," she adds.

Rosa says the situation has deteriorated since the government has been in power for a long time, since independence in 1980, and President Mugabe will not allow any opposition.

"They'll rig the elections; they'll do anything it takes to stay in power. And, most countries, like the donor countries, don't like him. And he has the habit of saying anything he wants, so he creates more enemies. So, we don't get as much aid as we used to do. And the situation is bad, especially for educated people!" Rosa laments, adding that the pay and the conditions and standards of living, if one goes to a neighboring country like Botswana, are much more favorable.

As a result, most Zimbabwean professionals have migrated to Botswana and South Africa, contributing a significant part of the professional workforce in those countries. "They get better pay, better terms; that's why people are leaving the country anyway, and it is unfortunate those people who are leaving the country are educated people, because they are the ones who can afford (air) tickets. The ordinary person cannot even afford a ticket; even if they were granted visas, they cannot afford tickets. So, all professional people are leaving. Three quarters are in the UK."

"Three quarters of Zimbabwe's professional workforce are in the UK?"

"Yeah, I think so," Rosa chuckles, and then adds dejectedly, "There're so many of them. So, we're all over."

"Was Zimbabwe that dependent on foreign aid?"

"No!" she states emphatically. "It wasn't, it wasn't! Another thing is, the weather pattern has changed; it used to rain. The Zimbabwean economy was based on agriculture. Now two things happened; it hasn't been raining so well, and another thing, Mugabe is trying to get back the land to the blacks. So, when he did that, the whites are not happy about it. So, they could not give blacks loans to start farming. The whites had money and the equipment, so that's why the farms were flourishing during their time. So he said, because 35% of the people got 65% of the land (35% meaning the whites), now they want to do vice versa."

"They want to do redistribution of land?"

"Yes! But while that's a noble idea, I think it is the way he did it; maybe he should have done some research to do it in a better way."

"How did he do it?"

"He would tell them, because you'd find a white farmer had three or four farms, so he would tell them, 'Sell your two farms and remain with one.' And if they don't want to, then he would take the land anyway!"

"And you're saying that they're in control of the economy, so if the land is taken from them, then they leave the blacks with nothing to develop the land?"

"Yes, that was basically what happened. Because, what is interesting is that, even in those farms, it was the blacks who used to work for them."

The case reveals yet another aspect of the impact of colonialism on African countries: the grabbing of fertile land by white colonialists from black Africans. The result was twofold: bitter wars for independence, such as was seen in Zimbabwe and Kenya, on the one hand. On the other hand, the newly independent states were left with a land redistribution dilemma that led to more chaos and confusion, such as is the case in Zimbabwe now. It can readily be seen that it is not fair for 35% of the population to own 65% of the land, even if they were considered natives of Zimbabwe as they are now. Yet, there is no easy way to redistribute the land fairly and equally without disrupting the already established agricultural system of the country, and subsequently the fragile economy that is directly dependent on it.

"Like right now, our Zimbabwean dollar (ZWL) is like one US dollar to 6,500 Zimbabwean dollars," Rosa declares unbelievingly. (Inflation spiraled wildly till the ZWL could not be used anymore.)

"That's incredible! Do you know anybody who got land under the redistribution program?"

"Yes, I do. Many people! The government trained people and gave them land, but they don't have implements, like tractors to develop the land. You know, somebody who wants to farm but has got maybe two oxen, you cannot plow a farm. These are big farms! So, basically that's the problem. Land is now in the hands of blacks, but they do not have farming equipment."

"So, the white farmers took their equipment and bought land in Zambia, and the Zambians are selling land to them?"

"They are! Before, Zimbabwe was so rich; it was like the breadbasket of Southern Africa, because we had more than enough. I remember there was a time when we used to export our tobacco to the United States. The white farmers would irrigate the land; they would build dams and what not. Now, farmers are only depending on the rain, yet it has not rained for several years. And they are not equipped to farm by irrigation."

"Does the government offer them loans?"

"Uh, the government has no money! They have no foreign currency; you know, everything is to be bought in foreign currency! There is no foreign currency!"

Rosa states that Zimbabweans are watching and hoping for the time Mugabe 'will go.'

"Everyone who is out of the country is just waiting. If he goes, I guess everyone will come home. We have so many educated people; educated people who can really do a better job. But, like last year we were very excited when elections were held. But they were rigged," she utters with exasperation.

Rosa is referring to the controversial elections recently held in Zimbabwe, which Mugabe and most of his party loyalists 'won' by landslide margins. When international observers criticized Mugabe's election-rigging practices, he merely laughed it off, saying they were much fairer than the American one, which brought George Bush to power in a thinly veiled reference to the Florida fiasco of 2000.

"Now, going back to education as one of the reasons for your coming to the US, you said you're still pursuing the G.E.D.?"

"Yes, and also…," she hesitates, "when I came, I was going to (name withheld) University. Then, I couldn't get my transcripts early and I went out of status. I tried to go back but they wouldn't let me. That's one of the reasons why I'm doing G. E. D. so I can continue. So, when I'm done, I'll go back to school and finish what I had started. They stopped me and said they wanted transcripts, and it was difficult for me to get the transcripts from home."

"What makes it difficult to get transcripts?"

"It was difficult because they said they didn't have records of people who went to school before our independence in 1980, and I happened to have done my studies before then, because at that time there was only one university in the country. So, they didn't have all those records."

"That's unfortunate!"

"Yeah, it was so unfortunate and when I tried to go back," she recollects as frustration sets in again, "You know how it is..."

Here is yet another facet of the impact of colonialism on citizens of the former colonies, long after its demise. Not all records kept could survive the turbulent transition from one government to another. The outcome is far reaching in what may appear to be small yet quite significant ways, such as is the case for Rosa, who is trying to go for further studies but cannot find her transcripts from the colonial era alma matter.

"I understand. Now, I know you've not been here that long, but how would you compare life here versus life at home?"

"Ooh, life at home is good!" she declares, then laughs heartily.

"Is good, in spite of the bad economic and political situation?"

"Yes. At least you have one job, you go home in the evening, and you're home with your family. But here, we have to do the worst jobs anyway. You cannot get a good job like you want to."

"Meaning, jobs that are relevant to your training and experience?"

"Yes. So, you end up working two, three jobs to sustain the family. For one thing, we are not beggars. I would never imagine myself in a welfare office to ask for food. I cannot do that! So, that's why you end up working and working, and hoping that someday we may get legal papers, maybe. I don't know but (emphatically) *we hope to go back anyway!*"

The difficulty in getting a job that is commensurate with one's education and experience is a recurring issue in the experiences of many of the cases. It appears to have two faces: one is the perceived lack of respect for Africans and/or blacks in America, making it difficult to get suitable jobs or to be promoted once one gets such a job. The other side of it has to do with rigorous immigration laws that limit students to working 20 hours on campus. Alternatively, one can work for one sponsoring employer for several years while waiting for the slow processing of papers before qualifying to be a resident of the United States.

No wonder then that Rosa has mixed feelings of hoping both to get legal papers and to return home. She needs the legal papers to be able to meet her educational and financial goals, but also hopes to go back to her home where she can live with more dignity and not have to 'do the worst jobs,' or live in fear of the possibility of asking for assistance from welfare services, an action that would make her feel like a beggar.

"That's in fact my next question: what are you planning to do when the kids are done with their education that made you come?"

"Yes! We're waiting for this one (pointing at the singing daughter); she is in high school and the other one is in college. Once she is finished with her first degree and is doing the second one, once she is able to look after herself. And the other one. Once they're settled and we have assessed that we can leave them, oh we'll go back home."

"Mugabe or no Mugabe, you want to go back?"

Rosa laughs heartily, then states more assertively, "Yeah, *by all means* we're going. I know, right now we're trying to invest at home."

Rosa discloses that she and her husband are buying and building houses in Harare, the capital city of Zimbabwe. "A house in Harare will be like a job. If we can secure three to four houses, then even if you go back home, you don't need to work," she muses hopefully.

With a severely devalued Zimbabwean dollar, Rosa is better situated to buy houses in Harare than an ordinary Zimbabwean would be. They have already started buying what Rosa calls 'beautiful houses' when compared to regular houses in the United States. "Right now, we're building another one where we know we're going to live. That's going to be our home. So, we're almost finishing. There're two houses there because there's a big house and a three-bedroom cottage. So, when we finish, we intend to buy two more houses in Harare now. If we do that..." she pauses for a long time, and then continues to outline her plans carefully, as if she is making them just now. She probably will leave the little girl in a Christian boarding school to avoid exposing her to a culture shock, like happened when they got to the United Sates. Rosa also plans to work for the United Nations to supplement the expected income from houses.

"You'd be living a very privileged life! What do you see the future holding for an ordinary Zimbabwean who has not had similar opportunities that you will have had?"

"You know there are survival skills. Those people work hard. God has given them…, the economy is so bad, but they are surviving! They are surviving. You know when you are in a bad situation, you try to live, and you find means and ways."

"You become creative."

"Yes! And so, you know what's happening is, those who are poor, are very poor now; those who had something, some are filthy rich now. So, that's how it is. So it is not surprising that when you go home if you don't do anything, you find that people who were at your level, they're much above you, because they're doing something. One thing about our Zimbabwean women, especially women, they're so hard-working. You will find them in all countries; they go everywhere selling things."

"Now, such an economy as you have described can be very scary, when the rich ones are filthy rich as you say, and the poor are desperately poor. There could be a lot of crime! What's the crime situation like in Zimbabwe?"

"It was, before it wasn't much, you know we didn't have delinquent homes like we have here, but now we have some incidents of crime. But when I left it wasn't so bad. But you know, changes occur. It's possibly going to be worse."

"What do you see as the short-term or long-term future of Zimbabwe? If Mugabe were to retire and be replaced by a more democratic government, what would the future hold?"

"When he goes, we'll rejoice, I think. Things are going to get better. We pray and hope so."

"You think more Zimbabweans abroad will return?"

"With a new leader, things will be better. Because when he started, Mugabe worked very well! That's when we prospered. That's when we prospered! Then I think as he got older, he became greedier, and I don't know..."

"'Absolute power corrupts absolutely!'"

"Yes, yes. We plan to go back, we've given ourselves like ten years from the time we came, then the Lord willing, we'll go back. We're hoping within that time we'll have accomplished what we wanted."

Rosa has their return plans vaguely mapped out in her head, and she and her family could have a wonderful life in the future, if only everything materializes as envisioned. The thoughtful pauses and reflections betray the risks in her hopes and aspirations, most of which are dependent on circumstances beyond her control. She hopes to successfully build the four houses, hoping house values remain stable. She hopes to finish her G.E.D., re-enroll in a university, and obtain a degree in nutrition; then the UN will possibly hire her. Rosa also counts on President Mugabe's old age as an indicator that he is about to go and will likely be replaced by a more fair and democratic government. All these are possibilities but without any guarantee.

"Do you think by going back you'll be helping the country more, or helping yourselves more than by staying here?"

"Home is home! We will help them, you know, hopefully with the knowledge I have, probably I'll be working with the people. And hopefully, the kids might come home, they'll be educated, and if the situation changes, the people will return home."

"What is the educational system like now without so many professionals?"

"You know, the funny part is that they have expatriates," Rosa proclaims, laughing. "Whereas we go out of the country, they have people come into the country, and we have some professionals who are there anyway, who did not even think of leaving. That's what's happening. I know the country has lost so many educated people.

"You know what was happening is that during the first few years of our independence, we had so many expatriates, and within the first five years they had to leave because we didn't need them. There were enough Zimbabweans to do the jobs. You know how the British emphasized education," she adds with more laughing. "There was a lot of educated Zimbabweans. But now when you call home, they tell you, 'so and so has left to such and such a place.' But the universities are still open, and students are still enrolled in them."

"What are the prospects for your kids should they go back?"

"If they go back with their degrees and everything, I guess it will be easier for them to get employment. The very highly educated people are valued. And they can even start something on their own."

"Prospects for business are still good?"

"We're thinking once the government changes power, it will get better."

It is hard to imagine what poor governance and dictatorial regimes have cost African countries. Here is a well-educated family that could be contributing critically to the development of their country, yet their contribution is stifled by the quagmirical conditions created by an oppressive regime. Many other Zimbabwean families like Rosa's have migrated to various developed countries, especially to the UK, as Rosa states. Even if regime change takes place as Rosa hopes it will, it is not feasible for the numerous Zimbabwean professionals to return home and develop their country. They will most likely be already 'stuck here' or wherever they may be, as is the case with many other African professionals abroad.

"Is there anything you want to say in closing? What do you think is the most significant cause of brain drain from African countries, such as Zimbabwe?"

"I think in Zimbabwe it is caused by the economic and political situation. You are not free. If you join the opposition party, they can come and burn your house, they can kill you, they can beat you up, they can imprison you! These people are part of the system; if the economy is bad it affects them too. How come they support the government that is responsible for these bad economic situations?

"The thing is, these people like Mugabe, if their mother or aunt is sick, they take them to the UK for treatment! A doctor would be sent to their home, even in the village to treat them, because they have the money and power! But that will not happen to my old mother in the rural area. She will die because there's no medication and we cannot send a doctor like that."

"The hospitals are understaffed!"

"Yeah, so it is survival of the fittest. It doesn't bother them because their way of life is not affected. In any case it is now better for them because they exploit people and they get rich."

"I am asking mostly about the forces that keep him in power, such as the police, the military, those who beat up his political opponents; what do they get from it?"

"You know, Mugabe's ex-combatants, the ex-freedom fighters, he uses them and makes sure he gives them something. He makes sure they like him. And when he campaigns and goes to the rural areas, he will intimidate them and ask the people; 'Do you want war?' and our parents don't want war. So, they'll vote for him. You will find the opposition is mainly in towns where there're educated people who are saying, 'No, you cannot do this!' But he tries to intimidate the elderly in the rural areas and bribes the ex-combatants so that they are loyal to him and they will never want to hear anything against him."

"So back to what you were saying, that the main cause of brain drain is poor economy and dictatorial regimes..."

"Yes, the political situation."

"Mugabe is one person. How can you be sure that when he is gone there will be not another dictator like him?"

"Because there are strong opposition parties, and there are strong people who are challenging him, and we know he is the head of the Z.A.N.U. party. When the head of the party is not there, things will change. Because you will find that the present government is only a government of old people, Mugabe and his men. The ministers are as old as he is; some of them are older. There are very few if any young men. Therefore, there will be total change soon."[7]

"So, overall, you are hopeful that the future is promising?"

"It is! As soon as he goes, yes, it is promising. We have people working out of the country. They will come back to the country. They have learned. They have seen how other people do things, so they will help. And if you talk to anybody who is outside the country, they *all* long to go home!"

"What attracts them to go back home the most?"

---

[7] Mugabe has been overthrown and has subsequently died, yet inflation has peaked, again, sending doctors to a nationwide strike. They complain that they cannot afford basic necessities such as rent and food.

"Our country is beautiful! It has resources. It has so many resorts and sceneries you can enjoy. But most of all, home is home!"

By the end of our interview, the singing daughter has gone full cycle and is singing 'His eye is on the sparrow, and I know He watches me,' again. She is quite right as far as Rosa is concerned.

"The Lord has been good!" she declares. "We barely came recently but we have done more than people we found here. This house has helped us and will still help us. We're going to refinance soon and use the cash-out to buy houses back home. The Lord has been good to us."

11

CONTRASTING PRODUCTS OF APARTHEID

DR. NXUMALO

When I arrived for the interview, Dr. Nxumalo was already driving off to another function, a sign of his ever-busy physician's life. He came to the United States for the first time in the early 1970s to complete a master's degree at a parochial university in Indiana, went back to Africa and worked there, and then came back in the late 1970s to do a master's degree in public health at a public university in northern California. Prior to this, Dr. Nxumalo was a minister of the gospel who served his South African church in various leadership capacities during the notorious apartheid system of government whereby all sectors of society were racially segregated. Even Christian churches were divided along racial lines.

When he initially returned to South Africa, he continued to serve in various departments in his church, mainly as director of stewardship, promoting giving and philanthropy. Later he was designated to head the Health and Temperance Department, something he declares he had always wanted to do. It was then that the employing church organization suggested that he earn a master's degree in public health at a Northern California University.

"The church was going to give me full sponsorship, but they ran into financial difficulties. So, really, I can say they bought me the ticket to come over. But once I came over, we had to struggle to pay our tuition and boarding and so forth."

"Now, what are you doing currently?"

"I am now a doctor of medicine and practicing family medicine."

"That's quite a dramatic transformation—from ministry to medicine! From stewardship director in a church organization to publishing director, and public health, to family medicine!"

"Yes, although there is quite a lot in common between the ministry and medicine."

"You mean just like Jesus, combining the gospel with healing! How did the transition come about, from minister to medical doctor?"

Dr. Nxumalo laughs at the analogy of himself and Jesus. He then states that he had always wanted to be a doctor from the time he was a young child in elementary school, but he never got the opportunity. Then later he had the chance to study public health and saw an opening.

"When I was about to finish the Master of Public Health degree, I felt very dissatisfied with the content. I felt that I had learned enough method but not content. So, I knew how to do public health, but I didn't know *what* I was going to teach, I would have to depend on other people to come and teach. The university had a Doctor of Health Science degree at that time, which was very rich and full of content. But the prerequisites for the program were the same as the prerequisites for medical school. I actually started the Doctor of Health Science program and ended up having done the pre-med courses."

"So, you said you had always wanted to be a doctor from your childhood, but you became a pastor?"

"I enjoyed preaching also. I admired all the great preachers who came by. When I was in high school, my school principal and the people in my community put pressure on me to pursue the ministry. The principal talked to my father and said that I should take the ministry, even though they had rejected some other applicants who were older than me because 'they were too young' to join the ministry," he says with amusement. "He just about forced me to join the ministry."

Dr. Nxumalo is quick to point out that he does not regret the pressure and that he enjoyed every bit of his work as a minister. Evidently, he is quite self-motivated, yet his childhood environment in apartheid South Africa did not provide the necessary opportunities to satisfy his intellectual curiosity. He enjoyed the ministry, and still does; but if there had been an opportunity to join medical school, he would have defied the intense pressure from the principal and gone to medical school.

Dr. Nxumalo completed medical school and began to practice medicine in his early fifties. "I have no regrets; it was the best thing that ever happened to me," he states, reminiscing of his days in the ministry. "But I did not feel challenged enough by the profession. I always felt I had a lot of time in my hand; that I could still do more."

"How would you compare your present job as physician to the former one of being a minister?"

"There is a lot of similarity. In both cases you're dealing with people who have problems: in the ministry, their problems are more spiritual, but as a physician, their problems are in the most part physical, and you deal with them in a more technical way. But there is tremendous opportunity for witnessing. Medicine is much more intense."

Dr. Nxumalo finds no comparison between remuneration in ministry and in medicine. "I earned more in dispatch in the medical center than I earned as a minister with a master's degree in South Africa."

But money was never a factor in his decision to switch professions from ministry to medicine. "I always loved knowledge— almost worshipped knowledge, if I may put it that way. I always wanted to learn more. I was always in school. I mean, even when I was in the ministry, I was taking courses at the University of South Africa. And I wanted to go study here; I wanted to go study there! So, knowledge—knowledge was the main thing."

He remembers a doctor who gave generously to his church organization's projects, making him feel that "if there were more people like this, the Lord's work might go a lot faster. And I thought to myself, 'If I were a doctor, I would be able to help along, too, financially.' But finance per se was not a motivating factor."

He does now give in a similar fashion and is the stewardship director of his congregation, where he preaches creative, inspiring sermons with emphasis on giving. As noted earlier, Dr. Nxumalo grew up in South Africa during apartheid, a system of government that was introduced by the minority white South Africans who originated from the Netherlands centuries ago. Under apartheid, the minority whites ruled the whole country, while the majority blacks were restricted to run-down neighborhoods in the cities and reservations in the countryside.

He felt significantly limited by the apartheid system that did not provide opportunities for blacks to attend medical school. The United States, therefore, presented him with a golden opportunity to realize his dream—which he immediately seized, even if at an older age.

"I grew up in a small town. Black schools did not have qualified teachers in all areas, but especially in the sciences, which were a prerequisite to joining medical school. Teachers in black schools had mostly junior high school certificate plus two years of teacher training. We suffered in that area, especially in sciences," he recalls. "In junior high school, we had two teachers who were working on their first degree. It was the same problem at the high school: the math teacher didn't pass math himself."

Dr. Nxumalo recollects only one medical school that admitted non-whites, and this included blacks, *coloreds*, and Indians. "Coloreds were at least also admitted to the University of Cape Town, but the University of Natal was the only one that admitted black people. And there were 56 seats for blacks and Indians in the whole country! So, getting into medical school was really a far-fetched idea." So he joined the ministry partially due to principal pressure, but mostly due to limitations of apartheid.

"What was it like to be a minister under apartheid South Africa?"

"Life under apartheid—that is a story for another three volumes," he states laughing. "But the ministry saved me from much of the pain of apartheid. I was working for the church, a black union. The Southern Union was a black union because by the time I came in, the whites had pushed us out. But there were a few whites still working with us who were my colleagues, like the secretary and a few departmental people. These few whites who worked with us knew that they were employees of a black union. And with my educational background, I probably got treated very well, because I had more education than many of the whites. So, the ministry sort of protected me from the pains of apartheid.

"When you went to Bethlehem College, apartheid ended a little bit, although there, too, the white teachers had their section of campus with nice, big houses; and black teachers had a section with smaller houses. But at least we mixed freely. But outside Bethlehem College, there are many things to talk about.

"I'll tell you about an embarrassing moment when we held a camp meeting and had a white American guest speaker. At lunch time the women gave me food but did not give the white American any. When I started eating, the American asked unbelievingly, 'Are you eating that food while I don't have any?' I was very shocked and embarrassed, and the ladies who served the food were even more shocked that a white man was asking for our food! All white guest speakers had always gone back to eat in their hotels and not with the native black South Africans. We were used to white South Africans who did not come to our homes or eat our foods, although our mothers cooked for them in their homes."

Thus, apartheid had widely permeated society, even showing its ugly face in the religious circles. He recounts that the women quickly served the white American pastor food, and he liked and ate all of it as the women watched in disbelief.

"The story of apartheid is one of human depravity and human goodwill: the deepest depravity and the best benevolence," asserts Dr. Nxumalo, speaking deliberately and in a pained poetic voice. "Seeing a white person killing a black person in cold blood, killing a servant, or just beating up on people that you don't even know, that have done nothing to you, just for the fun of it—it's a sport—shows tremendous depravity."

He gives the example of an elderly woman who lived with her family. The woman was going to a camp meeting with her little children, so she went to the train station. She loaded her luggage, beddings, and camping supplies, while the white conductor watched her. Then the children boarded the train as people helped receive them in the train. "And when she loaded the *baby* into the train, they took off and left her there!"

The people complained to the captain, but he did not care. "The lack of feeling was so deep. It is not a lack of feeling; it is hatred that had no reason, because these were helpless people, very helpless people," he adds wistfully.

Dr. Nxumalo states that the South African police hated educated black people so intensely that they enjoyed rounding up teachers and ministers, putting them in police trucks, driving them all around town with thugs and all sorts of people, and then putting them in jail, simply because they did not have a passbook on them.

At one time the president of the South African Union (who was black) got into his office, took off his jacket, and started working. Later he went downstairs into the cafe to buy something. When he got down there, the police confronted him, 'Where is your passbook?' He told them it was upstairs in his office; but they told him, 'Pastor, you're supposed to have it on your person all the time! That's what the law says.' They handcuffed him and threw him in the back of the truck. Fortunately, a white pastor who worked with us saw him being driven away and said, 'That man is a minister; he works with me up here! What has he done?' They said, 'He doesn't have his passbook on his person.' The pastor said, 'Why didn't you go with him upstairs to see it?' They said, 'The law says it must be on him! We don't care!'"

"So, if you were a black person you had to carry your pass on you all the time?"

"Yeah, *all* the time. Yes."

"What was the rationale behind it? Some fear? Some...?"

"Well, probably fear, but also, I think fear is the beginning of it, but depravity, just depravity. Because now, tell me, my brother, what threat would a minister of religion be to the country if he does not have his passbook on him and can produce it right here in his office? What is that? So, the white pastor ran upstairs and found his pass and brought it back. It was then they released him. But if it had not been for a white man's intervention, if a black person brought it to him, they would have still taken him away and charged him anyway because he did not have it 'on his person,' as the law said. Another pastor and a friend of his were also arrested in front of the gate of the house where they were staying; and their passbooks were in the house, but they got arrested! OK! Now, the passbook system was also a way of controlling your movement. I could show you my passbook as to what it says."

"Please, do!"

He runs upstairs at the speed of a cheetah and soon returns, remarkable agility for a man in his 60s! His passbook, a brown passport-like document, shows signs of years of use. It is like a memento, an ironically treasured evidence of years of oppression under the reprehensible apartheid system. The depression in his voice while describing life under apartheid is noticeably different from his regular upbeat tone. It reveals the demeaning nature of the life Dr. Nxumalo and his fellow black South Africans endured under the outrageous racist system of government.

"This was my pass, and it shows that I was allowed to be in Southwestern Johannesburg as long as I was still employed by the

Church Union. And your employer had to sign every month that you were still employed by them! Could you read the lines in English? Do you have your glasses? It used to be *big*! Then out of (jeeringly) *mercy,* they made it smaller," he says with laughter. "Ok, now let me find my glasses. Go ahead and read the English portion now." It reads: 'While employed by the Southern Union of the (name withheld) church in Johannesburg, James Nxumalo is permitted to be in the prescribed area of Southwestern Johannesburg.'"

"Oh, so every day, or every given period of time, you're permitted to be in a certain place?"

"Yeah! I was living in Johannesburg; so this pass says that I was permitted to live in Johannesburg as long as I was employed by the church. And then, *every* month, *every* month, my pass must be signed, showing that I am still employed by the said Church."

Dr. Nxumalo shows numerous signatures and dates. "You see that? Mmh. And who signs it? Any one of my white colleagues." Dr. Nxumalo states that later they signed their own passes since most of the white policemen were illiterate. "And what do they know? The police, many of them couldn't even read! Those poor boys! Yeah, which means that once I stop my employment with the church, I have no right to be in Johannesburg."

"So, where do you go then?"

"That's a good question! That's a good question. Then I don't belong anywhere! OK? Then they came up with a homeland policy and made places of dumping ground, which means they would take me from Johannesburg and go dump me in some rural reserve. And they determine where to go dump me."

The doctor recounts how the police, at a later date, took the same lady who was left behind at the train station and dumped her several hundred miles away from where she had lived. "They dumped her there with her children, with nothing! Nothing at all! No house, no toilet, nothing! (Jeeringly) *They* determine what ethnic group you belonged to; it was bad! It was bad! I mean some people did not even speak the language of the ethnic group that the government had determined that they belonged to." Her father, who bought a few corrugated iron sheets, helped her. Then she bought some more and carried them on her head, then built a shack for herself and the children; and then it rained, and the shack came down.

"Now, do you know much about the *Truth and Reconciliation Commission*?"

"Yes. Remember I told you the story of apartheid is one that shows the depth of human depravity and the height of human benevolence? The *Truth and Reconciliation Commission* shows the height of human benevolence. The goodwill of the black people of South Africa surprises me! It looks like it is inexhaustible because in Mozambique, they ran the Portuguese out of the country; in Angola, they ran the Portuguese out of the country. But in South Africa, the whites are still enjoying the same standard of living they always had. They're not threatened at all, and those who committed those heinous crimes were forgiven! You know what the Nazis did in Germany? And up to today they're still hunting them to come and stand trial for what they did. In South Africa, they put a bishop in charge of a commission to forgive the perpetrators of heinous crimes. So, all those who came and confessed their sins were forgiven.

"Was it Bishop (Desmond) Tutu?"

"Yes. The commission forgiving them was one thing, my brother; but seeing the families forgive them was something else! Yeah, that was something else."

"Like the mother who adopted the white boys who killed her son?"

"Yes, they are so many, so many. I don't know how to put it but"—his tone turns very sad— "when these things play on TV, for us that was just normal life. For other people it is, 'Wow! What's happening here?' You know what I mean? Yeah for us, being killed by white people was normal life."

Dr. Nxumalo talks about journalist/filmmaker Donald Woods whose movie *Cry Freedom* helped to significantly bring the plight of black South Africans to the attention of the rest of the world. "He was the editor of *The Herald*. He was very outspoken and very brave, and he suffered for it," he states, referring to police harassment of Mr. Woods and his subsequent spectacular flight from the country disguised like a priest in a flowing robe.

"And he fled in a very dramatic way. All those people, however, helped the people to see the truth about the system. We had been raised to think that apartheid government was invincible and that it was watertight and that you could not say anything; 'the government will hear about it.' And they drilled that into your head.

"But the escape of Donald Woods sort of gave us some doubts about the system," he states with amusement, "that it was not as impenetrable as they were making us believe. The escape inspired boys from my hometown to start leaving the country and coming back secretly! When scared people asked them how they were able to accomplish such a feat, the boys said, 'No, we just depended on the inefficiencies of the special branch, the security police.'

"The daring Soweto children who started the uprising that helped the people to realize that "the system was nothing like what they made it out to be followed such brave acts. The Soweto kids were thousands; and these are just school children—elementary and high school, that's all, no college! And they organized a meeting, and these meetings were banned; they were illegal. And they organized and held this *big* meeting, and nobody heard about it! And when the police came to hear about it, it was such an embarrassment because they had to assure the white population that 'we got you covered; they can't do anything; don't you worry, we got you covered.'"

This made the white people want to know how these kids were able to organize a meeting under the nose of the security police who were all over Soweto. "In the meeting, the Soweto children planned a big protest And among the things they planned there was that they were going to march on Johannesburg, and," his tone lowered to whispering, "that was the white part of town, so you see few black people—today the whole town is black—so that was a big, big, no, no! And these kids organized; and then the morning of the protest, they dressed up in domestic servants' clothes and factory workers' clothes. And they *filled* the trains. The police were watching all over for school children, watching all the trains for school children; no school children were supposed to get onto the trains. And so they're out there in Soweto checking all the trains for school children, and they hear the news that there is a big march in Johannesburg. The school children are marching down the street! 'How did they get there?!'"

"Do you think apartheid would have survived without the support of Western governments?"

"No! I understand Dick Cheney voted to keep Nelson Mandela in jail! And America was using apartheid in South Africa as part of the Cold War. They said that South Africa was guarding the route around the Cape of Good Hope. So it was very important to support the apartheid government of South Africa because it was very anti-Communist."

Life under apartheid had a traumatizing impact on Dr. Nxumalo's life. He tells the stories with mixed emotions of anger, frustration, excitement—and a sense of triumph and pride, having won both moral and the ultimate physical victory over the evil system. But he also tells it with splendid restraint. One can still see the effects of fear inflicted by the regime on Dr. Nxumalo's demeanor as he whispers when talking about what would have been very sensitive issues under apartheid; what would have certainly led to arrest, torture, and possible imprisonment or death.

Asked about going home, Dr. Nxumalo humorously responds, "I think about it all the time" and that it is just a matter of time, if only he could persuade his wife to join him in going.

On a more serious note he says: "Let me put it this way, going home now is no more like going home in the olden days. Now we are citizens of two countries, so to speak. I can live in South Africa; I can live in America. My children are here in America, which means we will always spend some time in America and some time in South Africa. Since the children were raised here, they are truly speaking, Americans. So, I do not see them actually going back and being able to settle. Our children are already culturally too different. You don't notice it until they go by themselves; then you see that they are of a different culture."

"How do you feel about that? Does it bother you?"

The doctor ponders the question reflectively and then speaks, carefully, selecting his words, "You have mixed feelings; you have mixed feelings. Number one, we had to come to the United States for their sakes. We couldn't have raised them in apartheid South Africa. So, it was a good thing that they came here." He adds that the children do not speak any South African language, and so the people out there don't see them as South Africans. Instead, they see the children as Americans. His daughter Thando had a two-year stint in South Africa, during which time she worked with disadvantaged children in the community and married a South African young man, who accompanied her when she returned to the United States.

In a separate interview, she states candidly, if not realistically, that she never was accepted as an African in South Africa, "…because I did not act, talk, or think like one."

"How can you say they never accepted you, when one of them even married you?" I ask curiously.

She smiles characteristically and answers, talking very deliberately but quite articulately: "My husband married me when knowing fully well that he was marrying an American woman. And so, our marriage does not negate the reality that South Africans did not accept me as one of them."

"Do you feel that the American society accepts you as one of them?"

Thando's demeanor suddenly shifts from calm and deliberate to wide-eyed excitement as she declares that she has actually changed her name from Thandolwenkhosi (beloved princess or literally "love of the king") to Jennie Johns in order to fit into the American society.

"I was virtually getting no calls back from prospective job interviewers when I used my real name, Thando. But since I started using Jennie Johns, I have actually been called back quite a few times, and even got a job offer."

Thando is referencing what Tammy, another subject in a later chapter, and her other African friends in the US have colloquially termed as the use of their "pizza names." She had ordered pizza one time and waited for eternity to be called, but nobody called her. Instead customers who came after her were served one after another. Finally, Tammy, who had used her African name for the order, went to inquire about her order, only to find that it had been ready for a while, but the delivery man was unable to pronounce her name and skipped her, more out of embarrassment than malice. She and her friends therefore each acquired an American name of convenience when ordering pizza, etc., thus a "pizza name."

The question of returning home to Dr. Nxumalo is not a matter of "if" but "when." He has already recently bought a monumental mansion there, in what used to be a white neighborhood. But his children were reared in the United States, and so he feels that they are more American than South African. He has mixed feeling about having reared the children in the United States since they missed out on growing up among relatives at home. But he does not regret removing them from the toxic apartheid environment that would have gravely limited their freedom and educational as well as career opportunities.

Dr. Nxumalo's experiences with apartheid were so contemptible that, rather than raising his children in his own homeland, he would have his children raised in a foreign land and acquire a culture different from his own, if that would remove them from the humiliations of apartheid. It was necessary then to take his family away from apartheid; but now the children are rooted here and are too Americanized to fit in the South African setting, even without apartheid. The children would be more like missionaries among his own people. And if he were to do it over, he "definitely would do it again."

"What are some of the problems of living in post-apartheid South Africa?"

Dr. Nxumalo believes that his quality of life would be better in South Africa than it is in the United States. "Doctors there don't carry beepers," he says with laughter, referring to the old practice of paging doctors, before the cell phone era. "When they are done at the office or hospital, they are done, okay?"

He adds that one's overhead is very low because doctors don't have malpractice insurance "and all the other ancillaries that we have to pay for workers that we employ, and that type of stuff."

Besides, the cost of living is much lower than that of living in the United States. "And the pace is a lot slower." But South Africans are oblivious to the idea that their quality of life is better than the quality of life in the United States.

"What is the crime situation in South Africa today?"

Dr. Nxumalo responds that crime is reportedly increasing, while at the same time statistics show that the crime rate is decreasing. "Well, there is one little book that says how to lie in statistics," he states, laughing.

He recalls how he went to Johannesburg recently with his daughter after hearing these reports of terribly increased crime rates. "I told my daughter: 'Let's go stand somewhere in the street and see how people behave with this terrible crime situation. Are people uptight? Are they tense?'

"So, we went to the busiest part of Johannesburg around Commissioner Street, and we watched people. And people were standing all there in line late in the evening, waiting for taxis, others waiting for buses, others walking over their business. Old ladies carrying stuff on their heads and in their hands also; nobody clutching to their handbags or anything like that," he adds with more laughter.

"And I looked at the situation and said, 'This doesn't look like a tremendously high crime area,' you know. And people were busy traveling and doing business. I think it probably looked a little bit better than New York! People were very relaxed." he adds, tongue in cheek.

He states that he has read about high crime rates in his hometown, but he has not witnessed any. "Now, there are two problems; one is reporting. Now that apartheid is taken away, there is freedom of movement. During apartheid, the police would immediately stop a black person seen in a white suburb, okay? Now that cannot happen anymore. But you know how people are—just seeing a black person means 'bow wow!'

"And number two, the curtain has been removed. You know when you have poverty, you're going to have a lot of crime! Now the curtain has been removed, and white people are for the *first* time able to see what actually happens in the (poor) townships. And the reporters are now reporting crime statistics for the whole country instead of just reporting on their little areas. Yes, and the jobless rate isn't helping any. Of course, when you have a high jobless rate, of course you're going to have more crime."

When asked what is causing the high jobless rate, Dr. Nxumalo identified various reasons. "The main thing is during apartheid," he narrates, holding his passbook, "this book and the group areas act removed people out of the system. If I lost my job, they would take me and dump me somewhere, so I do not count anymore as unemployed. So, the statistics were kept low at that time."

"But how did you get the job in the first place?"

"Oh, the law was at first that you could only get a job in the town where you were born. But later they even changed that, and you could even be deported from your hometown because the areas in which we were born were designated white areas. So, we were black spots in white areas. And then, you remember when companies were divesting from South Africa in order to fight apartheid. So, a lot of jobs left there, and they haven't all come back yet. Like Port Elizabeth was the Detroit of South Africa, or the Detroit of Africa, really! And those companies left: Ford, Chevrolet, Chrysler. They left when they were trying to bring down apartheid." So, a program that was intended to end apartheid for the good of the people has turned around to hurt them.

"Are there any chances that they might come back?"

"Well, they are coming back slowly; Mercedes Benz is back. BMW—the largest BMW showroom in the world—is in South Africa. BMW and Mercedes are manufacturing cars in South Africa, and I think Toyota is assembling cars in South Africa. So they're gradually coming back."

Dr. Nxumalo acknowledges many advantages to living in the United States, especially when one considers the relatively low rate of unemployment versus the high rate of 27% in South Africa. But he is quick to add that South Africa offers better opportunities for the man on the street. "Anybody can buy into the telephone franchise without a huge outlay of funds, for something like 1,500 Rands, which is about US$200. You buy the equipment and they sell you airtime. And so people come to you to make telephone calls, and they pay you for the calls they make."

He states that cell phones are paid for in advance. The consumers buy airtime; and when it is finished, they go buy some more. Therefore, one does not get a bill at the end of the month.

Anyone in South Africa could buy and sell electricity. "They have some gadgets whereby you buy a coupon, and then you punch numbers into that gadget, and that gives you electricity for a period of time, for the coupon that you bought. Anybody can get into that business; whereas here, a little man like you and me cannot get into such a business. It is so controlled! So, for a man of the street who really wants to do something, with a little bit of capital, they can make it. The business of eggs, chickens, I understand is extremely popular; there are opportunities there too. But of course, America is the greatest economy in the world; it offers the most opportunity."

Dr. Nxumalo thinks that Africans living in the West can help their countries either way, by staying here and investing their earnings in their respective African countries or by returning to Africa and personally making contribution to national development. He cites the example of a younger fellow doctor who recently went back and established a thriving private medical practice. On the other hand, people who choose to stay here can still be of help.

"The last time I was home, I helped three people establish productive businesses in the energy and cell phone sectors while I am living and working here in the US. Next time I go back, I hope to help some more people get started."

He asserts that if more Africans could do that, they would still be helping their economies and creating employment. "My vision for South Africa is that more professionals abroad will get involved in similar projects if they choose not to return home immediately. In South Africa we are lucky Nelson Mandela laid a sound foundation for the country by establishing a constitution that respects the rule of law. You see, Mandela was a lawyer."

Dr. Nxumalo argues that Mandela set a good example for South African and other African leaders in general to follow, the example of ruling for a limited time and stepping down. "Mandela is a great statesman!" he asserts with great admiration for the condemned freedom fighter turned revered president.

Mandela was followed by Thabo Mbeki, an outstanding economist with a vision for Africa. "He came up with the term of African Renaissance. When I was back home, I spoke with my nephew, who is high up in ESCOM, the electricity generating company; and talking to him, I got a feeling that the future of Africa is brighter than its past."

"The future of Africa is brighter than its past!"

"Yeah! I think that things are in the offing; well, I can't go into those details. But South Africa is going to be supplying electricity to all of Africa, but they will have enough left over to supply Southern Europe. So, someone I know personally is negotiating with different countries with regards to that, so we'll be selling electricity to Europe very soon. And energy coming from just two rivers, the Congo River and one river in Tanzania—just those two—will supply all of Africa and Southern Europe."

The doctor believes that soon electricity everywhere will be, even in the remote villages of Africa, and foresees an extended positive outcome. "Wherever electricity goes, development follows. Because once people have power, they do things. It doesn't matter whether it is the remotest village, if you put in electricity, people do things. I believe that Africa is going to develop very well *provided* we continue to have people with leadership and vision like Mandela and Thabo Mbeki."

He declares that Mandela's number-one personal strength is character, and secondly, he was an outstanding lawyer. "So, at the time when we were drawing the constitution, we had a lawyer as president. And when we were finished with the constitution, we had to turn to the economy, we had an economist as the president."

Dr. Nxumalo hopes that the trend that Nelson Mandela started will continue not only in South Africa, but also in other African countries, thereby helping the continent rid itself of dictatorial governance and corruption—the two evils that have plagued the continent since the end of colonial rule. It would indeed be a blessing to see the trend sustained in South Africa and adapted by other African states. But the key factor is, "*provided* we continue to have people with leadership and vision."

PASTOR FOSTER

After several attempts to reach him by phone, I finally found Pastor Foster and scheduled a meeting with him. He is a white South African immigrant who is now senior pastor of a Protestant church in San Diego, California. His position is reflected in the very busy schedule he maintains, which makes him turn down a weekend interview because "that is the only day he has for his family. Our interview in his coastal church's lobby, therefore, took place on a Tuesday night. Pr. Foster's friendliness and easy rapport with me contradicts the disreputable hostility and suspicion between black and white South Africans.

I arrived at the church just in time to find Pastor Foster opening the church gates after a hospital visitation. He had evidently had a long day but welcomed me warmly and gently to his church compound, pointing to a parking space. We were the only two souls on the then deserted and eerie church property.

Pastor Foster said he came to the United States in the early 1990s for a "twofold reason: number one was family reasons, and the second one was for political reasons."

"Could you elaborate on each?"

Pastor Foster replies that he moved to avoid getting into a top leadership position of his church organization. "In 1991 I was the secretary of the regional Conference of my church organization, and I was almost 38 years of age. I knew the next move would be into the presidency of the conference. And I was not particularly interested in continuing in administration."

In addition, he wanted to resume pastoring a church so that his children would have an opportunity to attend a church-operated high school without going to boarding school.

"It sounds also more of professional concerns?"

"Family and professional. Then, of course, the political situation with the fact that South Africa was, you know, on the brink of moving from the kind of governance that we had experienced through the years, with a white government, to a government of one man, one vote; and nobody knew, politically, what kind of stability there was going to be. And I did not want to bring my kids up in a more violent society than what already had existed in South Africa."

"So it was more of political uncertainty, not knowing what the future held?"

"Right, right!"

"Okay, in the first case, it's quite interesting that you were determined to not be promoted to the position of conference president!" This prompts him to laugh heartily.

His professional concerns are intertwined with family affairs. Most people would probably look forward to being promoted to the presidency of a conference; yet Pastor Foster was evading this fate. One wonders what makes him so confident he would have been made president, and what would have happened if he had said no to such a proposal if it indeed was made to him. He is quite earnest about his desire to continue working as a pastor to enable his children stay in a Christian academy.

"What was your experience? You mentioned government under a political system, which I believe was called apartheid. What was your experience under this type of government?"

"Well, obviously for me as a *white* South African, I lived off the fat of the land," he declares somberly and honestly, embarrassed of his white privilege. "But in that situation, to take six percent of the population and make them responsible for the whole population was not the right thing to do! But it was never transitioned in a way that the nationals could actually assume responsibility in a meaningful way. Almost the whole world turned against South Africa before they made any changes!"

"And that was pretty scary, as you say!"

"It was very scary."

"In your own words, you belonged to the six percent that 'lived off of the fat of the land.'"

"Mhmh!"

"What did that feel like?"

"Well, not knowing any different, it was my homeland where I grew up. In fact, my parents were missionaries to Rhodesia, which is now Zimbabwe. And my parents were born in South Africa, and their parents were born in South Africa, and their parents also! I think we were about fourth generation Africans."

"You pretty much consider yourself African?"

"Yes! Absolutely, absolutely! And we knew nothing different, because that's the way that we were brought up! And as Adventists, we considered ourselves to be apolitical; and as a matter of fact, I never voted in South Africa. The only time I voted for a South African political party was when I got to America, and they had a referendum as to whether we wanted to continue with the white government or move in the direction of multiracial government. I went to Seattle and voted in absentia," he recalls, with laughter.

"So, the church discouraged members from getting involved in politics?"

"They did not discourage us; we just never did! It was not part of the economy of our church; we just never voted! And we're very proud that we were apolitical."

"How come?"

"Well, we did not align ourselves with what the government was doing; and realizing that apartheid was not an appropriate thing, it kind of helped my conscience to be OK!" he explains, laughing as cell phone rings.

"That's an interesting way to put it; it kind of eased your conscience."

"Yes."

"And I wonder if anybody complained. Let's say, I don't know how your employing conference related to the black conferences. Did they complain and ask why the church did not speak up against apartheid?"

"Our conference was the first one in the South African Union that actually encouraged non-white members to join our conference and to become party to it. And under the leadership of the president of the time and me as secretary, we did merge the Colored Conference and the Asian group. The Indians and the coloreds we brought into our conference. And the next move would have been, the president and I said, to merge with the Black Church because we thought it was very important that *that* happen. And we felt that it was not a case of *whether* it would happen; it was a case of *when* it would happen. And we were quite proactive in that process; but I'm sad to say that even now, it hasn't happened."

"It hasn't happened?"

Speaking quite solemnly, Pastor Foster says, "It hasn't happened at this point. In some of the other geographical areas in South Africa, it has. But in the Transvaal, it hasn't happened at this point."

"Did the proactive steps to integrate the racial groups in your conference in any way jeopardize your standing with the rest of the white South African community?"

"I do not think it jeopardized my situation in any way because the president and I were very convinced that *that* was what God wanted for the church there."

It is quite impressive and commendable that Pastor Foster and his conference president took proactive steps, even if small ones, to end apartheid in his jurisdiction of his Protestant Church, merging the coloreds and Indians with whites. What would the reaction of the white segment of the church been if they had moved ahead and merged with blacks? At the same time, deliberately staying apolitical is disturbing. His church thereby missed out on the opportunity to confront the government along with the Anglican Church under Bishop Tutu, and "call sin by its name," as his church teaches. Instead, staying away from politics was a means to "help one's conscience be a little bit OK."

"Pastor, you said you had some fears of the transition from a purely white government to a one-man-one vote kind of government. Looking back now at the way things have turned out the last ten years or so of one-man-one vote rule, how do the expectations versus the reality compare? Has it turned out as bad as you feared, or is it better than you expected?"

"In certain respects, it turned out worse, and in other respects it turned out better. There was no violence when the first free elections took place; there was very little bloodshed. Nelson Mandela did an incredible job of leading the country in a very positive direction. But violence and crime got totally out of hand; and within a few years, and I don't remember how many years it was, Johannesburg was considered the crime capital of the world! Our family and friends ended up living in homes that have six-foot walls with electric wiring on the top and electric guides to stop thugs from getting in! And they basically became prisoners in their own homes! And that was immediately after the elections. In fact, the police were quite fearful of trying to curb crime because they would be killed! But now, when we were there at Christmas time this past year, things are definitely much better than what they were before."

"You mean in terms of the crime situation?"

"The crime situation. The police seem to have a better handle on what is going on. But there is reverse apartheid! Whereas in the past whites were able to get into the universities and get really good jobs, the politicians have now prescribed that a certain percentage of the work force should be a certain ethnic group."

"Sort of a quota system, a type of affirmative action?"

"Correct, right! Affirmative action! And the people now being discriminated against, rightly or wrongly, are the white minority. And if you are a white male in South Africa now, it's *very* difficult to get a job. And there are glass ceilings; and one would expect that. You could not run a nation the way that it was run before and discriminate against the majority and now not expect the majority to discriminate against the minority. To every action, there is an equal opposite reaction. But the South African government has done a tremendous job of weathering the storms. And hopefully as one moves deeper into the future, things will improve even more."

"What would you say was the cause of the increased crime after the fall of apartheid?"

"The folks did not know how to process their freedoms," Pastor Foster quips promptly.

"They didn't know how to process their freedoms. You think it was revenge oriented?"

"Well, part of it may have been; that's why I say I'm not sure that they realized how to process their freedoms; that was one aspect. The second aspect was the fact that, for years, the ANC had told that generation that they needed violence to free themselves. Now, how do you take a whole generation that has grown up using guns and weapons and violence to effect freedom, and now suddenly when you have a new party in power, now you tell them, 'Oh! Stop! Now you are not allowed to resort to violence anymore'? It runs very deeply in the blood, and I think it is going to take at least a generation for that inherent hatred and fear and sadness that led to ANC's revolt to work its way out of the system. Does that make sense?"

"It does make sense, yes!"

This fascinating perspective on the crime situation in South Africa suggests violence had been an acceptable means of fighting for freedom, and thus will take time to flush out from the system. In a way, this view confirms what Dr. Nxumalo and other black South Africans say about the subject— that crime had always been there, but the apartheid system shielded the minority whites from experiencing it by tightly controlling the movements of the desperately poor majority, including those who commit crimes. The end of apartheid exposed white South Africans to the crime that had always existed but which they did not see before.

The ANC government's view is affirmed as well by this statement that "now the police are getting a better handle of it." Their view is that police were trained under apartheid to oppress blacks and protect the interests of the minority whites. When apartheid ended, this need became obsolete, and the police found themselves unprepared to meet the new challenges of combating crime and enforcing the law equally among all South Africans. Who is right is hard to tell, but both views make sense. The question, however, is what to do to curb crime. Fighting poverty and making educational opportunities accessible to all would be the best way to start. The country's vast natural resources ought to evenly benefit all citizens.

"That's purely my perspective."

"I'm interested in your perspective, so I appreciate that. Yes, and I was also wondering if it might have anything to do with economics."

"Yes, absolutely! The scene after the ANC took over the government: 50percent of the population was unemployed because a lot of ANC members came back from foreign countries now having no jobs. A large proportion of your whites, as you indicated, the brain drain, started leaving. And so, there weren't as many jobs available as there had been. A lot of the wealth of the country had moved off. Many of the big corporations that had been run by the government, like the railways, the airways, ESCO, which is a big iron- producing concern, all of those were denationalized and privatized; and so, the private companies were not employing due to the fact that many people had gotten golden handshakes that amounted to millions of Rands. And so, the system had nearly collapsed."

"You mean the majority of white South Africans got millions of Rands?"

"Not the majority, but many of them."

"They got golden handshakes so they could leave?"

"Yeah. Some of them left, but others stayed because they had plenty of money!"

"Was that because the government was trying to cater for their impending uncertainty? 'Here is the money if you want to leave.'"

"That was part of it. But they moved whites out of the jobs, so that they could be filled by blacks."

"So, which government did that?"

"The nationalist government, before the new government took over—a kind of cleaning house ready for the new era."

Pastor Foster is describing what is comparable to the "white flight" phenomenon in some American communities: as minorities move into white neighborhoods, whites move on to new ones, disgracefully "running away from problems," meaning blacks or other minorities. The winds of change were blowing so strongly that the white minority South Africans knew that they would no longer hang on to power. Was it out of fear or malice that they depleted the economy to near collapse and gave lots of money to whites before blacks could take overpower? This underscores the degree to which racism and hate had taken root in the South African society.

Pastor Foster argues that many white South Africans left after the fall of the apartheid system of government that favored the minority white population. "I would say that the larger proportion went to Australia; some went to Canada; some to America; and later, a *large* group of them went to Britain," he asserts.

He does not know what percentage of whites remained in South Africa, but of his college graduation class he says somberly: "I think there are two of the eight of us still in Africa. The rest of us moved to other countries."

"Now, in the light of what you have said, under the circumstances that prevailed, what would you say is the single most important cause of the brain drain from South Africa?"

"The single most important cause of the brain drain was economic uncertainty—the fact that you don't want to bring up your kids in a country where you don't think there is a future! I have two daughters. I certainly don't want to bring up my kids in a country where I'm not sure they're going to get jobs or not; so, for the future's sake. And, our eldest daughter wanted to be a pastor, but women in ministry was not in vogue in Africa at that time. And so, we wanted to give her an opportunity as well to do what she needed to do."

"How was it for you to transition from pastoring in South Africa to ministering in the United States?"

"Tough! It was tough!" says Pastor Foster urgently.

"Tough! What was tough about it?"

"Culture shock! Even though one spoke English, the American culture is very, very different from the African culture, very consumer oriented. The hardest thing for us was to leave family and friends and move into an area where it was just my wife, myself, and our two kids, and no family other than the four of us in this country. And that's the way it still is 13 years later. We still are the only… [but] we do now have a son-in-law and a grand-baby."

Like black Africans in America, Pastor Foster's main reason for coming to America, in addition to fear of the unknown consequences of black rule in South Africa, was educational and professional opportunities for his two daughters. Although he was bound to get a promotion at work, he still found it necessary to move to create better prospects for his children. Since moving to the United States, Pastor Foster has been hospital chaplain, associate pastor of a church, and is now senior pastor of his church, where he has been for two years.

They try to return to South Africa every two years and visit his mother and his wife's family, his father having died two years ago. "But my mother is in South Africa and my other siblings (we were five, but my older brother died four years ago), and so my two brothers and my sister are still in South Africa. And then my wife's people, her mom and dad and three brothers and their wives and children, still live in South Africa."

"And so, as you were saying, it was tough transitioning to the US, leaving these people back in South Africa."

"Very tough! The other thing that was really tough is, uh, Americans (I know this is a generalization) but Americans do not seem to accept that education from other countries is up to the same level as what theirs is. My wife was a trained teacher. But she had to go back to school, do a degree in Nursing, and then do her NCLEX. She did not particularly want to teach in America, and so she had to start from ground level."

"Did they tell her that her teaching credentials from South Africa were not acceptable here?"

"Well, her teaching credentials were not acceptable here; they wouldn't accept them. She decided that the kind of education that was provided in the elementary schools was very different from what we were used to in Africa. Discipline for one thing, was totally different!"

"Tell me about it!" I exclaim as we both laugh simultaneously. "OK, what else made it tough?"

Pastor Foster looks through the window into the eerie darkness outside, then speaks reflectively: "Being away from family and friends, and familiar things, you know. I had worked in my regional conference for seventeen years; the church mainly knew me, and I knew the church. To come to a country that you were not educated in the ways that people act and react was quite an assignment. But we did adapt quickly.

"One of my South African friends who lived in Portland told us, 'You mustn't make any rash decisions until you've been in the country for two years. Then you can decide whether you can go back or not.' And we decided that *that* was an unwritten expectation: that we would spend two years and then decide whether we were going to go back or not. Thirteen years later, we're still here. We haven't decided to go back," he concludes as we share a mutual hearty laugh.

"Now, you were talking about your difficulties as you moved from South Africa to this place. Is there any specific example of how it impacted your work? Any specific experiences that you might want to talk about?"

"You leave a country where you are well-respected, well-thought-of, where you are making a significant contribution to a church and its economy and its theology and its whatever. You come to a place where you are virtually *nothing*. You know, I sat on executive committees; I was highly respected in the areas that I functioned. And you come to America and people kind of look you up and down. You never went to school with any of the folks that you're working with. It takes a while to build the trust level and for people to learn to know you, and to respect you and trust you. So that was the toughest assignment, to adapt to the American culture and the American church and work [my] way back into a position of trust and respect."

As George, Laura, and Mr. Chibanda expressed feelings of lack of respect sometimes experienced as Africans in America raise definite implications of racial discrimination and prejudice, now Pastor Foster, who is white, as well laments how tough it was to come from Africa and try to fit in the American system and culture, making him feel like he was "virtually nothing." Therefore, the discrimination and lack of respect appears to transcend race and encompass differences in cultural backgrounds, accents, and mannerisms.

"And so, how does the lack of respect affect your role as a senior pastor or as chaplain? Do you, for example, find when you're dealing with a situation [that] you encounter lack of acceptance?"

"I think initially that was the case; but the longer I have spent in the US, I think that I've changed some of the strategies that I use and some of the approaches. I think that the trust level is there, and the people know that we're prepared to work hard and that we *are* trustworthy."

"Right! Briefly, how does your work now compare with your work back home?"

"I worked very, very long hours in South Africa. I never had had the privilege of pastoring just one church in a district. I think my smallest assignment was two churches. [Now] to be able to pastor one church in one community is really fulfilling, and I get a lot more done. I felt in South Africa that I was spread like marmite on bread; whereas now you can concentrate more on doing ministry in a meaningful way rather than just trying to hit the surface and keep running. For instance, my first district that I was in, in South Africa, I had four churches; and I preached every Sabbath, but never in the same church two in a row. Here I preach virtually every week in the same church. And you can build up good relationships and grow the church."

"I see, Pastor. Now, what are your plans for the future?"

Pastor Foster speaks quite passionately in response to this question: "My plans for the future are to get ready to meet Jesus and to get people ready to meet Jesus. I want to do everything that I possibly can to expose people to the grace of God. Every Sabbath that I preach, I feel that it is an honor and a privilege to help people develop a healthy view of God and what He is about. The church organization now is working hard to share that with the membership. It really is gratifying to see it happening in many, many churches at the present."

"And you mentioned that 13 years later, you're still here!"

He laughs as he affirms, "Yes, I'm still here!"

"Do you think that might change? Do you think you might go back?"

"Although one thinks nostalgically that that might happen, I doubt that it will *ever* happen because everyone has moved on. Not only have we grown and moved in different directions, but I think the people back home have grown and moved in different directions too. Many of my colleagues that worked with me in the Transvaal Conference are now in Australia and New Zealand, and some of them are in Canada; some of them are here in the States.

"So nothing will ever be the same, even though nostalgically you think that it may be. To be realistic... I would not say we'll never go back because you never know what the future holds. My mom is aging; my wife's parents are aging. There may be a time when we may need to take some time out to go take care of them. I hope that *that* won't happen, but for their sake, one may have to make a little change in where we are and what we're doing. But the plan at this point is that we've naturalized. We are American citizens. We're not here on work permits, and we are American citizens by choice and very proud of it!"

"What did it take to get that citizenship?"

"It wasn't easy! You had to work really hard! Five years of naturalization and then two years of interesting stuff," he states while laughing, "that we had to do to get it all sorted out. We are proud to carry American passports and to become parts and parcel of this great country."

Apparently, the fear of post-apartheid life in South Africa was a significant factor in driving Pastor Foster and many other white South Africans away from the country to adjust to a tough new life in America while leaving loved ones behind. They feared a possible outbreak of violence against the minority white population that had been hitherto protected by the apartheid government under the white Nationalist Party. It seems they expected that blacks, who had been oppressed by apartheid, would take massive revenge on the whites, but this did not happen. Instead, Nelson Mandela's government instituted the Truth and Reconciliation Commission that promoted confession and forgiveness between whites and blacks, thereby avoiding prosecutions and reactions based on vengeance.

The South African "white flight" was prompted not only by fear of the unknown, but also by what Pastor Foster identifies as "economic uncertainties." The privileges of guaranteed college openings and jobs would no longer exist under the new government of majority rule. Life in South Africa was, therefore, good for whites only when apartheid lasted. While apartheid and its oppressive policies drove blacks like Dr. Nxumalo from South Africa, the end of apartheid now has driven white South Africans out. Granted, reasons are different: fear of what black rule might hold for whites as well as the fear that economic opportunities would be limited for them and their children under majority rule.

"Oh, okay. I was going to ask what your vision for your country, South Africa, is; but now you are American!"

"Oh, Zimbabwe was my fatherland! I was born in Zimbabwe, but I grew up in South Africa. I would really like to see the country develop spiritually, economically, and socially. I think there's plenty of room for development there. This is a great country and I would like to see it thrive!"

"Do you see this happening? And if so, what would it take for this kind of development to take place?"

"The church, particularly the Adventist Church—and I am obviously speaking in context of what I know—the Adventist church has a very crucial role to play in South Africa. They can model what a truly unified church can be: that it can transcend racial barriers, political barriers, and economic barriers, and model what God's grace can accomplish in the lives of people, building relationships and building strong infrastructure that is based on healthy relationships. That may be very difficult, but I still believe it will happen," he concludes, his voice fading.

The Adventist Church was conspicuously silent during the apartheid era in South Africa, or *apolitical,* as Pastor Foster puts it. It would be interesting to see if the church will now turn away from its apolitical position of passiveness to play the "crucial role" in bringing about development in the country. Pastor Foster seems quite sincere in his hopes and aspirations for South Africa, speaking truly as a minister of the gospel who naturally looks at the spiritual sides of issues first. But one wonders if the fading voice denotes lack of conviction in his vision for South Africa, or if it merely betrays the fatigue of an evidently long day for a committed servant of God.

"It is very sad!" adds Pastor Foster somberly. It is sad that people have left South Africa. South Africa was a very strong country; I mean, the first heart transplant was done by Professor Christian Barnard in Cape Town! And they led the world in some very, very interesting research and medical stuff from South Africa. It is a country that is richly blessed with resources and with people. But the brain drain has certainly affected what happens back there. The whites that could leave did leave; and the blacks were left at a disadvantage because they had not been educated and trained to pick up the slack and to move in. How can you have an election, take a people who had virtually been enslaved by the political system for over 400 years, and suddenly take Nelson Mandela who had been in jail for twenty-six years and tell him: 'Now you can be president!' The transition needed to be gradual and more calculated more than it was. But Nelson Mandela did an incredible job. If he had been fifty years of age, we would have seen incredible things happen in that country. Nelson Mandela is one of my heroes! He did a great job."

12

AFRICAN MISSIONARIES IN AMERICA

DR. MALEKHA'S BATTLES

D r. Malekha is a professor at a parochial university in Illinois, from where he had also earned his Master's degree in the late 1980s. He then moved to a reputable university in New York and earned a Ph.D. in science and research. Dr. Malekha taught briefly at two universities in the United States, and then returned to teach at his alma mater in Southern Africa. He has almost repeated this dramatic trend by coming back to teach in Illinois, doing research at the same university in New York, and then going back to teach in Illinois. He says he hopes to complete the cycle by returning to teach in Southern Africa someday.

Dr. Malekha informed me that he originally returned to teach in Africa because his church-operated alma mater had given him 'a small bursary' to come to the United States and pursue a master's program. He had signed 'a non-binding promissory note' to the effect that he would return home and work for them upon completion of his master's degree.

"They had just given me a small bursary. They didn't have money for a full sponsorship. And so, because I really needed that money at that time, I promised that if they gave me a small amount of money, I would also give them my service in return. But it wasn't an obligation; I felt that I had taken that money *hoping* that I would go back and help. So when I went back, I decided to not just stay for the five-year term we had agreed on; my intention was to serve throughout my professional life."

But Dr. Malekha expresses his frustration with the university he had purposed to serve for life. He had expected professional growth via research and participation in professional development activities, but that did not happen. Instead, he says, "When I went there, I found that the mentality was that we were there to teach."

The university only encouraged research in theory but not in practice and did little if anything to facilitate research. "Research, especially in science, requires an infrastructure and the organization of coursework that does not excessively burden teachers. But over there we were teaching *every* semester, including the summer, with *no* holidays! And each of us was required to teach at least 12 credit hours, as department chairperson," he laments. "Deans could teach four to eight. And ordinary teachers, up to 17. A professor could carry four classes of four credits to teach in one quarter."

"How does that compare to your teaching load in Illinois now?"

"In Illinois I was teaching only two classes, just about eight credits, before I went back. And I was just an ordinary lecturer, with no other administrative responsibilities. When I returned home, I found myself teaching 12 credits per quarter, and I was also Department Chair. Yet I did not have any secretary; we had just one pool secretary for mathematics, agriculture, and biology, all of us. So, (frustrated tone) it became *very* difficult for me really to become productive other than to teach."

"You couldn't do research!"

"I couldn't! I couldn't do research, because there just wasn't any time! By the time you teach 12 credits a semester and you're running the department, you have to write, you have to attend several standing committee meetings as a chairman. Every week you're in Academic Standards Committee, you're a member of Admissions Committee, and you're a member of other internal committees."

Lack of time for research also meant lack of professional advancement since one could only advance by being published, yet the teaching and meeting schedules did not leave room for research and publishing.

"So many people are down here, and the whole university had only four professors and two associate professors; the rest were either lecturers or senior lecturers, or tutorial fellows. So, without publishing, I could *teach all I was teaching* but I would never advance from where I was, because when you become an associate professor, you must have a number of publications. That's almost mandatory."

"So, professionally you found this to be limiting and not satisfying!"

"It became very limiting, and besides limiting, I did not feel self-fulfilled professionally, even though I was giving my services. I felt like it was too early for me to almost give up on my career, when I still had the potential for doing more. So, that became a concern. However, my commitment to the university continued being so strong that, even though I felt like I was not advancing professionally, I did not feel like, 'Oh I need to leave this place.'"

Dr. Malekha sounds very frustrated with the system in the university which he decided to return to and serve his country. He left a comparatively lucrative position at a university in Illinois to return and serve at one in Africa at a salary that could easily be less than one quarter of his Illinois pay, while his responsibilities more than doubled in the form of excessive teaching load and responsibilities of department chairmanship. His tone is full of disillusionment and frustration as he tells of the poor work conditions, which he implies triggered the poor health which later plagued him.

"Then what happened?"

"Now, I got sick in the process," he declares, his voice becoming more subdued. "Part of it might have been due to some other stress, work-related stress, some internal politics in the school, and some prior problems that I had. So everything gravitated together to make my medical condition serious. Now, when my medical condition became serious, the university started hesitating to pay for my medical bills because then the bills were very high."

"They knew about your medical bills?"

"Oh yeah; the doctor referred me to a hospital when my illness became very serious. But, ah," he sighs deeply, "the university did not want to spend too much money on my medical cost. As a result, they could not even agree to take me to the hospital. I was so seriously ill that I could not myself drive a car. It was risky, and there was no way I could arrive in the capital. And we tried the nearby town but there was no hospital capable of handling my case. It was determined I had to go to a referral hospital at the capital. That's where they had the technology to be able to diagnose my illness. But to get me to that hospital became a problem; the university would not give a car. So, I had to get a driver by myself, hire a driver to drive my car to take me to the referral hospital, about 250 miles away."

"At your own expense?"

"At my own expense. But the driver I found used to be a university driver. I had met him first when I was a student there. He chose to drive me, but when we got there, the university refused to have me admitted."

Incredibly, the university administration literally abandoned their very committed worker at his greatest time of need. Then they left him at the mercy and charity of a former driver, who offered his free driving services, and the chief physician who admitted Professor Malekha at the referral hospital "on his own account and said he was going to follow it up," like the biblical good Samaritan.

"He did this out of mercy, because he just couldn't take it. He couldn't take it when he looked at my condition and that the university is dilly-dallying. And what irritated him most was that he was also the personal doctor for a senior university official. He felt there was a double standard, because, here was a man in very critical condition that could not be admitted, but the official comes here, and he can get any services he wants. So he called and got me admitted and my condition was diagnosed, and I got treatment, but that wasn't very (tape inaudible.) From there, I was put on long-term therapy that started costing me much more money. My family was now financially straining, and during that time, God opened the door and the university in Illinois called me, and they said, 'Well, you said that you wanted to go back to Africa because you had a contract to fulfill for five years. Now you have been there for six years! Do you think now you can come back?' And I thought, to, me that could be God opening a door for me..."

"God, In His time!"

"In His own time, because I did not apply, I had not known they had an opening, I had not heard from Illinois in six years; that possibility never even existed in my mind that I would ever come back to the US. So, the fact that there was an opening, and they called me before I initiated it, and the fact that they sent me a ticket to come for an interview, and everything else, a series of things, followed each other. And I went actually before I had even been offered the job, I went to my father's friend, who was a member of the university's governing board, and asked his advice, and he told me, 'If God opens this door for you even without you applying, I suggest you should take this job.' Then Illinois called the President, and then even he said they were willing to release me. I think they were also getting fed up with me due to my medical costs."

The deep sighs make one wonder whether Dr. Malekha is regretting his loyalty that made him go back to Africa to satisfy the terms of "a small bursary" that he had received, at the expense of his health and professional welfare. Even though he says he has no regrets having gone back, he might be thinking what might have been, certainly with regards to his health condition which is likely to require long term care. The same university that might have contributed to the deterioration of his health was not willing to help with Dr. Malekha's treatment. The university's refusal to invest in his healthcare and professional advancement was Illinois' gain.

"You were talking about internal politics."

"Well, the internal politics had to do with the administrative system; the way things were very personalized. So that, if one made an order for something, the determination whether the application was ruled in favor of or against you was more based on your relationship with the leadership, than on policy or anything else."

"It was not based on merit?"

"Not based on merit. So, you were either in or you're out; you're either with us or not with us. Those people who were close to the administration almost got whatever they wanted. Those who maintained some level of independence, almost never got anything they needed."

"So, were you in or out; close to the administration or not?"

"No! No!" he utters urgently. "I was never close to the administration myself, and it had nothing to do with me personally but just because I had friends who were not close to the administration. But these were friends that I had even long before I went to that institution. So, the idea that I could just drop friendships so that I could become close to the administration was just ridiculous."

"Did they ask you to drop the friendships?"

"Yeah! In fact, there was a lot of pressure at first, for me to. I was so astounded by the university president warning me against my association with so and so. And given some of these people were very close to my family and close to me, for more than ten years before I went to the university! I said, 'No!'"

"You mean he called you to his office and asked you to stop being friends with…"

"He called me to the office and told me that he 'was concerned about my relationship with so and so because so and so is undermining me,' and so he was giving me counsel 'to be careful.' I took that to mean, 'You better get out of that relationship.' I didn't heed that counsel. I did not undermine the leadership either, but I just didn't stop the friendship. But the interpretation was that, if you didn't heed advice, then you were against the administration."

"And what transpired?"

"What transpired was that you had no support; whatever you requested many times was denied. You are a chairman of a department, you request certain supplies for the department, you are told there's no money. You file your request for a field trip, sometimes your field trip is cancelled by the administration."

"So they deliberately try to frustrate you?"

"It is sabotage. It became frustrating for me. For some time, I could take it. But it reached a point where, I believe, that was what amplified my illness. That's what precipitated it when I really felt like I was hitting a dead place. Either you have to choose friends, or you choose the job!"

"So, what happened when he called you to his office?"

"Two of my friends were very close to the Deputy President. Now, the Deputy President was in conflict with the President; that was their internal politics; power struggle. The Deputy President has many friends within the faculty, and among his friends is my friend. You know they say, 'A friend of your friend is your friend,'" says Dr. Malekha with a chuckle.

"So, because of that, I was in relatively good terms with the Deputy President myself. Now, my friend and the Deputy President would share secrets. The Deputy President and I had not reached that level of sharing anything, but since he was the one in charge of academics, I could come to his office and tell him if I was frustrated, and he would listen and work with me.

"Now," he proceeds with a deep sigh, "there came a time where the relationship between the President and the Deputy President reached a crisis point. So, the President decided to get rid of the Deputy President. But he is not the one who had hired him; the council that runs the university, had. Now I have no details how he did it, but there was a lot of rumor that he ended up influencing the political system of the government, so that when the Deputy President came for a meeting in the US, he could not be allowed back into the country. He was told that he was a security threat. So, one gone! Once the Deputy President was locked out, now the war began on the rest of the 'dissidents.'"

"War on those who were the Deputy President's friends?"

"Yeah, war on those who were his friends! During that time, this is, actually this is something I do not want on tape. It is a sensitive issue."

(Tape switched off as he tells of protracted conflict between the President and staff who were perceived to be for the ousted Deputy President, many of whom were subsequently fired.) Dr. Malekha was caught up in this conflict by association. In the end he was summoned to the President's office where the President threatened to 'dehorn him,' and to fire him. To which Malekha retorted, "Professor Sir, I do not have any horns, and if you'll fire me for following university policy, go ahead and fire me."

Then he walked back to his office, ignoring the President's calls to come back. When Dr. Malekha did not return, and instead went and wept in his own office, the President followed him and knocked on the door, considerately asking for a father-and-son-like dialogue. After another heated confrontation, they made a truce under which the President would respect Malekha's department, and he in turn would not 'undermine' the President.

It would be fairer to listen to the President's side of the story; but if these allegations are true, he and his Deputy President, the staff, and students and their parents who sacrifice much to pay the high tuition are all trapped in a quagmire of systemic flaws that could use major overhaul. Such inadequacies resulted in student unrest at this very institution, an unrest that culminated in what came to be known as 'Resolving.'

"Tell me more about 'Resolving.' What was it?"

"Resolving was something! The student council elected a very radical leadership," Dr. Malekha explains with laughter. "At the same time, the university leadership was becoming very autocratic and was squeezing everything from students. For example, at the cafeteria, they were reducing the variety that the students used to get, the food quality was deteriorating. They used to give them bathroom tissue but stopped, so students had to buy their own. They used to have hot water in the shower rooms, then they stopped the men's hot water supply, especially in the dorms with no solar heaters. So, it was a combination of a lot of things, aimed at saving money. All field trips, which departments used to sponsor, students now had to pay for. That became like extra taxes. Students were paying the same tuition but receiving significantly reduced services."

"And so, what was the students' response?"

"Students said this was ridiculous. Those were the same issues the student leaders had campaigned on and got elected to resolve. But they were not very diplomatic; they started holding meetings in the dorms, forming caucuses, and were becoming rowdy. I was their sponsor, so when we realized what was happening, we called a meeting with the students and the President asked for a discussion. The students who asked questions were very rough, especially with the President. They took him head on, and everyone cheered as they talked. So, he called these students later and told them they were to go through the disciplinary process. The students said that could not happen because they had been told to ask questions freely and openly. Eventually, the students decided to not go to class. So, the President called a general assembly, and we decided that the issues the students raised were very serious, but we did not want them to dictate the terms of how the issues would be resolved. So, we told them to go back to class and we would work on sorting out those issues step by step. But the students said, 'We're not going to class until the problems are solved.' So the thing became a crisis.

"The assembly voted to give students an ultimatum, to either go to class or go home. The students did not go to class and gathered behind the auditorium at night and were becoming rowdy. The university authorities called the police, and then invited students to the auditorium. Now, when the President stood up to talk, nobody could even listen to him; the place became rowdy and they started booing him and all that. So I looked here and saw the police and the students, and what came to my mind is that if the police begin to use teargas in this building, there will be total chaos and disaster. The students would have to be dismissed to go home at night, with no buses or taxis running. I knew the next thing would be that the girls would be raped.

"As their advisor, I could not stand these thoughts of the effects of a clash between the police and students. I decided to take a risk and address them. Now, when I stood up, fortunately, they listened and I asked them to calm down, which they did. I was trying to help in good conscience, but it turned out that I was accused of having instigated the whole thing!"

"Like Saul has killed his thousands..."

"That was the problem!"

"How did that affect you or your work?"

"It further damaged the already bad relationship between the President and me and made it harder for my projects to get approved or funded."

"So, looking back in summary, what would you say is the cause of brain drain from Africa to the west?"

"There are several factors, but I would say the first one is underfunding. Research, especially in sciences, requires proper funding, but we were working with a very limited budget. There is so much more we could have done but couldn't due to lack of money. There are therefore feelings of lack of professional fulfillment and that's why most African lecturers have gone to other countries."

"What else is causing brain drain?"

"The economy; poor governance has ruined our economy, and professors are poorly paid. Take the example of Dr. ..., I can't remember his name, but he is the best technology professor in the country; the best electrical engineer. He testified before the commission that was set up to examine professors' and lecturers' remuneration after they went on strike at the public universities. He was paid the equivalent of US$450 per month. After paying his mortgage, he was only left with about US$20! He could not even put fuel in his car. His wife divorced him! And here is a man who is well qualified, the best in his field. He is very committed to serving in Africa; he doesn't want to leave. Yet he's not compensated adequately for his work. So, when you have people spending their own money, training to be professionals, then you do not reward them properly, they'll leave."

"How does pay at the public universities compare with pay at the private university?"

"At the private university where I worked, we were very well paid! Oh, yeah, we were well paid. I was even shocked about it," he says in jest, laughing. "In fact, that's one area where I must give the President credit. He made sure we got paid well."

"How did he do it? Does the private university have more money than the government?"

Dr. Malekha laughs some more as he responds, "No, not quite. You see, it also had to do with his personal experience," he declares, with more laughter. "He did it for his own benefit, too. You see, he had a missionary for a secretary, so his secretary got paid more than himself. And the President didn't like that! He didn't like it. So he called a meeting, looked at the allowance the missionaries were getting deposited in their home country accounts, and found out that it was 200 dollars a month. The meeting decided that everyone would get the equivalent of 200 dollars allowance every month. Now, my wife and I got the same, plus our salaries, and that was a lot of money!

"So, salary at the private university was OK. I couldn't complain. We were paid much better than professors in public universities. The result was that professors wanted to get out of the public University to come and teach at our parochial university. So, we hired them as adjunct lecturers. Some departments were completely staffed by adjunct lecturers, which brings another problem, because these adjunct lecturers are not modeling Christian lifestyle. You did not recruit them based on faith; you recruited them purely due to their professional qualification. So they may not even profess any faith!

"When they are the ones teaching your students, you are not necessarily advancing the mission of Christian education. In fact, maybe you are undermining it, which is a big problem! You had two factors in the university: a very high non-Christian student population, nearly 78%, and a professorship, and lecturers that had no interest in Christianity. Departments of Technology, Languages, and History were all dependent on lecturers from the public university. I was dependent on them too, but by God's grace I hired a teacher who was a Christian," he adds with hearty laughter.

"Interesting! What other factors cause brain drain?"

"Poor health services. None of the universities back home has a working health care system! In fact, professors at one public university could not get health care at all because they owed millions of shillings to the insurance company. And, think of my experience: my institution did not care about my health condition; but the one in Illinois hired me even after I told them I was not in good health. They invested so much in me, and now my condition is much improved. That's why I'm saying, even if the NYU system wants me, I won't go to New York."

"You feel a sense of loyalty to your employer."

"Yes, a sense of loyalty and gratitude. Another problem that causes brain drain is poor administration, as I have said. The leadership should be more professional. As it was when I was there, they made decisions based on personal relationships, based on loyalty, rather than on policy."

"How did the children do? Did they like it in your home country?"

"The last-born was OK with it, but the first two weren't amused. You see my daughter was already six years old when we left and was accustomed to living here. They couldn't take it there."

"What aspects of life at home could they not take?"

"Life at home, man," he shakes his head, laughing again mirthlessly. "There're many things. But take public transport for example: many people cannot afford cars, so they rely on public transport. Road carnage in Africa is at epidemic levels. As you may know already, I lived in Kenya for some years and then returned to the south, and it was not any different. There was a bus company called, was it *Safari*...? I don't know, Safari something. This bus would leave Kakamega at 8:00 pm and be in Mombasa by 4:00 am! By 8:00 am it will have gone to Malindi and back to Mombasa, ready to go back to Kakamega! Did you read of the incident where a bus hit another, which then plunged into a river, killing 57 people?"

"I read about a terrible bus accident a few years ago."

"I think it was the one. Another time a bus from the same company was driving to Mombasa and had just passed Nairobi, going toward Athi River, when it came across some *Maasai* cows crossing the highway. Twenty-five cows and several human lives later, the bus stopped. It hit 25 cows before it could stop! There was a public outcry, and that's when they started the public transport reforms that are now being enforced. I'm glad *matatu* passengers now have to have seat belts."

"*Matatus* used to be reckless and dangerous."

"They were, and still are, but at least reforms are taking effect. One time I was sitting in a *matatu*, which was driving on a dusty road. A passenger was complimenting the driver, saying how fast the thing could go. The driver said, 'this thing is not even going yet! It can go faster still.' And the road was dusty; we couldn't even see that far ahead. Suddenly I just heard, 'Boom!' This thing that could go faster had hit the guardrail at a T-junction that we had not seen, and rolled, and rolled again, and by the time it rolled the third time, the sliding door had opened and almost everyone was thrown out.

Maasai cows cross a major road in Nairobi South.

Maasai herdsmen drive their cattle and sheep to a spring of water at the heart of Amboseli National Park, near Mt. Kilimanjaro. City or park makes no difference. Both photos by the author. July 2017

(The narrative in this next paragraph has graphic content that might be disturbing to some readers; reader discretion is advised.) "It finally rested on the side with the open door. Man! I looked and saw a leg that the car was lying on. I wondered, 'How do I get out of here?' Then I realized there was a window that had been broken, so I took my briefcase and squeezed out through that window. I looked again and saw a head in the cornfield. Leaves of corn were shaking left and right, shaken by blood from the body that the head had been severed from.

"I walked a distance from the scene and sat down on a rock. Moments later a vehicle stopped, not like an ambulance or anything - the emergency response was non-existent! It was just a Good Samaritan who stopped and took the injured to the hospital. Then the people, the on-lookers, said, 'That man over there sitting on a rock, he is also a victim. He was in the *matatu,* too! Take him to the hospital.' So they came to take me to hospital, but I just said, 'Uh, I wasn't in that vehicle! I am OK, I don't need to go to the hospital!'"

"Were you confused, like many accident victims usually are?"

"Maybe I was, but I just didn't want to see any more blood after seeing the (decapitated) man and his head. I took another vehicle and continued my journey, but whenever the *matatu* hit even a tiny pothole, or turned sharply, I clung to the support bar with all my might; I thought we were overturning again. When I got home and opened my briefcase, I just saw and smelled blood; everything I touched looked like and smelled of blood," Dr. Malekha concludes the horror story, wincing like Lady Mc Beth after conspiring with her husband to kill King Duncan.

Matatus are communal taxis that ferry people from one place to another for a fee. They are an informal public means of transport, which has helped the transport sector in an economy where owning a car is a luxury only a minority can afford. On the other hand, *matatus* have proved to be quite reckless and dangerous as they speed on bad roads, competing for desperate passengers who often have not much choice. *Matatu* drivers usually defy virtually all traffic rules but get away with it due to the corruption that prevails in the traffic police system. They operate non-roadworthy vehicles, overspeed, overload the vehicles, but easily bribe their way through the numerous traffic police roadblocks. Their conductors or touts, known as *manamba* are also usually rude to passengers. The result has been untold road carnage, maiming and killing thousands of Kenyans per year. A newly hired university lecturer was killed in one such "accident" as he traveled from the capital to the university, barely after finishing his studies abroad. Reforms have started but the dangers still loom.

"Did this experience and lack of safety on the roads contribute to your decision to return to the US?"

"No, that was before, that was before. But yes, especially when I became ill and had to travel frequently between the hospital and my worksite, I was concerned about my safety on the road because there were many accidents, and I was on the road a lot. And as I said before, public transportation problems in Africa are just about the same. So, yeah, brain drain is there, and it is a problem. But that's because our economies cannot really sustain well-trained, qualified professors. And within the church organization, we do not want people to do business while they're also working for the church. We had to sign a conflict of interest form."

"You had to sign a statement that you can't do business while working for the church?"

"That you cannot do business while working for the church there! And yet in state universities, they were encouraged to do business. In fact when I lived in Kenya, Moi told them, (mimicking former president Moi) *'Kama wewe na fanya kazi wewe tafuta njia yakutengeneza exthra mahni.'* (If you are an employee, you find ways to make extra money.) In fact Moi used to talk nationally saying, *'Ate hawa profesa nafanya kilele; kama wewe profesa wewe pata njia ya kupata kitu.'* (Laughter.) *'Wacha kilele, Moi apana zuia wewe!* (more laughter.) (I hear that these professors are making noise that they want better pay! If you are a professor, find ways to get something. Moi has not stopped you!)

"Wow! You know Kenya more than a Kenyan and speak Kiswahili quite fluently! How long did you live in Kenya?"

"*Najua kidogo tu, ya kuomba ugali*" (I know a little bit, just enough to ask for cornbread) says Dr. Malekha, laughing heartily. "*Miaka mitano* (five years). You see, as a Bantu language speaker from Southern Africa, it was not difficult for me to pick up Kiswahili quickly."

Thus, a highly qualified African scientist is back teaching and researching in Illinois, while his heart is evidently in serving in Africa. But out of pure frustration with the system that would not even care for his health when it mattered the most, he had to leave and is now part of the brain drain to the West. And he is just but a sample of many like himself.

DR. POINDEXTER: A THEOLOGICAL AND PHILOSOPHICAL PERSPECTIVE

Dr. Poindexter is a white South African professor of theology at a parochial University in Virginia. He has such a busy schedule that to make an appointment with him for an interview was quite a challenge. Luckily, he found a little time when a planned meeting was cancelled, and he gladly scheduled our interview in place of the meeting.

"Well, I essentially was born and raised in South Africa, of South African parents. So, I imagine that makes me an African in very focal sense of the term," he states pragmatically.

He did his high school and college education in South Africa, and then taught at an academy in South Africa for a few years. After that he served as Youth Pastor, as well as Senior Pastor of various churches. Dr. Poindexter then taught at a church-owned college before going to the United States for his PhD, after which he returned to South Africa and taught at the same college for some years.

211

"I was then given an Inter-Divisional call to come here, so I'm actually here while still maintaining my divisional status; my citizenship is in South Africa. And I am, therefore, on the church headquarters list as official missionary from Africa to the United States."

"So, you are here purely as a missionary!"

"Well, 'purely' is an interesting term. I mean, I'm here as a tenured professor but my coming here was an interdivisional transfer, so I did not leave the country on independent transfer to come here."

His church has its headquarters in the United States known as The General Conference (GC). It has regional headquarters around the world called Divisions, under which there are Unions and Conferences. When a church worker is *called* from one Division to another, he or she is considered officially as a missionary. Dr. Poindexter is therefore essentially a missionary from Africa to America—a phenomenon that reverses the traditional trend of America sending missionaries to the rest of the world.

"Right! *Unusual* thing to do! Normally when people leave a country it's just that they want to leave, but I was given a call through the GC and through the inter-divisional call to be here."

"Sounds interesting! And how was your work there..."

"Rewarding! Some of the best years of my life! The difference of course is—I'm just talking about my teaching experience—was that, being a department of about the same size, we had about 60 students in theology, but only three teachers. So we saw students for a lot of the times, and I would have a four-year period of training with intensive engagement with people and their lives. Obviously here it is larger, so you don't see as many students for as much of the time.

"I also went back to South Africa at the point when apartheid was not finished because '91 rather than '94, it was unraveling; Nelson Mandela had been released from prison; the dye had been cast. So, I was in fact participating in the transformation that happened there."

"So you actually lived and worked there under apartheid?"

"Oh, yes. Up until I left the country in the early 1990s. So obviously my whole life was under that regime, and it was impacted by the experiences. But, the later years, the final years of apartheid I was out of the country."

"How was your life impacted by apartheid for the little time you were there?"

"In three basic ways, I mean, fundamentally, everyone's life was stratified, so that the way you lived, and what you did, and although Adventism was sort of one church, the same basic problems of apartheid, the isolation of people, and the unfair distribution of resources impacted everyone. Of course, being white I am on the right side of the railway line and therefore obviously benefited. But gradually my own experience was of gradual recognition and realization of the fundamental problems with the system. Shifting from a person growing up..., although my parents were never, we were always English-speaking, that was positive, that never supported the nationalist party, and so I grew up with that tradition."

"The nationalist party was the white ruling party?"

"Right. Well, white ruling party but whites were divided into those of Dutch descent (who invented and spoke *Afrikaans*) and English descent. The English descent had power up until 1948, and although they were colonialists, they were not proponents of apartheid. So, I grew up in a family that had always opposed apartheid, but nevertheless benefited just because if you were white, you benefited from the country. But my journey was one of growing up in a white opposition party, finally to the point where I identified with the liberation struggle itself and voted for the ANC and therefore, the change, part of that movement at the end. So, my whole life was a journey of discovery and shifting loyalties, to the point where, basically, my own people thought of me as a traitor to them."

"They thought that you were a traitor to the system?"

"I think that would be correct to say of some of them, because now, nobody ever supports apartheid now, because of changes, but back then it was the norm."

"So how come they considered you a traitor? And as a perceived traitor, how did they treat you?"

"I'll give you a simple example. As a young pastor in Durban, pastor of a church in a big town, some of the younger pastors at that stage tried to make some movements on the racial structures in the church that had molded the country. There were three different conference structures: one for whites, one for Zulu-speaking Africans, an Asian Field, and South African coloreds (people of mixed races).

"The first step we took in breaking down the system was [to] bring all those who used English or Afrikaans as their main Language, because it was difficult to..., the Asian, colored, and white conferences merged. Now, in the new system, people still belonged to their different racially based local churches. And so, my church was actually the first to have people transferring from a non-white church, into a white church. I lost members over it, but we went through, and saw a church with multiracial people worshipping together. And I, you know, was considered a troublemaker."

"Did some members revolt?"

"I actually lost members; in fact, it was a whole family of German background. I sat in the lounge, explained to him that this was the right thing to do; I even remember the name of the family! That we need to welcome them into our church fellowship. He got so angry with me! He even sat there in the lounge and said, 'I come from Germany, and the Germans have the right solution to this thing, and I will not set a foot in your church if you do this.'

"But we did, and he left! That's the level of racism that, to be honest, I didn't see with all white South Africans. It's just interesting that a German immigrant was saying this. But we did lose that family! They never ever returned to the church. But it was the right thing to do. That family, colored man's family, later he became head elder in the church. We still stay in contact. A wonderful family! And many others followed them."

It is noteworthy that Dr. Poindexter starts some thoughts but does not complete them. For example, in response to the question about the German's 'right solution,' he states, 'They have the right solution to, to…,' and diplomatically moves on without expressly stating that the German church member wanted white South Africans to treat blacks and coloreds the way Germany, under Hitler, treated Jews and other minorities.

This episode reflects the intensity of the conflict he went through to promote his revolutionary position. His progression from a whites-only church to a racially mixed one and voting for ANC is quite remarkable. He seems to have strongly believed in breaking the color bar under the apartheid system to the extent that he was willing to stick his neck out, even to the point of losing church members, while bringing coloreds in. The level of racism that prevailed in South Africa is apparently embarrassing to Dr. Poindexter, and he is eager to declare that not all white South Africans, including himself, were party to the alarming racist practices.

"And you mentioned three ways, so that was one."

"Yeah. Later, when I returned after graduate studies, we were helping the church in transforming Hillside College from essentially all white institution, to a point where it is now: 70 percent of the student body is black. What does that mean for local governments, you know, for student organizations or faculty changes? You see, one of the reasons that I was willing to leave South Africa was to make way for a black person to teach in my department. I mean here I am, as I said, we had one black South African on the faculty, of the four of us who were teaching at the college at the time. But unless somebody goes out, how are you going to transform the faculty racially to reflect the country?" he asks, explaining the dilemma of racially integrating society after it has been segregated for so long.

"The other thing that we were involved in was making an apology on behalf of the church, and a statement of intention with regards to the Truth and Reconciliation Commissions (T. R. C.) They invited churches to respond, to reflect on their involvement in the apartheid era—what they did do and didn't do. Some churches did worse than us, and others were better. We were first ignored, and eventually we wrote to the Truth and Reconciliation Commission and asked, 'Did you intend to ignore us?' And then they invited our response. It was quite a process. I have talked in many places at length about the process and the final document that we developed a nine-page statement. You can get a copy of that. You can also get it on-line."

"What's the crux of the statement? What does it say in brief?"

"Briefly it is the use of our church theology, the famous Revelation fourteen, verse twelve: 'Here are they that keep the commandments of God, the patience of the saints that keep the commandments of God and the testimony of Jesus,' and unpack that confession by showing how we failed in the whole apartheid era, by not really standing up to what we believed, and betraying the gospel. And there is language there of apartheid being a heresy, and about fundamentally betraying the gospel. We spell it out, and in the end a vision of commitment for the future. And that is an officially voted document by the South African Union Conference."

As stated before, Nelson Mandela's ANC government instituted the *Truth and Reconciliation Commission* to promote reconciliation between blacks and whites and all races in South Africa after the fall of apartheid. People on both sides who had committed acts of violence or torture or any form of oppression and violation of human rights could appear before the commission and confess their crimes to Bishop Desmond Tutu and his fellow commissioners, and they would be set free without any prosecution. At the inauguration of the commission, Dullah Omar, South Africa's former Minister of Justice said, "... a commission is a necessary exercise to enable South Africans to come to terms with their past on a morally accepted basis and to advance the cause of reconciliation."[8]

The appearance of Dr. Poindexter's church before the commission is seen as an admission of guilt either by commission or omission. They promoted and benefited from, or failed to condemn, apartheid and its racist practices under the system. This action also helped, as Pastor Foster would say, 'our conscience to be a little bit OK.' In the document, the white South African Adventist Church pleads guilty before the commission: guilty of failing to condemn the injustices of apartheid mainly because they benefited from the system.

Such injustices included oppression of the poor, brutal killings and beatings, and separation of families, among others, as Dr. Nxumalo states; "For us, to be killed by a white person was just normal." All these practices are against the commandments of God, which the church purports to uphold. Dr. Poindexter and his church thus presented a document to the commission which says in part: "We have to confess that, in appearance and reality, our practice in South Africa gave lie to the very intent of this tenet of our own fundamental beliefs. We were out of step with the stated principles of our worldwide church... We resolve to be more biblical in relation to the balance between the spiritual and the social in the future." (TRC Confession Document, p. 3.)

"Very interesting! Now, you lived in South Africa for five years after the fall of apartheid?"

"Oh, no! It depends on what you mean by "end of apartheid"; I mean apartheid was already finished by '89, when discussions were beginning… but if you want to say after elections- in '94 elections as an indication, then yes."

"Or we could say you lived there both during and after apartheid."

---

[8] http://www.justice.gov.za/trc/ Accessed 14 October 2019

"Yes."

"So, how do the two periods compare? You were in a very privileged position at first. Then after apartheid, I believe it probably wasn't the same. How was it different?"

"Well, white people still have massive privileges from the sheer economic advantages they had, and so I wouldn't say I was getting into a disadvantaged position. I'm a professor at a church school, teaching. So, I would not be experiencing any kind of a personal disadvantage.

"Of course, a numerous white South Africans in the church and elsewhere are worried about the future because it is much harder for their children to get the benefits of automatically getting into medical school. It's much more competitive; strong affirmative action goes on. That's why people feel concerned."

Dr. Poindexter points out that white fear is a product of the legacy of apartheid which created an economy for a minority white population who were "always guaranteed access to the best jobs," regardless of their qualification or lack of it. The railways, the post office, and other parastatal organizations where they had been almost always guaranteed jobs now strongly practiced affirmative action with the aim of rapidly building a black middle class, "and so, these people are left hanging." He states that the private sector is still thriving and creative white people who are willing to work hard still have opportunities to make lots of money.

"There's also a breakdown in some of the controls that prevented criminal activities and security issues. It has been a problem. I mean, political violence in South Africa ended; and when I went back, there was no stoning and killing of people on roads into Cape Town. We're in convoys, and all that ended completely. This was a benefit. But, I mean, we personally were burgled three times in our home on campus, which indicates the level of economic deprivation and crime that's happening there! I didn't consider that a disadvantage."

"You considered it a result of economic deprivation?"

"Obvious. It is a general result of apartheid, because what it did was break down the bonds of the family because men would go off and work on mines, and families would be shifted to tribal areas. And so it created a system, even the period of resistance created a climate in which legitimization of the use of violence and non-civil means of bringing about change, which could be understood. In a way it is a legacy, a tragic legacy, because there are countries that are for tourism like South Africa in the rest of Africa, where there is one culture basically of civil order and not a breakdown of social structure, even when you think it happens because poverty is all worse. But that's breaking down in the rest of Africa, too! You've not been in the city of Lusaka for a month or more and seen the problems facing the people. And they're traditionally a very peaceful society. I've been to Kenya this summer and seen the tragedies in the country. So, the whole continent is facing the problems, yet in South Africa I still think apartheid is the main engine to produce the violence today."

Dr. Poindexter's views on the crime situation in South Africa are quite balanced. On the one hand, he agrees with Pastor Foster that the situation is largely a result of poverty or economic deprivation of the majority, created by the apartheid system of government. And he also cites the black majority's use of violence to fight apartheid as propelling continued violence since they had grown accustomed to this as an acceptable tool for change. Yet he politely points out that apartheid is not the only cause of poverty and crime, since such crime is found in other parts of Africa, too, parts that were never under apartheid as we know it.

"What was the general reaction of the white population to the changes that took place in 1994? I understand that a lot of them might have left the country?"

"Um…, yes! There may have been an upsurge in '94 because it was almost a euphoric situation in '95. Ninety-four was the general election, was Mandela's reconciliation stance. I would say that during that period there was in fact influx of people coming *back* to the country; more than those leaving!"

"Oh, so people who had left came back?"

"Many, many, including many whites. There were many Eastern Europeans looking for a better life who flocked to the country, so the net immigration loss was probably reversed during that period. It got worse in the decade or more since then as the fundamental problems are still there; and many, many whites fear that there is little future for their kids as stated earlier.

"But a lot of people are feeling afraid," Asserts Dr. Poindexter, listing three main causes of white fear in South Africa today as "the lawlessness situation, characterized by high levels of carjacking, burglaries, and violent crime!" he pauses reflectively, then continues; "Maybe there is more fear than actuality, but that's a prime factor. Secondly, there is a fear that there's no future for their children, which is probably not true but is a perception. And, thirdly, and this is fairly speculative, but there is still many who have grown up with a kind of colonial outlook and are materialistic; and on top of that many who have an apartheid kind of racism. Although I think racism is not the real engine of what apartheid was; apartheid was really a form of nationalism. It is exactly what's happening in Northern Ireland and in the Middle East. It is a small minority worrying about a huge majority, and they're trying to protect the interest of its power base.

"That's essentially what's happening and a feeling of threat. But they were racist, and racism is still alive and well in the world as in South Africa. Those with that kind of outlook and just can't live in a new order have left. But they were leaving in the seventies already! There has been a brain drain for whites from the beginning of apartheid, probably for political reasons, others for purely personal advantage reasons. They saw a future they didn't want to live in, the brain drain was there. It hyped in the eighties, and the nineties."

"And so they feared those three…"

"Right! For a time in the seventies, the South African Rand was stronger than the dollar. It was one dollar thirty-two to a Rand! And in those days the economy was strong. As the economy seemed to get worse, people looked elsewhere..."

"What was making the Rand and the South African economy that strong?"

"Gold, diamonds, huge and powerful infrastructure. Unlike anywhere else in Africa, South Africa has a first world infrastructure: telephones that work, roads that are well-kept, hospital systems— all that is in place."

"I see. Now, professor, what're your plans for the future?"

"Well, my primary vocation is to serve the church, and I was willing to accept a call to come here to this university, after spending altogether just over a decade teaching in South Africa."

"For a change?"

"Well, mainly for three reasons. For me it was not to get a better life for myself. I already had job security and had a wonderful place to live and bring up my kids. But first reason: I was in a very isolated part of world Adventism, a little corner of Africa. And my location as a systematic theologian... I'm one of a handful in Adventism. I have a degree from Princeton Theological Seminary. My sense was to try to help Adventism grapple with modernity and post-modernity and to work on the huge challenges that face the church with respect to its theological vision for the future. To do that in isolation was very, very difficult! I thought I needed to be here to be able to deal with colleagues and to be able to have the opportunities for writing, for research, and for involvement with the church; so that was one factor."

"Have you had that opportunity?"

"I feel I have had it, and it definitely has been good to do that. There are many things that I miss, but that has been a valuable opportunity. The second factor was, I already told you I felt time had come for me to make it possible for a change in terms of the makeup of the faculty. If someone sits there in faculty position, what are you gone a do?"

"Expand the university!"

"There's no budget for that!" he exclaims, then laughs. "There's only so many slots that you can fill. So, the only thing to do was for somebody to move."

"Right. And the third one!"

"I mean the third one was, it has been good for my children because they have been able to stay home and be in church education for their college life, which would have been more difficult to do because of the limited offerings at a small school like Hillside College with a total of 300 students."

"What do you see as your future? Do you plan to continue here or to return to South Africa?"

"This is a permanent move. We moved here with a commitment to this university to stay here and to work here until retirement. However, (and the school has been very good) I have kept with their blessing my contact with my work in South Africa. So, I have been back to Africa in one capacity or another almost every year that I've been here. And I continue to work on research projects back there, we continue to be working on plans to assist graduate education in Africa, be a partner with the new graduate school, and helping in the training of ministers. So, I'm still very much involved in what's going on back home, and fortunately, the university has been able to support that. I'm still doing work there. Also, I still maintain my citizenship in South Africa; I'm not a US citizen. I'm here on a green card, and I will maintain my status until retirement as an inter-divisional worker, and then I'll decide what to do. My family is in Africa."

"Your family is in Africa! Who is there?"

"My parents are there, dozens, and dozens of uncles, and others. And I have two siblings with citizenship in African countries."

The professor has mentioned a number of reasons here as possible causes of the brain drain, namely: fear of the future for white kids under black rule in which they may not get guaranteed jobs as before; fear of an outbreak of violent crimes; taking advantage of opportunities for personal gain; and a weakening South African economy and currency. But Dr. Poindexter's reasons for living and working outside of South Africa are quite different from the reasons he mentions as causing the brain drain. While others left for fear of the future, violence, and economic advantage, he left South Africa for professional fulfillment, which he has now found, matters of conscience (to create room for a black faculty member), and to provide opportunity for his children to obtain Christian education. The last reason is in sync with other subjects' reasons, which involve seeking educational opportunities for themselves and for their children.

"A commendable family history of commitment to the church," I observed as we mutually laughed. "And what do you see as the future of South Africa?"

"I'm optimistic about the future of South Africa. My son has also been very involved in thinking about the future of the country, very involved in grassroots activism. And his point of view needs to be noted; he believes that there still awaits a real radical transformation in South Africa. That what we had, the end of apartheid was a shift from a white oligarchy to a black oligarchy; from a white middleclass to a black middleclass and that there's still a huge challenge of absolute poverty on the part of many, many people.

"If you go to South Africa, despite more than ten years of black government, what you find is a good tourist South Africa that … (tape inaudible) and increasing number of Germans and other Europeans who have bought property and are actually making a killing in huge amount of money. And poverty is still there! Yes, there has been some progress—water is being supplied to some townships—but the vast bulk of people still live in extreme poverty.

"In certainty, the legacy of apartheid economics still exists, and the question is, 'Is there a revolution still brewing to tackle that?' Now, Mbekki won an election with an increased majority. So, politically South Africans are clearly still willing to trust ANC even though they have been very slow to deliver on the changes being made. And South Africa has really bought into a kind of globalization vision, in South African terms called 'Gear.' When the ANC government first came to power, we had an office we called the Reconstruction and Development Program (RDP) which was a kind of a national socialist program meant to lift up the poorest people. Five years when Mandela retired and Mbekki took power, there was a whole shift; a shift from that to (what might have made white people happy) a basically structural readjustment so that South Africa would be competitive in the world market, to try and do what's happening in Asia. And I think Mbekki's vision was that South Africa would kind of try and play a leadership role in Africa, and, he is quite committed to a growing black middleclass but really neglecting the social agenda, and I'm not sure that that's a good thing.

"But still, I think the future of South Africa is bright. My advice to white South Africans is not to leave but to be engaged; to simply come to the psychological acceptance that you are a small minority in a community, but you are a minority that has a huge significance and responsibility even in a country that has enormous power way beyond your five million numbers, in a forty million country, but to be involved and to play a constructive role in the future of the country. And I urge the white South African Church to do that as well. Sometimes the church seems to be lagging society in general, which is a tragedy."

"Mhm! Now, professor, is there anything else you would like to say about the brain drain?"

"Yeah! Let me quickly say a couple of things. I think the brain drain is one of the greatest challenges to the future of Africa in general. It certainly has been a massive problem in South Africa. It's not only what I obviously can speak to in the sense I'm part of it, which is, white South Africans who have left in vast numbers and in many cases, along with their expertise, particularly medical doctors... (tape inaudible), medical assistants. We have just lost hundreds of thousands of people. So much so that the new South Africa had to invite Cuban doctors to come to South Africa, to work in the rural areas where you couldn't get South Africans to do so.

"There has also been significant brain drain of black talent, some of that because you could understand people didn't want to live in a country with the political system that they had. So, many people have left. Some came back, but not all. But if I look across the whole continent of Africa, I think it is one of the *huge* challenges.

"The only way of stopping it is to reverse the practice of uprooting Africans, training them in a western environment, and then expecting them to go back after their families and their children have become Americanized. There's a huge culture shock. Africans need to be self-reliant in developing institutions, partnerships, the kind of thing we were talking about, where we can assist but rather lead to indigenous programs in Africa to try to reverse the pattern.

"It's a huge process; and, one last thing I'll say is, in terms of Christianity in general and Adventism in particular; what we're facing, already an accomplished fact is, in the last 50 years, a complete change in the face of both Christianity in general and Adventism in particular. It is no longer a northern phenomenon; it's a southern phenomenon."

"It's a southern phenomenon?"

"The growth of the Adventist church, for example, is in all the same areas as it is for the rest of the Christian Church: Latin America, Africa, and Southern Asia—Africa more than anywhere else. Christianity is just growing in leaps and bounds; people worry about Islam, and Islam is growing, but Christianity is growing just as fast. By natural growth, as well as by...,"

"Evangelism?"

"Evangelism to some degree. And Adventism is growing very fast in Africa, and here is the challenge; we here in North America and Europe represent less than ten percent of the world Adventism mission. White Adventism is a dying phenomenon. How are we going to grapple with the enormous challenges of a new Christendom and a new Adventism, which is a southern Adventism? And it is an Adventism that is poor, an Adventism that is largely non-sophisticated and uneducated? That's the huge challenge on the agenda. So, the brain drain is working in the exact opposite direction from where the center of gravity of the church is moving. So, you're studying a very important problem."

"Thank you!"

"And I look forward to seeing the results of your research, to know what we can do about it."

"Well, thank you very much! I really enjoyed speaking with you."

"Thank you! I appreciate you."

Dr. Poindexter has taken a very theological and philosophical approach to addressing the subject of brain drain from Africa to the West. No doubt his highly academic and scholarly background informs his position. His greatest concern is the potential impact of the brain drain on the Christian church in the world. Like Tammy whom we'll meet in the next chapter, who pleads guilty of the brain drain, Dr. Poindexter feels the same: "I'm part of it." But he, likewise, is stuck here in a mishmash of psycho-sociological, professional, and educational circumstances, much like the rest of the subjects.

13

THE SECOND GENERATION

IT WIZ: MABUTI

Mabuti is an information technology (IT) specialist from Zambia. He first came to the United States in his early teens when his parents were students in the United States and Canada and then went back with them to Zambia where he completed his high school education. Mabuti then attended a parochial college in Zimbabwe for two years before transferring to a similar university in California. I asked him to tell me his perspective on the brain drain: what causes it and what can be done about it.

"For me personally I think it was my ambition to come here since I was about nine," he states with laughter. "I knew that I would come and graduate from a university here. That's how I planned it and, fortunately, that's how it worked out."

He surmises that his parents' western education exposed him and his siblings to the western world at an early age. Mabuti missed a golden opportunity to attend a top-rated high school after earning a scholarship, because it was his mom's time to return home.

"I was 13. And in fact, while I was out here, I got a scholarship to go to Brown, a prominent high school out in the East Coast. But my parents thought I was too young for them to leave me here," he says laughing heartily. "Brown is a very prominent school; that's where, for instance, John F. Kennedy graduated from. They were granting scholarships to gifted students in inner city schools, right on the edge of Harlem, in Manhattan."

"Well, congratulations! You're gifted and talented!"

"Well I was, at least then," he jokes with another hearty laughter.

When he went back home, Mabuti decided he would come back for university education, and his parents agreed to that. He had wanted to join an HBC in Alabama, but his parents refused, thinking that he wanted to go there for the music, not for the education. They objected, and Mabuti ended up attending college in California. "So that was always my goal, to come out here and work in this economy, mainly because this country really supports and facilitates ambition and drive. As I grow older, I realize that's the main reason I wanted to come out here. And so, I did; I went to school here, as you already know."

Mabuti does not regret missing the prestigious Brown scholarship. "Thinking back now, I appreciate that. I think it was the right decision, because, I have always been a type 'A' personality," he states with a spirited laughter. "I'm not sure that at that age, without close parental influence, that it would have been the right thing for me to be in high school here by myself."

"I see! What do you do now?"

"Right now, I manage databases for a certain corporation. They make defibrillators and pacemakers and catheters —heart technology medical devices, basically. I am a project lead for a certain segment of their technology."

"That sounds like a highly technical field!"

"It is! It is very, very technical. Very, very technical. Yeah, I spend probably, I'd say, two out of three hours in front of a machine," he chuckles. "I'm always on call, so I always have to be near a cell phone and near my laptop," he adds with more titter.

"Wow! How long have you done this?"

"At this level, almost six years, and before this I was doing it at a junior level for another five years, and then for three years prior to that I was a programmer."

Mabuti is one of the numerous skilled African IT specialists who live and work in the United States and other western countries, providing the much-needed expertise that keeps the Western world's economies vibrant. One wonders what would happen if such specialized knowledge in this and other areas were to be employed in Africa: would they help accelerate the growth of the emerging African economies? Are these economies in a position to absorb and meaningfully employ all such highly skilled labor?

"You were saying that this country supports your ambition. If you were in Zambia with your kind of technical know-how, what would you be able to do with it?"

"Well, the good news is that things are changing now, at least from what I'm reading in the newspapers. But it was very discouraging a while ago. Let me give you an example of a very good friend of mine, Charles. This guy graduated from Zambia's top university at the age of fifteen! Or was it sixteen?"

"He graduated at the age of fifteen or sixteen!"

"Yes! Kilembe, the ivy league of high schools in Zambia. He immediately got sent off to Oxford to study engineering. And by the age of twenty-four, he had his PhD in engineering. So he goes back to Zambia to work for the mines. He looks at their smelting process, and within a few days of examining what they do and running some calculations, he realizes that the current process wastes about 30 percent of the usable ore. So he walks into his boss' office and makes a suggestion, saying, "I have been thinking about this process. If we make just one, two, three, four changes, we could have a yield that's 30% higher!' And the guy listens to him and at the end of his presentation says, 'So you go to school for a few years, you come back, and you think you can tell us how to run things! Get out of my office!' Within a year and a half, he had left and now is one of the top engineers at one of the most prominent engineering firms in the UK. He's doing well. That was typical of many, many stories, my parents included."

"Your parents included!"

"My parents, as I mentioned, they came here on scholarships and did very well. My mother is an Ivy League graduate of Columbia University."

"She is!"

"They went back; my father was one of the key designers of Zambia's privatization program."

"He's an economist?"

"He is actually trained in public and business administration, but he understands economics very well. He was, for instance, managing director of the National Import and Export Corporation, which is the main import and export procurement wing of government in Zambia, for some years. And then he got into the privatization program after the new government came in.

"But after all of that, when their primary tasks were done and when they refused to do certain things that certain leaders wanted them to do, they were forced out of those positions and were very frustrated, so much to the point that they finally said, 'We're not doing this anymore.' The best thing I think is they went and started working for the church and have worked for the church for the last 15 years or so.

"But the mentality of leaders back home, that of suppressing new ideas and viewing ambition as a bad thing and also to a very large degree, looks down on upright people who do not want to do corrupt practices—all of that contributes to underdevelopment and brain drain!"

"Do you have examples of some things that the government wanted them to do, which they did not want to do?"

Laughing generously, Mabuti says, "Oh, yea! My father, for instance, as I mentioned to you, was in Import and Export Corporation. A senior member of the government walks in and says, 'Listen; we've got this procurement of tractors coming in from China, but I also need a few tractors for my own personal farm. If you're willing to do this, we can split this thing out so that we purchase more than the actual amount, and we split the extra. And if you want to, you can sell yours,' and so on. My father refuses and within a few months after that he is asked to resign."

"Was this under previous or present administration?"

"This was under a previous administration; but the same thing happened under the present one as well. The privatization program that my father also co-designed was supposed to look for buyers of the parastatals[9] in three different levels. They were supposed to look at Zambians with means, first: those who have the cash and have a good business strategy. Secondly, they were supposed to look for Zambians without means, but who could be financed either by government or by banks. The third choice was foreign investors with means, and then everybody else after that.

"Because everybody in government was barred from participating in the program to try and eliminate graft, what the government did instead, all these ministers and the president himself included," he states with a chuckle, "is they set up companies which are just shadow companies. (That's why he is being prosecuted now, if you've been following Zambian news. They're coming after him for that.) These companies would submit their bids, then the leader would come and put pressure on the privatization agency to sell the parastatal to their company. So, my father protested that, and again within a few months, you know, he was asked to resign."

"Who would ask him to resign?"

"In this case it was the minister of finance himself, and it is believed he was under pressure from the president. In fact, he might even get called to testify in the case against the former president. That is the corrupt aspect that hurts people with good intentions. People are there to get rich quickly. You see people especially in this government who were living very simple lives, and within two years of being in government they were buying multimillion-dollar

---

[9] A parastatal is an organization or industry that is partially owned and run by the government in many African countries. Examples include the post office, the railway systems, and electric power companies.

mansions, and five or six each. That's a typical Zambian politician's story. Everyone is there for personal gain, and they ultimately do very little for the people. When you think about it, with the resources we have in Africa, there is no reason we should be the poorest continent in the world! Frankly we should be the richest continent on earth!" he asserts, then laughs.

The theme of Africa's rich resources as it contrasts to its poverty is a dominant one. Dr. Uche, Dr. Omari, George, and now Mabuti, have raised it and often almost using the same words. Africa indeed has very highly skilled human resource as seen in Mabuti's high-tech skills as well as in other subjects' expertise in various fields, and these individuals are quite successful in their respective occupations in the United States and other western countries. Besides, Africa is rich in minerals and other natural resources. Yet the continent remains afflicted with poverty and underdevelopment.

So, what causes the underdevelopment and poverty on the continent? Mabuti's description of attitudes of the establishment in the civil service—where ideas are rejected due to age and education of the sources—and his specific examples of graft at the highest levels of government may hold the answer to the question: it is greed and corrupt leadership. If this can be rectified, Africa would develop and get out of self-inflicted poverty woes. Shortly after this, a social-media video went viral; it decries how Zambia has sold her copper mining industry to China at a throw-away price of US$25 million, only for the Chinese to turn around and make a profit of US$75 million within weeks and pay off their loan without having had to make any capital investment. If true, it is a striking example of appalling mismanagement of resources by African governments. And it is mismanagement that does not necessarily result from lack of qualified human resource; rather it results from the practice that does not give a chance to African experts to apply their expertise in the best interest of their countries.

I posed this question to Mabuti: "Where does this culture come from? Are we Africans more corrupt than other peoples?"

"I don't know, but I think there are certain things about our culture that made it that way. Let me... (tape inaudible) this by saying that I'm very proud of my African culture. But the element of the culture that made modern economic growth impossible, at least with the current thinking—and I've been called all kinds of things for this— first I think it is "the chief" mentality. The idea that it is disrespectful and unacceptable to suggest that leadership is wrong... and I'm not sure where this came from, because I'm sure that in the old days, people may not do it openly but the elders were always free to speak with the chief," he asserts, laughing again. "And they would tell him frankly where they thought he was wrong."

"Probably now we have "the chief" without the elders to apply the brakes!"

"And we have this hero worship of our leaders throughout Africa in this present generation, I believe. Kaunda for instance, *nobody* could say anything against him in public, *nobody*. This is why it was such a big shock when *Mutenge* came in the early 1990s, which finally took him out of power. Otherwise if you said something against him in public, even without his prompting, the police would take you away and you'd never be seen again. It was that simple. Anybody who dared speak out was either arrested or completely suppressed.

"A day came when a new crop of leaders came and after what we called the old guard, the ones who led from independence on, took over, at least in Zambia that seemed to happen. I follow Kenyan politics a little bit and that seemed to happen there also, after Moi left and Kibaki came in, and now Uhuru. So people are speaking out a little bit more, but unfortunately the corruption side of things didn't change very much. In fact, in the Zambian situation things got a lot worse. The Kaundas made many mistakes due to lack of experience and lack of good advice. I mean Kaunda was a Form Two dropout when he assumed the leadership of Zambia. He assumed a two-billion-dollar rich treasury, which was all squandered by the time he left. But very few people can accuse Kaunda, at least in the monetary sense, of being corrupt. Now, he was oppressive politically. He suppressed opposition, he suppressed alternative voices, but he didn't enrich himself."

"He didn't enrich himself. So, you would say that Kaunda's case was more of incompetence due to lack of education?"

"I think so, yeah, while the next groups of leaders were just there to rape the economy. The new guys who came after him, I mean, they came in to get rich and get rich quick! Now, the third generation, Levi Mwanawasa, he is really pushing for change. He's trying to prosecute the corrupt practices of the previous government officials, including the ex-president himself. But he has a very tough journey ahead of him because most of the political leadership are not behind him, as far as fighting corruption. I'm reading news reports from Malawi; the same thing seems to be happening to the leader there. He wants to fight corruption, but he doesn't have the support. So, change is coming very slowly. I think it will be a few generations before we actually have meaningful change."

'A few generations' is a long time for Africa to wait and change from corruption, poverty, and underdevelopment to efficiency and progress. The cost is too high, and the other continents are not waiting. Africa is losing human and other resources to these continents. The best time to change is now. It is increasingly amazing how the subjects use similar phrases, such as, "African leaders are raping the economy," which is used by both Mabuti and Dr. Uche. It gives credence to the belief that Africa has enough resources that could be tapped to enhance the continent's development and progress if only such resources could be competently and honestly managed.

"Now, you were saying that we have resources enough to be the richest in the world. What different approach could be taken in managing these resources to enable the continent of Africa realize its riches potential?"

"Well, when we got our economies back after colonialism, we didn't really invest ourselves; we kept the status quo. I mean we kept mining diamonds, copper, and gold and shipping them to Europe. Look at what happened...," he pauses uncharacteristically of his eloquent self.

"That's what the colonial governments had been doing!"

"That's what the colonial governments had been doing! We just changed management, really," he chuckles. "But we kept shipping the wealth out, instead of using it to build locally. Look at the East Asian model; they don't have much in terms of resources! They import copper at however many dollars a ton. They turn around and create these JVCs and SONYs and Hitachis and sell these small components with little bits of the copper that we shipped them so cheaply. And we buy them for two or three hundred dollars as we import them, thereby enriching their economies.

"If we stopped thinking that way and started building factories and start creating manufactured, finished goods, and start exporting those instead, we'd do a lot better! Because we're using very little resources in this complete product! And we ship that out and sell it at a much higher return than if we are shipping the raw material out. So, that's the first change in mentality that needs to happen," Mabuti affirms, his gaze still fixed on the television set in front of us. The TV has been on since I walked in, tuned to a news channel, but volume turned to a bare minimum as Mabuti multi-tasks – talking with me attentively while also watching news; a testimony to his generation X status.

"What would it take for us to manufacture, let's say those transistor radios?"

"Here is the paradigm; we talked earlier about suppressing new ideas and ambition. People who can come up with ideas and walk up to a bank or the government and present a business plan should get a loan to set up that kind of thing. But that kind of thing is not encouraged!

"There was a guy that my father ran into some years back. He was creating stereos in his home! Using wood for the outside covers and getting all these transistors and dials and whatever he needs to put them all together. And he even made the speakers by himself using cardboards for the actual air moving portions. He had a magnet and coiled wire and literally created everything—an amplifier with speakers. But it was radio only (no tape recorder). My father looked at this guy and said, 'This is really something! If we could get some funding, we could actually get something that could be comparable to a finished product.' He worked with him, made a business plan for him, and helped him prepare an application to the bank. He went to the bank; he was turned down. They literally laughed at his idea!"

"They laughed at his idea."

"That guy went back to the village and became a cattle herder in the rural areas. But in the US, that kind of thing would be looked at positively. So, people with ambition are suppressed, and they have no avenue to express that creativity. It would take those kinds of people being funded by the government and being encouraged. But that kind of thing will take a lot of time."

Mabuti's story reminds me of a cousin in Kenya who, for high school science project, created a radio waves transmitter. Its radio signals were detected by the country's then only radio station, which was run by the government. The government panicked and frantically searched for the source, till they found him. The special branch —the intelligence body—confiscated his project and warned him to refrain from such endeavors. Now he is one of the African IT specialists in the United States. Maybe, as Mabuti suggests, if the government encouraged innovation rather than discouraged it, such individuals would go a long way in contributing to national economic and technological development. Kenya would indeed be exporting radios, not importing them as is still the case now. So, would Zambia, and many other African countries that are primarily consumer markets. Another video has gone viral on social media of a Malawian young man who has assembled bicycle tires and motor-bike engine, brakes, and gears, and made a rudimentary car out of it, to the great admiration of on-looking villagers. It would be helpful to seriously consider Mabuti's suggestion that such talented individuals be mentored and funded.

Children in Nairobi's Pumwani Estate rummage through half-burnt trash, salvaging discarded electronic parts to reassemble for toys.

Against the backdrop of politicians asking for votes with large posters, this boy has found enough material to begin his assembly.

With the keen eyes of an expert, this child has embarked on the assembly process, having found enough material. Imagine what would happen to Kenya's economy if politicians invested in educating and providing opportunity for these children instead of filling their own pockets, amid desperate poverty! Maybe we'd be at par with our "age-mate" – South Korea? Photo by the author, July 2017 (Face obscured to protect minor.)

"Is there anything else you'd like to say about the brain drain and its causes?"

"Yea! I think another thing that affects the situation back home is our dependency culture. Not only dependency as in how our economies are dependent on aid from IMF, World Bank, and the G-8 and so on; but also way down to the individual level. You've noticed that in families there's one individual who does well? And as soon as that one individual does well, a host of others move in," he titters again.

"And they're expecting that one person to take care of them. And not only those living with that individual, but also the ones back home expect some money to be remitted back home every month and so on and so forth. And often, a lot of those dependents don't work, as they should! Well, that has multiple effects: number one, it drains resources for the one person who is doing better. If you look at economies like the US, the people who succeed do so because they are able to reinvest their returns. But back home what ends up happening is that any little extra cash that the very ambitious and successful people make ends up being drained by supporting extended, expensive family and friends. Now, on a humanitarian level, that's a good thing; but economically, it is negative because what ends up happening is, we become a consumer culture. We're spending and never investing; never investing! Constantly spending.

"And so, you find that a lot of these people when they retire from their good jobs, they actually have nothing! They may have built a house and that's pretty much it. They don't have anything that they have put down as investment that can *grow* and create jobs. That's another thing I think people try to get away from, because from here they can work and support their families by sending money back, which goes a lot further. But also put it in other things that will secure them in the future, not only in terms of having savings when they retire but also in terms of having investments that can actually grow, and they can even build a business. So, I think that's another area that really affects us.

"Now that is on the micro level. On the macro level, it is the same mentality as far as how the government manages the economy. I'm not sure that there's active thinking on 'how do we get rid of this debt and how do we not borrow more and still sustain ourselves?' I think the mentality is still, 'we'll borrow so much from the IMF and we'll get so much from the World Bank, and we can meet our budget requirement that way.'

"I think there're simple things that can be done to make a very big difference. For instance, why do African leaders have to drive

Mercedes Benz cars? Honestly!" Mabuti asks with a chuckle, puzzled. "They don't really have to! We can't afford it! During the Chiluba government I remember they ordered 90 X Class Mercedes Benz cars, direct from Germany! The shipment cost alone was estimated at 25 million US dollars! Just the shipment cost; forget the actual cost."

"What were they going to do with them, the Mercedes cars?"

"Ministers, deputy ministers, and so on and so forth, for just driving around. You know, that probably is a small portion of the cost, because when you look at the roads in Zambia and you look at the maintenance cost of those luxury vehicles, it is extremely high! Changing tires on a BMW Sedan is an 800-dollar task! To buy the tires and get them realigned and all of that! Eight hundred US dollars! Forget the more expensive parts of the vehicle. And with those roads back there, the maintenance cost is very high because it is done more frequently. So, if they thought of driving vehicles that will do better on those roads, maybe smaller SUVs, like the Hyundai SUVs that cost US$15-16,000, make that official government vehicle. I think that will cut a significant amount of money."

"Do you think somehow we may be under pressure from the donor countries to buy their products, so that they're really giving us this aid but also boosting their economies?"

"It's possible that that's also a factor! But lately I have seen some protest from the western world on those kinds of purchases. But yes, you are right that is possible. The western governments have been really mute on those issues. It's only recently they have started pushing for what they call 'good governance.'"

Mabuti has raised a thought-provoking question, similar to what someone else once asked, wondering why African government officials drive expensive cars, such as US$50,000 SUVs. It would be interesting to have an answer from a government official; an answer to the question, *"Why do African leaders have to drive Mercedes Benz cars? Honestly! Can we really afford it?"*

It is a shame that African leaders have to wait for donor governments to demand 'good governance.' Why don't they demand it of themselves? They owe it to the people they govern. They owe it to the children in Pumwani, Kibra, Mathare, and all the sprawling slums where people live under squalid, less than human conditions. How do they feel when a western leader calls their countries, "s#@t-h*#e countries"? Do they realize they are the ones being so described? And why don't the people demand it of their leaders? It is their right to have good governments, with services that work. The 'chief mentality' that puts leaders above those led may be the reason, and it must change.

For this to happen, the leaders must realize that they are there for the people and not vice versa. They cannot exist as leaders without the people but the people they lead can exist without them. The peoples of Africa ought to hold their leaders accountable and demand good governance from them. But this change may take generations to happen, in the absence of deliberate and persistent education of the people. Thanks to social media, there are signs of citizens holding their leaders accountable.

I remember my elderly uncle and his peers had a scheduled *baraza* (community meeting) with the location chief at 2:00 pm one Tuesday. They bought crates of sodas and snacks to welcome the chief. 3 o'clock, no signs of chief; 4 o'clock, still no chief, and no message of a meeting postponed or cancelled. At 5 o'clock my uncle, as the village headman, addressed the other elders and dismissed them, stating that it looked like the chief was not going to come. I asked him, "How can the chief, a man twenty years your junior, keep you elders waiting for hours and then he doesn't show up?"

"*Ooo, Wuodwa; kon odoko wuon piny!*" (Oh, our son; he happens to be the owner of the land!) In my uncle's and his fellow elders' minds, the chief, by virtue of having been appointed chief, was the 'owner of the land' or community and therefore could do as he pleased with it. He could, and did call meetings and then not show up, thereby wasting many potential development hours. Each elder could have been engaged in some productive activities, but instead they sat there for hours, waiting for 'the owner of the land.'

And this phenomenon was common to many government offices where one could go to get a document signed, but end up spending the whole day waiting for the officer, who had either stepped out for personal business or was just sitting there chatting on the phone or waiting for a bribe. Therefore, "the chief mentality" as Mabuti calls it, is a reality that hinders progress and development in many parts of Africa.

"Do you know many Zambians or Africans in your area of specialization, the field of IT, who work in Western economies?"

"Yea, Quite a few! I'm on a list of professionals and students called 'Zambia net.' We exchange e-mails every day, as many as 50 in a day. These are Zambian professionals not only in the US but also in the UK, Australia, and Japan. We have a network of 300-400 members on that list, just within this area, I know three other Zambians who are in different areas of IT. One is in networking, one in systems administration, and another in the business end of IT."

"Do you think that if many of you returned home at once you might overwhelm the corrupt system and bring about positive change?"

"Yes, it might work, but there is only one major hurdle that I see: the system back home is set up to grease the politicians. The only way you can do something is by giving something to the politicians. You want to set up a business, you have to give a percentage to the politicians. If all the professionals went back to Zambia today, they wouldn't form enough of a majority to overcome that one factor.

"The politics," he chuckles in frustration, "would be the biggest obstacle, and I'm not sure how one would be able to get around that. Even if you had the funds to set up something, you'd still have to apply for a permit to do business. Even if you were to set up a business on land you already own, you still must apply for a permit! And that's the agony. That's what the politicians use to get the greasing that they want. And so, if you refuse to do it that way, they'll say no! You agree to it, you could part with as much as 30% of your profit! Maybe you're already thinking, 'Is this going to be profitable enough for me?'"

One can logically conclude that one major cause of the brain drain from Africa is graft in government. It has permeated society from highest to lowest levels, making it virtually impossible for an honest person to do business and succeed. As Mabuti states above, it is next to impossible to set up any business venture without having "to grease the politicians" or government officials by giving them bribes.

He echoes what Dr. Kanuma said regarding professionals returning from abroad to change the system: "If all the professionals went back to Zambia today, they wouldn't form enough of a majority to overcome that one factor."

You can hear the frustration and anguish in the tone of his voice and repeated chuckles of frustration as he narrates the hurdles that one has to overcome to bring about positive change in his country. It may truly be a long time before such change is realized. It could actually take a generation or more, as Mabuti suggests.

IT specialist Mabuti sits in the corporate jet of his company enroot a business trip. Courtesy of Mabuti

TAMMY

Tammy is a dentist in her early thirties who just graduated recently and is newly married. She was born and raised in an affluent family in Uganda, but her humility and self-discipline belie her upper middle-class background. She engaged in odd jobs to pay her way through college, thanks to her father's philosophy of the benefits of hard work and achievement. She came to the United States in the early 1990s to pursue a degree in biology, which was to prepare her for entering dental school.

"I actually wanted to become a dentist at that time so that's why I came to do that," she states confidently. Previously she attended a private academy in Uganda and then proceeded to study French literature in France for six months. Subsequently Tammy came to the United States, where she enrolled in a Historically Black College (HBC) in the south. "it was a huge culture shock! Huge!" she recalls.

"You mean the French experience or the Mississippi one?"

"No, not the French experience; the Mississippi experience. This is very strange; I experienced more culture shock in Mississippi than I did in France!" she states with laughter.

"How come you went to France?"

"You know, I took French in high school, and I really, really enjoyed it!"

"So you speak *Français*?"

"*Oui,*" she responds in French, laughing heartily. "I learned to speak it, and there was a program I learned about and told my parents I was really excited about it."

"So it was your idea to go to France?"

"It was mine! It was like a bargaining chip, because I wanted to go to England for college; but my parents wanted me to go to the US. So it was my bargaining chip," she explains, laughing some more. "At least go to France, then to the US."

Tammy remembers how hot Mississippi was when she first arrived that summer. She experienced severe culture shock as it relates to interacting with African Americans in her new college. "I thought they were really loud; the women were," she recollects.

Tammy's parents accompanied her to Mississippi, gave her just US$2,000, and then left for Uganda, saying they would come back for her college graduation. They were not sending her any more money for the expected four years of study. She acknowledges that even though two thousand dollars was hardly enough for one quarter of private college education, she was much better off than most Ugandan student who came to study in the United States. "Many students did not come with anything," she muses. Besides, in Uganda Shillings, "that was *a lot* of money."

Several African students in the United States indeed do not "come with anything," as Tammy puts it. They end up working two or three odd jobs to sustain themselves and pay tuition. Many end up taking longer to complete their courses, while others do not finish at all. For those who complete their studies and manage to secure professional jobs, the temptation to stay on and make up for years of toiling may be great.

Tammy could not take the loudness, which also made her fellow students appear unfriendly. By November of the same year she was determined to go back home. "I didn't think they were very friendly, and then, I also got tired of constantly being corrected!"

"Being corrected?"

"You know, pronunciation, because I was used to the British way, so they couldn't understand you, and the constant question was, (and I was probably speaking just the way I do now!) 'Where're you from?' I don't sound Canadian, but they thought I was Canadian. I decided by November I'd be going home; definitely going home!" Tammy seems to have been quite frustrated by the "where is your accent from" phenomenon.

Most African and other international students have had to endure this experience upon entering America. Many of them had hitherto not realized they spoke with an accent. At one point an African student asked her fellow African students, "Have you been taught how to say your (first) name?" Everyone laughed as each shared his/her story. It turned out everyone had been corrected on how to say their western first names by some well-meaning Americans, and other not so well-meaning.

Some other African students had been called aside by a professor who told them, "The people here like you, but they say you have a strong body odor. It may help if you buy some deodorant..." The students were tongue-tied as they asked themselves, 'Wait! We are dressed up in suits, and someone is telling us that we smell? No way!'

"But then you didn't go home!"

"You know, my parents said to me, 'If you don't like it that's fine. Go ahead and stick it out through the whole year, at least finish one year. If you don't like it by the end of the first year, go ahead and transfer somewhere else. No big deal.' And so, believe it or not, I had a couple of friends who were at Southeastern College, and so I was going to transfer there. And probably about a month before my scheduled transfer, one of my mother's friends—I had met him once or twice—and he came to me and said, 'I had a dream last night that you wanted to leave this college! Is that true?' And I told him, 'That's true, in fact I'm leaving!'" she recalls, laughing.

"Did he really have a dream, or your parents told him?"

"You know, my dad didn't even know he was there! I don't know, but I told my mom about it and she said, 'I think you really need to stay.' So, I prayed about it and decided to stay."

"Wow! So, his dream and encouragement, influenced your decision to stay at the Mississippi college?"

"I knew it was a *call* in a couple of months," she says, heartily laughing.

"So now, in retrospect, what do you think of your decision to stay in Mississippi?"

"The best decision of my life! The best decision! It was definitely worth it!"

"What makes it the best decision of your life?"

"Because I came out with a certain pride I don't think I could have got anywhere else! The college is a unique one; it is a Historically Black College that teaches you everything they possibly can to make you feel that you can do anything, and they really hammer into your head that you can. But they also really equip you for the fact that when you get out of there, you will not be treated like you can, but to know that in spite of the people, you can do it. And it was kind of the best thing."

"Has their prediction come true since you left the south?"

"Are you kidding me!" she exclaims then laughs vigorously.

"Or, let me take you back a little bit: after you left Mississippi, where did you go?"

"After I left, I came to Washington, to a private dental institution under a new program, since there weren't a lot of black students coming to their dental school. And...," she speaks haltingly, her characteristic articulate confidence fading, "they wanted to get a couple more black students, and they had a partnership with my previous college...and they have a fairly unhealthy reputation; the black students. But anyway, I got into this Early Selection Program. The funniest thing again, I didn't want to come to Washington," she exclaims, again beaming with laughter.

"They say 'man is naturally resistant to change!'"

Tammy laughs more generously and says, "I think so! And I got in, and that's how I came to Washington. I got in the first quarter and took classes free. They said, 'If you like the classes, or if you don't, no big deal.' So, I took classes the first quarter, and they paid for it."

"And you're still on your two thousand dollars from your parents; you were surviving by working?"

"I'm still on my two thousand dollars," she affirms with amusement.

"When do you work, when do you go to class, and when do you make the grades?"

"It's a struggle! I remember when I was in college, if I wasn't sleeping, I was in class or studying, I mean, those are pretty much the only things beside work. Sabbath was the best day of the week because that gave me from sundown to sundown to rest and sleep without working or studying."

"What work did you do?"

"The first job I got was in housekeeping. It was so hard! That motivated me through the eight years of school," she laughs even more. "That was very hard, and then I worked as a receptionist for another year and then taught Biology Lab for two years."

"Wow! That's quite commendable! I wonder if many people with your kind of background would have been able to do that. I mean, I know socially, you were very well-highly placed back home, at least from the point of view of most people (more laughter.) Going from that to doing housekeeping…, and how much did it pay?"

"Below minimum wage. But we had to! We had to! My dad believed in education; it quite helps to have parents who value education. Going to college for us was not a question of *if* we'll go to college; it was taken for granted that we'd go. My dad did not care very much what you studied in college, but you had to go and also plan on doing some post-graduate work. And I'm glad my dad made sure we paid for it."

"You had to pay your way through college, even your siblings?"

"They, too, had to! My dad had this saying that, how does it go? 'For those who have to fight for it, life has a certain flavor the sheltered never know.' So, he made sure we worked for college education. That way you value it more."

"It is like what a certain teacher here told me; he had taught in Zimbabwe for one year with the Peace Corps and is now back teaching here. When I asked him to compare the experiences teaching there versus here, he said, 'I wish I had the African students with the facilities I have here; for they desire to learn but do not have much. Students here have much more facilities, books, and supplies, but have no desire to learn.'"

"I would like to reverse that though, especially at college level. As a college student here, I don't remember ever sitting down to rest or relax except for sleeping time and on Sabbath, which I luckily got off. We were always working."

"University students back home seem to have more free time?"

"Oh, yes! They do! They do," she asserts, laughing again. "We went to one of the public universities in Zimbabwe; that was my sophomore year. There was one professor who got funding from World Health Organization to do a research project there. So we were all excited and went there, working hard. But after every few hours the local students would sit down and take a tea break. And they would be asking us, 'Why are you guys working so hard?' And I'm like, 'Someone is paying for this, for us to be here and do this!'"

"And do you think this attitude spills into the workplace once they graduate; it continues?"

"It does, it sure does. Before our project was over, they rioted," she states with laughter.

"What did they riot for?"

"Oh, I don't remember but it could be disagreement with the government over allowance, food, or some political issues. If university students back there worked to pay their way through college, they would value the education more and riot less."

Tammy makes quite a significant observation: many African public universities offered free education to the few that made it to that level, some even paying them allowances, while students in secondary and/or high schools had to pay tuition. Yet those very universities are traditionally plagued with student riots, which sometimes shut them down for months. Would the situation be different if university students were made to pay tuition? Would their college education have a 'certain flavor' to help reduce the riots and eliminate lost time and revenue? Yet many see their rioting as being a direct result of government inefficiency and institutional corruption.

College students are often the daredevils who are willing to take the risk of speaking out against oppressive regimes in Africa, some to the peril of their very young lives. This may also be because they are better informed than the average population. Thus, while some of the rioting is a product of idle minds and lack of the said "flavor" in free education, other causes of rioting include perceived injustice by government officials or embezzlement of funds by university personnel. Or sometimes, as seen in the experiences of Professor Malekha, lack of effective communication between students and administrators is a key factor. In fact, in the latter case, students paid high tuition at the private university but still rioted to oppose perceived injustices. Students in many African public universities now pay tuition, and it would be interesting to see if this has impacted incidents of riots in any way.

"And, could you tell me about your experience at the dental school in Washington. You said you didn't want to go there."

"Yes. I didn't want to come to the university because I had heard that, uh, as far as...," she pauses and sighs deeply, "racially, they were not very accepting of black students, you know, and...," Tammy takes another long pause.

"Which is why they started the Early Selection Program?"

"Yes. And in my first year I had a pretty bad experience with an instructor. I remember I walked up to him and he said to me, 'You know you're probably here because we need a black student!'"

"He told you that!"

"He did. And I just stood there and looked at him, and he continued, 'There's a black lady in my class, and she didn't do very well; you probably won't either.'"

"He said that?"

"Yes, he did! He told me that. And I remember the feeling, 'I knew that, I knew it!'" She laughs heartily. "And there is a lady who had a mission, (name withheld); she grew up in the South. And she is the one who actually pushed the whole thing, of getting black students. Her parents were activists in the, uh..."

"The Civil Rights Movement?"

"In the Civil Rights Movement! And the election was in Mississippi, so I always joked with her and told her she was the only white democrat," Tammy laughs energetically. "I mentioned the incident to her, and she said, 'You know what, hang in there.' And I'll tell you it's hard..., it's very, very hard because the dental profession, unlike the medical one, is not accepting of women. And they make it very clear."

"And, how come?"

"Ah, it is a very conservative, I don't know how to put it and not sound terrible, but it's a chauvinist white male club. We often got this comment in class that, 'I don't know why they accept so many women; they're going to have children and drop out of the profession anyway.'"

"They were saying that, the teachers were saying that?"

"They were saying that, they'd often say that. And it was hard."

"You were a double minority. Here you are, a woman, you're black, the teachers are saying black students will not make it, and also saying women should not be in the program."

"There we go, you know! And you had some teachers who were very encouraging and would tell you to hang in there, but they were very few."

"And is that where your Mississippi experience came in handy, that you can do it?"

"Yes! That's when it really did. Because I was determined that, if nothing else, I *will* graduate from the college. I *will*, definitely."

"Wow! Any other experience that you had that proved the Mississippi prediction true?"

"I had a couple of them. One was when we had to do a research project. We were only three minorities in the class, so we grouped together to do a project. And this project is judged by professors and teachers, and they have prizes at the end of the presentation. You also had to have a display, and you know there must be criteria for research. We had to do this and that; everything is fine. We went through all the steps and made the presentation as was required. And we ended up creating a video production of our project. Three prizes were to be won; and to cut the long story short, our project was evidently unique. We had to get special permission to do some things, because we really wanted to make a good production. Our topic was wonderful; I thought it was wonderful. One group did not even comply with the criteria for research project; it wasn't a minority group. It got down to a point whereby there was one more prize to be won, and the only groups left were mine and the one that had not followed the criteria for research projects. And they just decided to give it to that group, and everyone was *so* shocked!"

"Not only was their project accepted but they also won a prize!"

"They won a prize, and in all honesty, our project was really great, and you could tell that we really put it together. At that time, I was close to graduation."

"You got used to it!"

"Not even a big deal. But even with graduation requirements, one teacher tried to keep me from graduating because of one procedure we were supposed to do. I couldn't do it because they could not find me a patient with this condition. I tried, they looked for it for a month and everything, but they couldn't find one. So they said, 'We can't find one, and so we're not gone a sign you off.' I'm like, 'It's not my fault that you can't find me a patient!' I prayed about it, and I had a faculty member that was assigned to me. He was from India, and he happened to be at the department. He came to realize that two other students, who were Caucasian, had the same problem, but they were signed off - no question! And he became *very* angry about it and asked, '*Why* are these being signed off but *she* isn't?' And of course, the department had no answer."

"They had no answer! If you had not known about these two, they would not have allowed you to graduate?"

"No! So they said, 'We'll let you march, but you're not technically going to graduate.' And he said, 'No, you're not gone a do that.' I said, 'Why don't you give me a test of the skill in question, since it is the skill you want me to master?' And I asked, 'Are these people gone a take the test too?' And they kind of (tape inaudible) and said, 'Yes they, too.' But it was quite unfair, I mean, and even when they gave the test, they gave the two guys a different test than they gave me. It is so trying, but you just ignore that and realize you're gone a get through. Yeah, you're gone a get through!"

"That must have been very difficult to deal with!"

"It is very difficult!"

"Probably when you experience it outside the church is one thing but experiencing it in the church is a different thing!"

"It is very tough. It was a very tough time there."

Tammy moved from one form of culture shock in Mississippi to a totally different kind in a university in Washington. She must have been very strong both academically and otherwise, to be able to "hang in there" as her "white democrat" mentor told her to. Her long pauses seem to be filled with pain in a quick recollection of the unfortunate experiences at the dental school. The pain is particularly compounded by the thought that this was happening in an institution run by the church organization that she belongs to. Her bubbly laughter is a cathartic release from her internalized pain, more than an expression of genuine joy or happiness. Her determination to prove her critics wrong and subsequent graduation from dental school are noteworthy indicators of strength and will as she repeatedly states, "I will definitely graduate from the college."

"What would have been different if you had gone to college in Uganda? What other options did you have, say if you didn't go to

Mississippi, or if you had gone back after one quarter like you wanted to?

Tammy says she had wanted to go to a church-operated university in Uganda originally, but they did not offer a degree in Biology. Instead they offered Botany and Zoology, and she didn't want to take that since it would not qualify as a pre-dental program. "The only reason I would not have stayed in Uganda is that at that time, the School of Dentistry at the main university was having problems. And it wasn't so much their problem but the problems that universities have all over Africa, of frequently shutting down."

"What made the universities frequently shut down?"

"Due to riots. But there were also problems at the School of Dentistry, a couple of problems. I had a big fear! I had some friends who had been at the university for at least six years and they hadn't graduated, mainly because of riots!"

"What were they rioting about?"

Tammy laughs spiritedly and says, "I don't know, all sorts of things. I think at one time it was about some *meat*," she asserts, this time with derisive laughter.

"A lot of times it dealt with money, and sometimes they didn't have enough equipment. I was just determined to get in and out of school; I'm not one who enjoys the education experience," she states, laughing some more.

The riots at government-run universities is a phenomenal waste of human and financial resources. They would lead to the closure of the universities for extended periods of time, during which university employees would still have to be paid their salaries according to labor laws, while student admissions for the following year are postponed indefinitely. Such riots have also led to the injury and even deaths of some students at the hands of vicious riot police.

Although Tammy trivializes causes of student riots to being something as small as meat, there is more to it than that. It would be one thing if they rioted for meat or lack of it, but it is a different thing if the meat is missing because someone has embezzled the

STUCK HERE: AFRICAN IMMIGRANTS TELL THEIR STORIES

funds allocated for buying it. Thus, the fault does not lie with the rioting students alone, but with the corrupt administration that misappropriates funds and the system that allows this practice to thrive.

At the time of her interview, Tammy was a dentist holding two jobs: one with a group practice while the other was with another doctor in private practice. "The group practice job is very, very tiring; it's just too much! I see too many patients in a day. That's why I chose to work in the private practice one day a week just to get a break. And, believe it or not, I teach in the School of Dentistry at my Alma Mata," she declares, laughing.

"Well, congratulations! You are a very busy lady! So even though they have some discriminative practices, they can also hire you to teach there!"

"They do! You know what? One thing I really, really wanted to have black faculty there. Really, really wanted to have one; we had one black faculty, but unfortunately, he died. It was just such a sad situation. It's amazing: as hard a time as they gave me when I was there, in my senior year they asked me to be on the discipline committee, which I was very surprised at. They actually tried to get me to teach at the medical college. I didn't know whether to take it as a compliment or as a groan, but I decided not to teach (full time) at that place. They did actually get a black faculty who teaches there, but I, I hate to put it this way, but the main reason I teach at that same university is just to interact with the black students there and be there for them."

Tammy has had very conflicting experiences as a female black student of dentistry. She has been a victim of racial and gender discrimination, saying, 'The dentistry profession is not very accepting of women' and is more of a white male club. On one hand she was quite humiliated by a male white teacher telling her, "You're probably here because we need a black student." On the other hand, she has served on the discipline committee in the School of Dentistry of the same university that maltreated her and is now serving as part-time faculty. The negative experiences, however, have remarkably left Tammy more determined to succeed and to "be there for black students" and act as an encouraging positive role model.

"OK, that makes sense. So, what are your goals? How long do you plan to do what you're doing now?"

"Well, hopefully, so far my goal is to open a practice of my own, eventually hire a dentist to work for me. That way I get to work a little less. When I first came to this country, my first option was to finish school and go back home. The number one reason I've not gone home is, I'm concerned about the safety, I'll be honest with you."

"Your safety in terms of... crime?"

"In terms of crime! I am! I really am concerned about that."

"How come?"

"Living at home, growing up in the city, there is just something, I don't know if I'm being paranoid, but I don't think I am. But even growing up, there were sometimes that I'd be really afraid... Mainly, to sit there and listen to your neighbor being robbed, and nothing is done about it... people are shouting."

"Did you have an experience like that where your neighbor was robbed?"

"Mhmh! I don't think I had an exactly immediate neighbor. But they were within hearing, and several times! And that really saddened me. My dad was robbed at gunpoint, you know!"

Tammy goes on to narrate how her father nearly lost his car in that daylight robbery incident. A friend of theirs was traveling from one city to another, in the western part of the country. He was robbed and stabbed in the head.

"They have become so afraid. When I went home last time, I found it very hard to adjust. Don't wear this, don't wear any rings, don't wear any type of watch. After dark, people don't want to go anywhere. And I'm like, 'OK!'" She laments the crime situation back home, which existed before she left but now seems to have gone out of control. Her views make a striking parallel to those of

Dr. Poindexter, despite their gender, age, and racial, and regional disparity.

"What has happened to make the crime situation worsen?"

"I think a big part of it is unemployment. People don't want to be criminals; I don't think anybody says to themselves, 'I wanna go steal.' So many people with college degrees have no jobs. Desperation drives people to commit crime—lack of industry. I still believe that if some of the money that we have in Uganda, especially those who have a lot of money, was invested in the country, we'd have a lot more jobs."

Tammy thinks that many African leaders are corrupt and therefore feel insecure. They may be overthrown at any time, so they stash lots of money in foreign accounts to fall back on in case they are overthrown. Such money, she says, could serve the countries better if invested at home, thereby creating employment opportunities for the numerous unemployed young people. They, in turn, would shun violent crime and this would make the countries safer to live and invest in.

"You know what I believe? That if the environment would significantly change and if the government creates just enough jobs, it would be more stable. I remember in the mid-1980s, it was more peaceful and a lot safer. You create that environment, and I would want to go back! I like it here, but it's such a rough life, and I would not mind going back. In fact, I have a deep belief that if that would happen, a lot of professionals would go back, and with each professional returning is more jobs created. It would be like a domino effect in improving our economy. But when you have an environment that is so risky, you don't feel like being the one who wants to take the risk," she contends. This view is very similar to those of George and Rosa, who find life in America less than satisfying but are enduring it due to "the bad situation" at home.

"OK. What do you see as the future of Uganda, given the situation as it is now? Do you see things improving?"

"I don't know," says Tammy dejectedly. "I had so much hope at the beginning. But it seems like I'm not seeing as much change as I would like to. I was hoping there'd be a big sweep in the government."

"In the last elections?"

"Yeah, where a lot of the corruption would be at least lowered, not necessarily wiped out completely. That would be hoping too much!" She lets out an animated laughter. "But at least I was hoping we would have more stability. And, we do get a lot of aid, we get a lot of loans... And so, I was hoping that would happen. I have still not seen the change. but I still have hope. I still believe that," tone changing to frustration. "I don't know, I don't know! African countries have had *really* bad governance. It has been really bad!"

"So, if we have a change of leadership, and the economy improves, then crime will reduce?"

"I do believe so, yeah, yeah. When the economy stabilizes, crime will decrease! It's not going to disappear, but at least it will decrease. With that, I believe more people will go back, and more people will be interested in investing, not necessarily returning Africans, but even foreign investors. In fact, foreign investors can create more jobs! And that will stabilize the economy a little better. Yeah."

Here again insecurity is mentioned as the main reason for African professionals not returning to work in Africa, and the insecurity is seen as being directly linked to the poor state of the economy. The economic decline, too, is seen as a result of poor governance rife with corruption and incompetence. As the subject laments, 'it has been really bad!'

Tammy's perception is that African economies have the potential to create and sustain enough jobs to keep most citizens in gainful employment, which in turn would reduce crime rate significantly because most people turn to crime out of desperation. But the resources are mismanaged and misdirected. "We have the money to this end, but it is not being put into the continent. It is put into people's pockets," she asserts.

"Mhm! Is there anything else you'd like to say about the brain drain?"

Tammy laughs her characteristic hearty laughter and then says, "I'm guilty!" Then she laughs some more before adding more somberly, "I am guilty and I'm very sad, because my father is a true example of someone who came and whose mission was to come, get an education to go back and better his life. He has done that; he has stuck with it. Yeah, he decided he was gonna go back. He had friends who went back with him, and friends who stayed here, from what he tells me. And, there have been good times, and times when things have been really, really bad! I admire him because he has had a lot of really good international job offers, and he's turned down every single one of them."

"And what is his reason?"

"His reason is that he is needed in Uganda, and he believes that he can do something for his country. He has taught for many years, and he feels his mission is the big need in the country."

"So, he feels that he'd better be there to make a difference?"

"Definitely! And I admire that. I probably think at the back of my mind, I.., I.., must go back, I must go back! It is nothing… just… just because of what my father has done, I must go back."

Tammy expresses strong sentimental desire to return home, influenced by her father's decision several years ago to serve in Uganda after studying in the United States (and he has indeed served with distinction). But she says it haltingly, which is quite uncharacteristic of her typical eloquence. She is caught between powerful conflicting forces: the desire to do the honorable thing like Dad and go back and serve, versus the harsh reality of the situation back home, against the backdrop of the dental career and family that she has established in the United States. It feels very much like she is being 'stuck here' against her wish, like Waribah and other subjects, and like many other Africans living in America.

"Thank you very much! You said that your grandma lives here in the United States; does that mean your mom is from here? She's American?"

"Mmhm!"

"Do you consider yourself African-American or African?"

"African!" she declares urgently, then laughs spiritedly. "I consider myself African. It is really funny that you ask that, because I think…" she pauses reflectively.

"I'm sorry to ask a personal question!"

"Yeah, yeah, yeah! I do. I never really fit in the African-American culture very well. And so, no matter how hard I try, I just never really, really felt…" another long pause…

"Were you born here or in Uganda?"

"I was born in Uganda! I was born in Uganda, grew up there. We left Uganda when I was very young to come visit Grandma, cousins, etc. But I look at my siblings, and they're probably more African American than me, because they fit in better in the culture."

"They fit in better than you do?"

"Yeah, I think, better than they fit in with the Ugandan one. Anyway, it's strange because on the other hand, when I was in Uganda, I really don't think I really… (long pause) felt accepted there either, so it was kind of like a limbo. But yeah. I consider myself African."

"OK. What happened that made you not feel accepted?"

"Oh, at home? I think a lot of it dealt with people asking, 'Where do you come from?' I come from, you know, I'm very light. I come from the darkest ethnic group in the country," she states, laughing. I would say where I come from, then they would laugh and say, 'Really, what tribe are you?' They just wouldn't believe me."

"Do you think it might have more to do with socioeconomic background than where you come from?"

"No, more of where I come from. Because I was really made aware of it when I went to school! I am very minority, you know, my community are very minority in my church. Unfortunately, it goes back to church again. I mean, they made it so bad for me that I had to leave one of the schools early. It was so bad!"

"Who are 'they'?"

"Well, specific people. I went to school with majority (ethnic group identity withheld), and they would often mistreat me. They did very bad things to me."

"Like what?"

"You know, common… (tape inaudible) now. 'Well it's too bad you're not our tribe!' And then they would switch and start talking in their language. Teachers would come into the classroom and switch into that language so I wouldn't understand, a lot of times. And it wasn't just me; usually at least one other person could not speak that language.

"I had a cousin going to school with me for a while. They talked negatively about my mother—that's one thing I do remember as a child, always. I remember them always saying things like, 'Oh, your mother is American anyway, so you don't count.' I remember them, especially the women, I remember them coming up to my mom and dad, and they would greet my dad, but they would just look at my mom and walk away. I definitely remember that as a child. As I'm older, I kind of begin to understand, because I know sometimes the bitterness that is between… you haven't had a marriage, but you see a black man that has done well, and he marries a white woman. It looks like they're thinking, 'couldn't he find…' I think that's what was going on there."

"They are wondering why he did not marry one of them?"

"And I think as a child, I really…" (long, reflective pause.)

Lost in the labyrinths of her childhood memories, Tammy pauses in an apparent rekindled pain, wondering why she never actually felt accepted in her Ugandan community as a child. Now as an adult, she still does not feel that she is accepted in the American community either, the price of dual citizenship where one belongs to two countries on paper but fits neither here nor there in reality. It reveals the folly of human nature: we discriminate against people because they are of different races or tribes or nationalities. The result is the same—a negative impact on the individual but also on society. Many African countries would be much more developed if their governments and peoples did not practice tribalism. America would be much better off socially and economically if Americans did not practice racism. But we are trapped in what philosophers have commonly referred to as *the human condition*, and it is a condition of moral depravity.

"All the negative experiences I had were within the church, which is really sad," she continues after her long pause. "And in my mind as I really analyzed it, outside the church there's no big deal, but within the church there's a lot of animosity. I would say that to people, and they would say, 'What? Really!' It's hard for them to believe."

"You think maybe they were also fighting for positions?"

"I don't know, I don't know, I don't know," Tammy repeats, and then sadly adds, "but definitely, that was tough! It was tough growing up. Maybe that's part of life. But you know what? I think there's discrimination everywhere! Because if it's not tribal, then it is socioeconomic. We have discrimination. No matter where you are, there's discrimination."

"Well, thank you! And I hope in the new Africa we're going to have better relationships where it won't matter who is a Teso, Kisii, Kikuyu, Luo, Baganda, Yoruba, Ibo or whatever other tribe."

14

CASES COMPARED AND ANALYZED

Numerous factors push Africans from the continent to the United States and Europe, where equally strong forces pull them. Dr. Kanuma is quite emblematic of many Africans living and working in the Western World. He is a product of more than one of the several "push factors" such as limited educational opportunities and political instability at home. "Pull factors" for him are evidently better educational opportunities for himself and his family, as well as a steadier political environment in the United States; an environment which is socially and economically unappealing and challenging.

The socially unappealing factor results from one not being able to expect "to get a suitable marriage partner," which may impact his children. Besides, if he were at home in Africa, he would most likely be in company of more familiar peers and family than he is currently, staying by himself most of the time, mowing his own lawn, and spending the night alone when his wife has gone to work. Further, being in the United States is not satisfying economically since he cannot afford to employ as many house and farm workers as he would have if he were living in Rwanda. Rather, he now does much of the chores by himself, chores such as mowing the lawn, serving his guest drinks, and the like.

Dr. Kanuma is quite modest in stating that he does not use the Rwandan genocide as an excuse for not returning home; yet it is inconceivable how he would have gone home to such a hostile political climate in which his elderly neighbor had just been murdered in a politically motivated and retaliatory assault. What if he had been at home at the time of the assault? It is horrifying to imagine the most likely tragic outcome. Thus, even though staying in the United States is challenging, the benefits make it worth the sacrifices. Educational opportunity for self and for the whole family, safety in times of war and political turmoil at home, and reasonably comfortable living standards are apparently the major pull factors.

Whereas the United States offers Mr. Waribah 'a lot to learn' as well as reliable utility supplies and other services, he perceives the social environment as being hostile to the African man. Getting jobs that one is qualified for is often hard, and thus many Africans are underemployed. The conveniences are expensive as well and, as Dr. Kanuma puts it, "You are one paycheck away from being homeless here; at home (meaning in Rwanda or whichever one's African country is), I am at least assured of a home."

In addition, family ties at home are greater, and Waribah feels more accepted and respected. Housing is guaranteed, and one is less stressed. People, not money, come first. An example of respect is when he was invited to the national holiday celebrations in Cameroon, and he and his family were seated in the presidential quarters. The children were alarmed at seeing "so many black people" and to realize that even the president was black, and it was normal. It was quite a boost to their self-esteem to realize that as black people, they are not an insignificant minority, which they appear to be in the United States, but that they are indeed part of an overwhelming majority in their vast continent.

Waribah is "stuck here" in a hodgepodge of socio-economic, psychological, and political push and pull factors. He started out looking for educational opportunities in the United States but got tied down when he started a family. Dr. Poindexter makes a fitting illustration of the point when he states that "uprooting Africans, training them in a western environment, and then expecting them to go back after their families and their children have become Americanized results in a huge culture shock."

The political and economic atmosphere back in Cameroon has not been attractive enough to fully pull him out of his American mesh. Extended family ties have recently pulled Mr. Waribah hard enough to get him to seriously want to go back, but immediate family realities pull to the opposite direction. Nevertheless, cultural values, especially the desire to bring up children speaking their native *Douala* language has had a strong influence on Waribah; so much so that he is willing to defy the socio-economic and political drawbacks and venture into returning to do business at home.

Three months since our first interview, he has gone back to Cameroon, traveled across the African continent, and returned to the United States. The children remained in Cameroon with relatives. He states resignedly that he is going back to Cameroon, and this time when he returns, he will bring the children back with him. I asked him why he was bringing the children back while he had intended to go to Cameroon to start a business.

"What has changed? What makes you want to bring them back now?"

"Well, my goal has been achieved. I just wanted the kids to learn the culture, to speak the language."

"Do they speak the language now?"

"Oh yeah! The first two kids speak it; the last two are still learning but are making progress." Waribah declares that he has started the business and he has "a communication center going." But he plans to bring the children back anyway, because, "You can't just pack up and go; oh no, you can't do that! If you just pack up and go, you'd have to come back here to look for more money. However much money you take home, it will run out. So, until the business is established, and you have it generating money from within, you can't just pack up and go. Besides, I have to relearn the culture...Since I have lived here for so long, my mindset is different, my way of thinking and doing things is different... (sneeringly) I have to learn to go through the secretary of some stupid man sitting there... have to give them a tip to forward my papers to the officer in charge.

Otherwise the papers will be sitting there the whole day and won't get to be signed. So, I have to relearn that culture."

Mr. Waribah seems resigned to this aspect of the culture, though at first, he was optimistic that things would change. Now he realizes he might have to change himself and relearn the culture of tipping or bribing his way through, if he is to get anything accomplished in the country he nostalgically calls home. Instead of working with others to promote change, he himself must change to fit in the system. This quite affirms Dr. Kanuma's view that if "you go home, you would have to change to fit in the system, or else they would kill you." It also concurs with Laura's despair about the bribery situation in Nigeria, where one must give the tip before, not after the service.

"So, instead of packing up and going, you will bring the children back?"

"Yes, like I said, your money will run out, and you'd have to come back here to make more. Also, we want the kids to get established in a good high school and to go to good colleges here. In fact, that's *the main issue*; even though they are in a school that follows the American system in Cameroon, it is not as good as schools here. So, I will go after the kids settle down in good colleges."

"Did you say earlier that the system was quite competitive, and one of the children had adjusted by waking up as early as 5:00 AM to study, but now you're saying that it is not as good…?"

"Yes. Oh, yeah. The school is good; we have a few black and white American teachers, plus Cameroonian teachers. But it is still like a second-rate American school. They lack exposure. They don't have the Internet. The computer lab is not fully equipped. When they went to school here, there was a strong support system—teacher-parent association, library facilities, possibility of taking college courses in high school. These count towards admission to a good college. They don't have these back there. So, since we're planning to have them transferred here, it will be difficult for them to make the transition. We have had someone graduate from there, and they got a full scholarship to college. But mine are children, and we do not want them to be at a disadvantage, so we don't want the system to be too different."

"I see!"

"One thing I'm sure about is that I don't want to grow old in this country."

"What would be the problem with growing old in this country?"

"Let's say, if I got a stroke, my wife would have to put me in a nursing home. Back home you build the house, you own it, and you don't have to pay anybody anything. You'd be taken care of in your house even if you had a stroke. That would be very difficult and expensive here."

Staying here or going back home is a decision that Waribah, like many Africans in the United States, must wrestle with. The decision is a source of constant internal and external conflicts, including the conflict of choosing between better educational opportunities here for the children versus the desire to acquire and understand their cultural heritage. These conflicts have resulted in a vicious circle that Mr. Waribah and other subjects aptly describe as getting "stuck here." It is difficult for him to "pack up and go" home; he is wistful as he imagines what might have been, had he gone back.

"When you compare job prospects at home versus here, does that have anything to do with your decision or desire to return home?"

Waribah sighs very deeply, then with subdued eyes looking down honestly responds, "Yes! Part of it is. Part of it is. If I had gone home ten years ago, with my qualification, I would by now be a bank manager with a driver and a gardener..."

And if he stayed here and started his dream business, it would be located on the East Coast because "it is closer to my family. I have a brother in Georgia and another in Iowa. When we go home, the children will have to stay as a family, hold each other's hand as a family."

Waribah agrees with Dr. Uche and George that children's education "is the main issue." Likewise, he concurs with Laura's views on the significance of strong family ties and the fear of growing old here. Thus the dramatic attempt to live in two worlds separated by thousands of miles of water and land. Dr. Uche's concerns for his children's education and welfare have had the greatest impact on his decisions to move back and forth between Nigeria, Saudi Arabia, and the United States. While he points out all the problems and failures of the Nigerian society, he also acknowledges that he could personally "survive all that," but it would be unjustifiable to leave his children in the mess when he has a better option.

Listening to Dr. Uche reminds one of Chinwah Achebe's novel, No Longer at Ease, in which young Obi Okonkwo returns to Nigeria after studying in England and lands a prestigious job with the colonial government, only to find that his western education and good job are not enough for his survival in the new and complex Nigerian society. Expectations versus reality are poles apart. His 'large salary,' in the eyes of the less educated members of his village, cannot sustain the numerous responsibilities and lifestyle expected of someone with his educational and social background. While maneuvering this fine line, Obi is doomed.

For Dr. Uche and his generation, the postcolonial Nigerian society equally has multiple complications. The traditional ways of life have "fallen apart," as Achebe would say, while the new western ways that replaced them in Nigeria have broken down and stalled to the point that "over there, nothing works," and life has become "impossible" as Uche tersely puts it. A case in point is the oil situation. Oil has polluted the environment that supported the old traditional lifestyle, to an extent that local people can no longer gather adequate rainwater for drinking, nor can they get enough fish from the great ponds of the Niger Delta.

The modern running water system that was to make the people independent of river and rainwater has fallen apart. Revenue from the oil industry that formerly sustained livelihood does not benefit the people who are thus affected by oil mining and its devastating effects on the environment. The result is substantial desperation, frustration, and mass exodus of professionals and all who can find their way out of the country. Some of those who are unable to leave have engaged in a desperate war to sabotage the oil industry.

The futility of colonial boundaries in Africa is another apparent factor. Nigerians from the southeast perceive themselves as being a highly educated, mostly Christian society. They have been traditionally farmers and fishermen. The northerners are viewed as nomadic pastoralists and Muslims. Both groups view themselves as two distinct groups of people with little more than their skin color in common. For administrative purposes, the British combined these two culturally distinct regions to form one country called "Nigeria." This has resulted in tribal and religious tensions and several coup' d'états. A bitter civil war resulted in the 1960s when the East tried to secede and form a new state called "Biafra."

Overpopulation is another force behind Nigeria's problems. As life gets more difficult in the countryside and traditional lifestyles fall apart, more people are migrating to urban areas to seek jobs, which they do not always find. This increases crime rate, overburdens the underdeveloped and poorly maintained infrastructure, and leads to inadequate supplies of power, water, and other services. As a result, "nothing works." Some of the professionals like Dr. Uche and others with much needed skills end up leaving their countries for greener pastures in the West, "to get a breath of fresh air" where there is adequate compensation for their expertise while also enjoying a relatively comfortable lifestyle with public amenities that work.

Ken's case has a mixture of issues at play, the most significant apparently being socio-political problems in his home country. Ken considers himself Ugandan while Uganda does not consider him as her citizen. He does not and cannot possess travel documents, such as a Ugandan passport. Staying in the United States as a green card holder might be psychologically more comfortable to him—being a symbol of permanent residency which could lead to citizenship— than going back to a country which he considers as 'home,' but does not necessarily welcome him. Even though Uganda is relatively peaceful now for Tutsis, the future is quite uncertain. As Ken states, there is calm now that a Tutsi-friendly regime is in power in Uganda, but one day if a Hutu-backed government takes over, that regime might expel all Tutsis from Uganda, triggering a humanitarian crisis.

Thus, ethnocentrism is another issue at play. Ken could probably very well fit into the Rwandan society among the Tutsi people, but he does not speak the *Kinyarwanda* language fluently and may be very unwelcome since it is his grand parents' generation that left Rwanda several years ago. The people that he longs to "be close by as they age and die" are not in Rwanda but in Uganda. The persistent ripple effects of colonialism are still seen at play, affecting lives of the people in several little ways that may not be readily noticeable, but which have significant consequences and lasting impact on people's lives. Even if Ken decided to go to Rwanda, he may not fit in there as an English speaker—a product of British colonialism—while Rwanda was colonized by Belgium, and therefore has French as its *lingua franca*.

Other issues responsible for the brain drain from Africa to the West are lack of educational opportunities, economic issues, and political instability in the sending country. Having lived through two wars, Ken has no reason to believe no third or fourth one will occur. With children's future at stake, he has reluctantly decided to stay in the receiving country, for now. Lack of democracy threatens political stability and makes the future bleaker. The prospect of poor pay and witnessing the return of previous returnees is discouraging, so that people feel they are better off staying put.

From the interview with George, certain issues appear to directly and indirectly influence brain drain from Nigeria to the

West. Rampant corruption has infiltrated most government quarters, making normal function of government impossible so that necessary services may be delivered. Those Nigerians who have trained abroad due to inadequate educational opportunities at home, have seen how efficiently the system works elsewhere and are frustrated to the extent they cannot endure the failed system at home. They feel helpless in constituting change of a desperately corrupt system that is deeply rooted in tribal, religious, and ethnic resentments and can heartlessly eliminate anyone who gets in its crooked ways.

If George returned home, for example, his road building skills could be invaluable in improving the dilapidated transport system in Nigeria. But he would most likely find himself bogged down in the corrupt structure that uses his skills to benefit his superiors, as has happened to others before him. He could easily be asked to certify that a given road has been built to required standards, yet it has not. The builders usually use less building material than is recommended, thereby saving themselves millions of dollars. They will have bribed a powerful government official, who could fire or kill George if he failed to certify that the road has been built to specified standard.

As stated earlier, a major part of the problem appears to be inheritance of the colonial government by several distinct groups of people with different cultural and religious practices and values, who try to act as one nation. Achebe argues that the government is viewed as a foreign body responsible for one's wellbeing, and from which one needs to take as much as possible, while giving the least that they can get away with (Achebe, p.37).

Significant chunks of government money and foreign aid is misappropriated in many African countries, as many of the subjects have stated. Most officials who loot from their governments would probably not steal money directly from individuals; however, they do not regard it as 'stealing' if it is government money. They are merely 'taking' what is available.

Ethnicity and religious differences compound the problem. The south and east of Nigeria is mostly occupied by Yoruba and

Ibos. The north, on the other hand, comprises the Fulani and the Hausa, who are mostly Muslim, as noted earlier, and some of them have very anti-western sentiments. According to George, this phenomenon is responsible for poor governance in Nigeria, since no qualified leadership emerged during both democracy and military rule. The Yoruba and Ibo also feel that they are resented by the northerners and are therefore frequently targeted for political assassinations and murders.

Some elements in the Muslim north would like to enforce "*sharia* laws," Islamic laws that would require, for example, that one's hands be cut off if he steals or drinks alcohol. An example is when the 2003 Miss World contest had to be postponed and moved out of Nigeria as riots erupted in the north due to what was perceived as an irreverent comment by a western journalist who said something about Prophet Muhammad and the contestants. Many Christian Nigerians, who had nothing to do with these comments, were killed, followed by the killing of many innocent Muslims in retaliation.

Another example was when a lady called Aminah was sentenced to death by stoning by a *sharia* court because she got pregnant after a divorce. She was therefore presumably guilty of adultery, although the man who fathered her child was never sought and/or prosecuted. Human rights organizations around the world helped save Aminah's life, and an appeals court reversed the sentence due to *lack of sufficient evidence*, and not due to the recognition of any weakness in the judicial system. This and other events have negatively put Nigeria on the spotlight.

These incidents illustrate the problems inherent in the significant differences between the peoples of Nigeria, differences which exist between peoples of other African nations as well and often result in tragic social and political conflicts. They are part of what Dr. Uche refers to collectively as "the foolishness we inherited from the British," trying to glue together many different peoples as one nation.

The latest, current internal conflict in Nigeria is between elements of these two groups: the "Boko Haram" segment of the Muslim community waging Al Qaida-style deadly attacks on perceived "infidels," who in turn carry out revenge attacks. This group has currently stepped up their war against the Nigerian government and people, attempting to impose sharia laws as previously stated. Their tactics include kidnappings as exemplified by the recent kidnapping of 200 schoolgirls, followed by several women and children. In so doing they have created a tragic social and moral dilemma which resonates around the continent and the world.

Dr. Nxumalo is so far the most optimistic case in this study. Could it be that South Africa is different, having just overcome apartheid and having no major ethnic rivalries, or is he just a natural optimist? Nelson Mandela and his ANC party reportedly won more than 70% of the ethnic majority Zulu vote while Mandela was not a Zulu. Possibly, the British system of 'detribalization' of South Africans worked to some extent. It is also possible that having had a common enemy under apartheid, South Africans naturally united to defeat the foe, regardless of their ethnic backgrounds, at least for a while. But it is as well possible that traditions of South Africans worked in their favor. They tend to not care much about tribal loyalties and in fact traditionally do encourage inter-tribal marriages. As Dr. Nxumalo explains, the Zulu, for example, have a saying that, "a beautiful stick is cut from among the other nations." This is expressly used to encourage young men to marry women from other tribes, unlike in some other African communities where marrying from outside one's ethnic group is regarded negatively. For this reason, in South Africa, one is always related to members of other tribes, regardless of one's own ethnic group.

Dr. Nxumalo could amazingly find his family name among all six ethnic communities in Southern Africa. Mandela and Mbeki won elections despite their ethnic minority status, something that has not happened in Nigeria or most other African countries, but one that these nations could learn a lot from. Time will tell if the South African model will survive. So far it has been impressive, and credit goes to Nelson Mandela for setting precedence in stepping down after only one term as president. It gives other people hope that their turn could come in their lifetime and demonstrates to other African leaders that there is a life after being president and one does not have to die in office.

Dr. Nxumalo described apartheid as a double-edged sword that reveals the "depravity of human nature, on the one hand, showing its irrational hatred, which kills or beats a helpless person for sport," while on the other hand "portraying overwhelming human good will." As noted earlier, South Africa did set up the Truth and Reconciliation Commission, whereby all who had committed heinous crimes during apartheid could come and confess publicly to Archbishop Tutu's commission and be forgiven. And many did come with horrendous stories and received forgiveness. "South African whites are forgiven and free!" They can contribute to national development and keep their money circulating within the country's economy.

But unemployment and crime persist. One explanation might be that since scores of young people did not get quality education under apartheid, they have no skills to get meaningful jobs and now resort to crime. This is compounded by the fact that many white-owned companies fled when black rule began, thinking retaliation would be taken against them. Others left earlier to pressure South Africa to change its system of government. These phenomena caused unemployment to rise.

Also possible is that crime remains at the same level as before the end of whites-only rule, but poor blacks were restricted to their own neighborhoods and the realities of crime were hidden from the eyes of the rich white population, as Dr. Nxumalo theorizes. Now that people are moving freely, everyone sees 'the other side of town" for the first time. Blacks marvel at how beautiful South Africa is, beauty that they had hitherto not seen. Whites lament perceived increased crime, yet they are just seeing or experiencing what was always there but were protected from seeing by their privileged status and by the restrictions on movement of the poor masses.

While Dr. Nxumalo is very optimistic, Mr. Chibanda has quite a pessimistic outlook of life in his country and has resigned himself to the sad reality that he will not return to live in Malawi. While acknowledging that replacing professionals like himself would be hard for his country, Mr. Chibanda does not see the political and social situation in his country improving enough to allow him to return and make a meaningful contribution to the development of Malawi. He envisages having grandchildren in the United States, which would further seal his fate of being stuck here.

Dictatorship and political suppression have devastated many African countries such as Malawi in diverse and far reaching ways. Inefficiency in the delivery of services is extensive and results in misuse of resources and, subsequently, underdevelopment of the country. A ripple effect is felt through all the sectors of the country when professionals like nurses and doctors can no longer function and leave. As professionals leave, more underdevelopment occurs, and the cycle gets more vicious. Poor countries like Malawi invest much of their limited resources in training these professionals such as doctors, teachers, accountants, and nurses. When professionals are lost, the loss doubles, with devastating damages to the country's development efforts. The brain drain has serious consequences which compound its negative impact on African economies. The risk of being left further behind in the global economy is substantial and leads to the gloomy likelihood that more people will want to migrate to the West, in a perpetual vicious circle.

Joy is a living testimony to the numerous socioeconomic problems of postcolonial Africa. Her stranger-than-fiction experience is not just a personal tragedy but also family, national, and indeed a universal one, depicting the deplorable nature of human vice. It is inconceivable how any human beings in Rwanda, or anywhere else in the world, could possibly commit such atrocities against fellow humans, as narrated by Joy in her unbearable true-life story. Wanton and brutal killing of numerous innocent people just because of difference in ethnicity, and furthermore, training children to participate in such killings, is despicable and incomprehensible.

But Joy, too, is a symbol of hope for human courage, strength, and benevolence. The fact that she survived her gruesome ordeal is implausible. Even more incredibly admirable is her planning, although reluctantly, to set up a clinic in Rwanda "because there is more need." She is willing to equally serve the Hutu, the very people who brutally victimized her as well as her family who were not as lucky to survive. Is it possible that she is thinking of how a Hutu man risked his own life to save hers, carrying her in a bloody vehicle while speeding dangerously through roadblocks, an act which is a remarkable demonstration of human virtue? Or does she merely want to pour coals of fire on the enemy's head? Whatever the answer, war and strife are quite evident as major source of brain drain from Africa. This issue must be addressed comprehensively if the problem is to be resolved and reversed.

Apparently, Dr. Malekha is a case of someone who genuinely wanted to return, and he followed through with his desire to serve his country. Whether his aspiration to serve was born of a patriotic spirit or not is debatable. He states that he had a 'guilty conscience' for having received a small amount of money from the university and subsequently signing a 'non-binding promissory note' to go back and serve for five years after completion of studies. Would he still have gone back, had he not received the money, and/or signed the note? We don't know. But we do know that he remarkably and determinedly kept his word and returned to serve his country.

Malekha, however, was caught up in crossfire of administrative infighting in a greatly conflicted college leadership that was perceived to be totalitarian and high-handed. In so acting, if the allegations are true, the administration forced Malekha and other qualified personnel out of the university to other universities abroad, thereby contributing to the brain drain. Dr. Malekha's scientific research skills and experience will be difficult to replace, and not only his, but also the services of the Deputy President and his friends on whom "war" was allegedly declared. Ending such unnecessary wars may be a big step toward in eliminating the brain drain.

In trying to save money by adhering to a stingy health benefit policy, the university lost much more in the form of quality personnel, with rare experience in scientific research. Their loss was Illinois' gain, since Illinois was willing to invest in Dr. Malekha's healthcare and personal well-being. Again, this is one side of the story, but if true, it must have been a stressful experience for both parties, and especially for Dr. Malekha, who in fact believes that such stress added to the deterioration of his health. Although he is not saying so, it could have indirectly contributed to his decision to return to the United States.

African countries would be much more developed if only administration and faculty of their institutions declared an academic war on ignorance by providing top quality educational services, but not war on each other.

Moreover, organizational leaders need to work in environments that will make them feel most empowered to do their best, without feeling the burden of individuals or groups that are 'undermining their efforts' or working for their downfall. The church, and other organizations could be better served by a system whereby a leadership position is advertised, qualified candidates apply, and a search committee selects the most qualified and suitable for the needs of the organization.

The politicized system of voting for candidates based on popularity may be responsible for creating factions within the said university and other church institutions, causing the administrators to feel insecure and undermined. In turn the administration resorts to extreme measures to counter the perceived threats. The result is institutional malfunction and inadequate delivery of services to students and all parties as described here by Dr. Malekha.

So far, several subjects have talked about repressive and dictatorial African governments driving professionals away, thereby causing brain drain. Joy, Dr. Omari, Mr. Mbajah, and Tabby are prime examples in this study who directly experienced personal suffering and pain at the hands of such repressive governments. They serve as evidence that it is not mere talk but a ruthless reality that one has to either painfully put up with or fearfully flee from.

Dr. Omari tried to live with it, found it unacceptable, then became involved in a process aimed at bringing about change. He got mixed results of success and failure: success in the sense that one corrupt and dictatorial government was brought down, but failure in the sense that the subsequent governments have not been significantly better than the predecessor. The ultimate element of failure was that Dr. Omari had to flee the country for his life and safety, and his family had to suffer serious consequences due to his attempts to change the system. This is in accord with what Dr. Kanuma and Mr. Chibanda said: if you tried to change the system, it could crush you or overwhelm you. Such was the fate of Dr. Omari's law professor friend who was gunned down in his house in broad daylight for competently and persistently chairing the constitutional amendment committee.

Nevertheless, it is quite striking that Dr. Omari was brave enough to risk it all and, with a few people and very little at their disposal, bring about significant change in his country's political system. Hopefully the change will serve as a springboard for more improvement in governance and development of the country, for the benefit of the present and future generations. Just a few years earlier nobody could have imagined that the former leadership would leave office, especially after seeing the fate of anyone who dared oppose him politically. It gives a ray of hope, however thin, that with more committed individuals, and most likely and unfortunately with more lives on the line to be lost, African countries will emerge from the grip of dictatorship and totalitarianism and the corruption and economic ruin that goes with it. Maybe then the problem of brain drain will begin to be reversed.

Two months after initial interview, Dr. Omari invited me to his house to read and critique some ideas he has generated that would help bring about positive change in Kenya and on the African continent. He has followed through with his plan to stop lamenting and "gone back to the drawing board, to draw and address various tangible ways of bringing about meaningful change in Kenya." He has drafted a 20-page document advocating moral leadership based on Biblical principles. His argument is that if Kenya, and other African countries, can come up with morally upright people and train them to be political leaders, the problems in Africa can be overcome, the problems of corruption, avarice, and dictatorship, that lead to suffering and poverty, and consequently to the brain drain. Dr. Omari's rationale is that if leaders have a relationship with God, like Joseph, Daniel, and David of the Bible, then their countries would experience justice and prosperity. His next step is to obtain a list of committed young people with leadership skills who are willing to be trained to take up leadership positions in various African countries.

I also learned during our visit that when he joined different groups to press the Kenyan government for change, several attempts were made to bribe Dr. Omari and his team to keep them quiet.

"When the government realized that we could not be bribed they got very frustrated. They knew we were serious with our movement toward change." When those in power offered him money, land, and position as ambassador, he refused and let them know that he and his colleagues were pushing for change in governance and not money or position.

May be Africa's problems could be solved if only 'a few good men' like Dr. Omari, with genuine commitment to moral leadership, could be found. Then corruption, tribalism, dictatorship, and bribery would end or be significantly reduced, and development would take off. The need for people to emigrate from the continent would be minimized.

Mbajah's case is another example of brain drain caused by incompetence, corruption, and brutality of governments in Africa. Mr. Mbajah was determined from the beginning to return and serve his country, and he did. But he was pushed out much against his will by factors stronger than one individual to resist. In so doing, Kenya lost additional qualified human resources in Mr. Mbajah, and his wife, who is also a highly educated and qualified professional. African countries and their governments have more to gain by abandoning repressive policies that lead to this kind of avoidable tragedy and its devastating consequences.

Regrettably, Sylvia's hard-to-believe story has been excluded from this publication at her request. Hopefully it will soon appear in her own book. She represents a case of one who has struggled with unique determination to attain a high level of education and experience. She has gone through very challenging experiences including linguistic barriers, financial shortages, and personal tragedies but has prevailed by individual and family resolve and strong faith in God. She represents the so far minority group of Africans living in the United States who are quite optimistic about Africa's future. She is therefore set to personally get involved in improving the situation back in Africa in her own ways, big and small. Her country of Angola is a typical example of African states that went through bitter wars to gain independence, followed by protracted civil wars between the ex-freedom fighter parties for the control of the countries and their vast natural resources. No wonder then that Sylvia cites political strife as the main reason for her and her family to have not returned to Africa immediately after completing studies in the United States. Indeed, she sees this strife as the reason for many other African professionals working abroad, thereby contributing to the brain drain.

Sylvia is determined to contribute to her country's economic development even if she is living in the United States. She promotes and sponsors education and health services in collaboration with nongovernmental organizations that provide aid for international development. Thus, she can be part of the 'brain gain' instead of the brain drain.

Rosa's case is one of a complex nature, with no single push or pull factors but interdependent ones. The primary reason for her and her husband moving to the United States was to seek educational opportunities for their children. This pull factor is directly influenced by a push factor, namely the "bad situation" at home both economically and politically. The three factors influencing their decision to relocate are educational opportunities in the United States, or lack of such opportunities in Zimbabwe; poor, dictatorial governance; and a ravaged economy whose currency is worthless. The more logical order would be political misrule, which causes destruction of the economy, which in turn results in poverty and loss of quality educational services.

As a result, Rosa seeks educational opportunities for herself and her children while also aggressively seeking to establish a financial pillar in the form of buying houses back home, not just to live in but houses to rent out as a source of income. As she contends, "Four houses will be like a job."

She is as well quite hopeful that the oppressive government will soon come to an end so that she and her husband can safely return home, to be followed by their daughters. Rosa is relatively newly arrived in the United States, and her insistence on returning is consistent with the observed positions of most newly arrived immigrants who always think in terms of going back. Ten years after arrival, the very time she had set as her goal for going back, Rosa and her family are still "stuck here," much like the rest of us. Suppose her children get married and settle in the United States[10]; would Rosa still adamantly want to return to Zimbabwe? Would the desire to stay and be close to children and grandchildren override the

---

[10] One of her daughters is now married in the US

strong spirit of patriotism that insists, "home is home," even when many professionals are evidently leaving? Time will tell.

If she gets the United Nations job she is targeting, Rosa will have succeeded in establishing a strong financial base that will be added to her educational and social success as a parent. However, it remains to be seen if she experiences the fate that awaits other ordinary Zimbabweans as they return home from studies abroad, should she decide to do so. Political and economic uncertainties loom ahead.

Ostensibly, Laura is one of the subjects who are genuinely interested in going back to serve in Africa, even if not for altruistic reasons, but is frustrated by the deeply rooted and impenetrable system of corruption, inefficiency, and the subsequent economic deterioration that plagues her country. She is raising her children in the United Sates even though she clearly would have liked not to. Neither would she like to grow old here, but she is, in spite of herself. These outcomes are reflected in the fact that she has unsuccessfully tried to relocate twice, but each time was repelled by the frustrations of the bureaucracy in her original home country, to the extent that she ended up returning to the United States.

As she states, "It is very, very complex because people out there... have set up a system of government that is very complex, that is very tight, and nobody can get through. You cannot penetrate that to begin to want to make changes. And so, you're frustrated, and they are frustrated. We went home, tried to re-establish, it didn't work." One wonders what the situation would be if the "people back there" had been receptive to new and different ideas offered by those returning from studies abroad, like the Zambian mining engineer Mabuti mentioned. It is possible and likely that things would work much better than they do.

Despite her frustrations and disappointments, Laura joins the ranks of those who are optimistic about the future of Africa and see it as improving and not deteriorating. "I see a brighter future, though, for Africa in general, I really do," she says. Her optimism is based on the theory that privatization of services, which is already taking place. Change to the better is being forced by giving stiff competition to services that have been traditionally offered by the corrupt and incompetent government, such as telecommunication services. If such change does happen on a larger scale and in many sectors, it surely would give reason to believe that Africa may see a brighter future.

Tammy's case is a unique one in the sense that the subject is a second-generation immigrant. Her father came to study in the United States earlier, married an American wife, then returned home after studies. Now Tammy is back here herself, having originally come to study but is now practicing dentistry. She could claim to be either African or American, but states without hesitation that she is African. Ironically, however, Tammy had trouble fitting in either culture. As she puts it, "I never really felt accepted there either, so it was kind of like a limbo." But it is notable that she still has a strong desire to return to Uganda, if it were not for the perceived lack of security in the country, even though most of her immediate family is now living in the United States.

Consequently, in spite of her dual cultural heritage, Tammy shares the frustrations common to other subjects, such as feelings of lack of safety, an economy that is run down by corrupt and inefficient government officials, and poverty of the majority of the population in her country. Such frustration, mixed with her unhappy childhood experiences in school, makes it likely that Tammy will continue to live in the United States, or as she states, "So far my goal is to open a practice of my own, eventually hire a dentist to work for me; that way I get to work a little less." If she does meet this goal, which she could, it is very likely that Tammy will find herself "stuck here," very much like Waribah, Tabby, and Tito fittingly put it. She could find herself so much entangled in running her dental clinic and probably even working more than she plans to, while continuing to hope and think of "going back home."

It is lamentable that tribal animosities, like racial prejudice, should run so deep and wide as to cause someone so much pain and suffering anywhere, but especially inside church institutions. The experiences described by Tammy both in church schools in Africa and in American church colleges are loathsome and must not be tolerated in or out of any church organization. Conscious and deliberate efforts must be made to free the church and society of such evil.

Pastor Foster is an exceptional case mainly due to the fact that he is a white African immigrant who is full of ambivalence about his African roots. He sees himself as a true African, a fourth generation one, with nostalgic memories of the continent, but at the same time is quite emphatic in stating his pride in having acquired American citizenship. "We are American citizens by choice, and we're proud of it."

Living in Africa was only worthwhile as long as it lasted, in a privileged position under apartheid. But with the uncertainty of impending black majority rule, Pastor Foster did what most white South Africans did—leave the country. Was it a guilty conscience, as he says, "You could not run a nation the way that it was run before and discriminate against the majority and now not expect the majority to discriminate against the minority... to every action there is an equal opposite reaction."

Or was it a mere fear of the unknown, considering how poorly most African countries fared after independence, which prompts Pastor Foster to say, "You don't want to bring up your kids in a country where you don't think there is a future! ...I have two daughters. I certainly don't want to bring up my kids in a country where I'm not sure they're going to get jobs or not." While Dr. Nxumalo as a black African could not bring up his children in South Africa under apartheid, Pastor Foster as a white South African could not similarly bring up his children in post-apartheid South Africa.

In retrospect, Pastor Foster evidently does see apartheid as a social ill, a practice that "was not the right thing to do." At the same time, living in South Africa without the white privileges of apartheid would not be fulfilling. His relationship with Africa, its prospects or problems, will now remain at the nostalgic and well-wishes level. Even though life in the United States has been challenging for Pastor Foster since he had to start over, going from a position of respect and trust to that of being "nothing," he is now better settled and is more at home in America than in Africa. It is apparently easier for Pastor Foster as a white African to accept this reality than it is for most black African immigrants.

Whereas Dr. Poindexter is also a white South African, his situation is peculiar in the sense that he and Dr. Malekha are the only cases that are in the United States officially as missionaries from Africa to North America, having accepted "calls" to that effect. Even though he had some family and professional hidden agenda, he came as a missionary, is still one, and plans to retire as one. His insightful commentary on the brain drain situation reflects Dr. Poindexter's intellectual curiosity, which partially drove him to accept the call as a missionary to America to enable him to pursue research, writing, and interaction with professional colleagues in the prestigious field of systematic theology.

Quite evident is the fact that Dr. Poindexter has traveled widely around the world and has had education and other experiences to shape his open-minded view of world affairs. For example, though a white South African, he talks about apartheid and its negative impacts in the same way a black South African would. Despite having every opportunity to acquire United States citizenship, Dr. Poindexter has firmly decided to retain his South African citizenship, at least until he retires, while also maintaining ties with his former college and with colleges in other African countries.

Mabuti represents a choice group of African immigrants who, like nurses, are highly desired by the West; the IT specialists. They are readily granted visas to live and work in the host countries and are paid significantly higher wages than their African countries could match. His narrative about a young PhD graduate who could not contribute to the improvement of his country's mining industry due to ridiculous bureaucracy is quite disheartening. Through such autocratic and unreasonable managerial styles, Africa has lost some of its top brains, such as Mabuti and his friend, to the West.

His friend's regrettable story confirms another subject's statement that "once you've lived here for a long time then go back ... you have good ideas, you know it will work, but they won't take it. They think you think you know it all." After spending much money and time to send people abroad for further studies, government and corporate officials ought to be secure enough to accept any potentially useful innovative ideas the returning individuals may bring back, ideas that may foster development.

The following tables summarize the major factors influencing or pushing each subject from his or her country of origin to the United States. Such factors have been termed "Push Factors" after Odunsi (1996). Subjects or cases have been assigned numbers according to the order in which they appear in the publication. A closer look at Tables 1 and 2 indicates that most of the subjects were pulled by the need for more educational opportunities and later stayed for the same opportunities for themselves and their families, or for some other purpose.

Table I: Push Factors

Factor	ED	PL	CP	UE	WR	CR	EC	SF	HL	FM	MW
Case											
1	X										
2							X			X	
3					X						
4			X								
5			X								
6	X							X			
7	X			X							
8	X										
9	X										
10	X			X							
11	X	X									
12	X	X		X							
13	X										
14	X	X									
15	X							X			
16	X			X					X		X
17				X							X
18	X										
19	X										

Key to Table 1: Push Factors

ED	Educational Opportunity
PL	Political Persecution
CP	Corruption and Poor Funding
UE	Unfavorable Employment
WR	War and Strife
CR	Crime and Violence
EC	Economic Deprivation
SF	System Failure
HL	Poor Healthcare
FM	Family Separation
MW	Missionary Work

Table 2 has been designed to illustrate the factors attracting Africans to live in the United States. Such dynamics have been termed "pull factors," to follow Odunsi's model, and may be similar to, or different from the push factors. A subject might have been pushed from Africa by one factor but then settle in the host country after being attracted by a different pull factor. For example, Dr. Uche initially came to study but was attracted by a system where "everything works"—unlike in his home country of Nigeria where "nothing works." Dr. Kanuma was initially attracted to the United States by a desire to study but later remained here due to the educational needs of his family. Similarly, Waribah came to study initially but became "stuck here" due to family, education, and socioeconomic phenomena.

Table 2: Pull Factors

	Factor	EDO	SFS	PFD	FMT	MSW	ECO	RLS	EMO	SHC
Case										
1		X			X					
2							X			
3		X	X							
4		X	X				X			
5			X		X					
6		X	X						X	
7		X								
8		X						X		
9		X						X		
10								X		
11		X			X					
12					X			X		
13		X			X					
14					X		X			
15									X	
16						X				X
17						X				
18			X						X	
19								X	X	

Key to Table 2: Pull Factors

EDO   Educational Opportunity
SFS   Safety and Security
PFD   Political Freedom
FMT   Family Matters
MSW   Missionary Work
ECO   Economic Opportunity
RLS   Reliable System
EMO   Employment Opportunity
SHC   Superior Healthcare Services

15

CONSEQUENTLY

Tables 1 and 2 from the preceding chapter illustrate the factors initially pushing Africans from the continent to other continents, especially to North America; and factors attracting or pulling them to continue to stay in the host country. In both tables, the most prominent motives are lack of adequate educational opportunities in the subjects' African home countries and the availability of such opportunities in the United States. Most of the subjects in this study left Africa primarily for the purpose of further studies, in search of better and further educational opportunities either for themselves or for their children, and in some cases for both.

As Dr. Uche puts it, "I first came to the United States in 1958 from Nigeria in quest for what we then called 'the Golden Fleece', that is, education" which was considered the key to success and upward mobility in newly independent African countries. George echoes similar sentiments, as do Dr. Nxumalo, Mr. Chibanda, and Tammy. George declares, "Back then, obtaining a bachelor's degree was a sure ticket to middle class in Nigeria," and it is something that guaranteed one a job. Quite evidently and ironically so, is the fact that quest for education is the main cause of the brain drain. To curb the brain drain, therefore, African countries need to strive harder to provide adequate educational opportunities to satisfy the intellectual zeal of their citizens.

Ken laments the fact that African governments promote the education pyramid concept whereby only a select few make it to the top of the education ladder. The rest of the population is left out and cut off from the prospects of obtaining *the Golden Fleece*. Such practices need to be reversed so that quality education is made available to all. When that happens, African professionals abroad will not be reluctant to return home for fear of lack of educational opportunities for their children. They may, in the first place, feel no need to go abroad for further studies.

This position agrees with Dr. Poindexter's views that, "The only way of stopping it is... Africans need to be self-reliant in developing institutions...where we can assist but rather lead to indigenous programs in Africa to try to reverse the pattern."

For this to be realized, funding of the educational programs and institutions must improve. For example, Dr. Malekha and Dr. Omari decry poor funding of the higher learning institutions as having been a major source of their frustration while working in public and private universities in their home country. Professors feel limited in their ability to conduct quality research, which leads to feelings of lack of professional fulfillment. As a result, many leave for greener pastures while others stay on and endure adverse consequences. This reality is illustrated by experience of the technology professor who reportedly suffered a divorce because he could not adequately support his family on his meager professor's salary.

If African leaders and policy makers ensure that money and grants intended for improving education are truly used for that purpose, the institutions will be able to attract and retain quality professors. This step would be an important one towards meeting the educational needs of the people.

To their credit, some countries, such as Nigeria and Kenya, among others, have made impressive progress in the area of providing greater opportunities for higher education. Almost every little town in Kenya now has a "university," to a point where a university degree parse is almost meaningless. Expanded opportunities need to be balanced with relevance to developmental needs of each country, so that graduates from such universities will have the opportunity to contribute to the development of their local communities and respective countries and live fulfilled lives. In addition, funding and remuneration call for sustainable increments. Such expansions ought to be done responsibly and realistically, without diluting the quality and value of higher education, and with economic development plans to ensure that such graduates have access to gainful employment.

A possible alternative method of reversing the brain drain pattern is by using online distant education programs. Care must be taken, however, to avoid those that fraudulently offer substandard programs. According to a study by the World Bank (2003), "Distance education is an increasingly important phenomenon. So far, the largest use of distance education is in developing and middle-income countries, where a huge unmet demand for access to post-secondary education exists.... Little is known about their standards for admission or graduation. Distance Learning is the 'Wild West' of higher education." (P.337). Governments and their accreditation agencies must monitor such programs adequately to ensure college diplomas thus obtained are indeed authentic. Many universities now offer online courses and degrees in various fields, and the Wild West of education is already significantly tamed.

Another major factor pushing African professionals from the continent is war and strife. Dr. Kanuma, Ken, George, Dr. Nxumalo, and Joy are direct or indirect victims of war and strife in their respective African countries. Even though Dr. Kanuma insists that the Rwandan Genocide is not the reason he did not return, it certainly has had a negative impact on his plans as they relate to his professional choices. The private university at which he planned to teach was severely impacted by the genocide. In addition, it claimed the lives of some individuals who were very close to him and his family. Joy, with bullets and shrapnel still lodged in her body, is an epitome of the genocide in Rwanda in particular, and indeed the devastating and destructive nature of war and strife in Africa in general. While in Zimbabwe, Tabby had traumatizing and traumatic experiences perpetrated by government forces, both in high school as a student and later as a teacher.

Too many wars have taken place, and some are still active, in diverse parts of Africa. The cost of such wars in terms of human lives lost, the maimed and wounded, and the displaced, and stalled economic development, is phenomenal. Some significant examples of African countries that have recently experienced catastrophic wars include Mozambique, Angola, Uganda, Liberia, the Sudan, *Côte d'Ivoire* (or Ivory Coast), and the Democratic Republic of Congo. Most recently, Burundi, which is rated as one of the poorest countries in Africa, has experienced and is still experiencing political and civil unrest even as we prepare to go to press. The unrest has already claimed many lives with many more injured. The main cause of the turmoil is that the president wants to defy the constitution and run for a third term, but the Burundi people demand respect for the constitution. Somehow, the security forces like the police and the army still consider it their responsibility to keep presidents and rulers in power by brutally assaulting protesting citizens.

These wars have taken their toll on countries—not only stalling economic growth, but also destroying whatever development was in progress before. Loss of skilled manpower related to these wars is staggering. In order to curb the brain drain and its negative impact on Africa's development, there is need for African governments and peoples to deliberately work toward the elimination of endless, brutal wars and conflict. They must address the issues causing such wars through dialogue and compromise in order to better serve the interests and welfare of their people.

A few subjects did not personally experience war and strife in their countries as such; nevertheless, their governments are perceived to be repressive, dictatorial, and brutal in ways that indirectly impacted their lives. Many African leaders have held on to power by doing whatever it takes to stay in power and silencing opposition by any means necessary, including torture and unjustifiable imprisonment. Dr. Nxumalo, Mr. Chibanda, Dr. Omari, Mr. Mbajah, and Rosa represent individuals who have been driven away from, or prevented from returning to Africa by oppressive regimes in their respective countries. The Burundi conflict (Warner, 2015) is like a fulfillment of Ken's 'prophesy' when he said, "War can break out in any country at any time…"

As a result of these wars, many Africans have fled, and others are still fleeing their countries in search of safety in Europe and elsewhere. The current Syrian refugee crisis in Europe has only temporarily shadowed the plight of African refugees making the perilous journey across the Mediterranean Sea, barely at the mercy of human traffickers who care more about their profit than the fate of the desperate cargo on their decrepit boats (Poggioli, 2015).

Such totalitarianism promotes the brain drain and denies African countries the employment of very highly skilled manpower that are needed for development. It becomes a vicious cycle as the underdevelopment itself drives more people out in search of better educational and economic opportunities as well as security abroad.

Dr. Omari, who took an active role in pressuring the Kenyan government to change its heavy-handed approach to leadership, echoes Mr. Chibanda's feelings. He lost his job, narrowly escaped arrest and imminent toeture, and then fled to the United States due to lack of security and employment opportunity for employment at home.

By arrogantly refusing to dialogue with university lecturers and professors, the government initiated a massive brain drain of the highest trained intellectuals, thereby losing much more than they would have otherwise lost had they raised the intellectuals' pay. It is very likely that Dr. Omari's attempted arrest could have led to torture and subsequent death had he not fled the country. Mr. Mbajah is another subject who states that he experienced that torture and fled his country due to political violence which directly targeted him and his family. Based on her observations in Zimbabwe, where a tyrannical president threatened, arrested, and imprisoned opposition leaders and elections are regularly rigged, Rosa expresses similar views. Recently, Zimbabweans celebrated the dramatic ouster of Mugabe from power, but they quickly went back to lamenting the oppression under the new leadership.

For African nationals to not be 'stuck here' in the West, African governments need to move from the oppressive authoritarian modes of leadership, to more tolerant ones that accommodate and learn from different views. Just because one happens to be head of state does not make one right all the time. Meaningful democratization of African governments, so that leaders are held accountable for their actions, is urgently needed to resolve the matter.

An additional factor causing Africans to be stuck here is economic instability. Poor governance is the primary cause not only of economic instability but is also a major contributor to many other factors leading to brain drain. Corruption in governments, coup d'états, and war and strife in Africa all create a climate that is not conducive to economic prosperity. As Dr. Uche, says: "Nigeria has no reason whatsoever to be in the condition it is in" because it is endowed with lots of natural as well as human resources.

Similarly, Dr. Omari laments that Kenya is endowed with human and other resources but is not developed at a level reflecting this endowment after 50 years of independence. "All we have is failed projects, stalled projects, and numerous cases of misappropriation." Without the restoration of meaningful democracy and honesty and transparency in governance, it will be impossible for African states to make significant economic progress that can improve their peoples' lives.

Dr. Uche also reveals the bitterness of a helpless people whose resources are exploited for the benefit of the powerful few: "This is where oil is produced. This is where I come from. We are sitting on an ocean of oil, but our people are totally impoverished!" he fumes, blaming government officials who mismanage and embezzle funds. In fact, a protracted dispute rages between the Nigerian government and the ethnic minority communities of the Niger Delta where oil is produced as to who owns the crude oil there. The government claims ownership of all natural resources, but the local communities do not think so. Ejobowah (2000) argues that "the multiethnic structure of the country has led to the adoption of a differentiated political community: the national and the sub-national. This situation, therefore, requires the sharing of jurisdictional rights within the country, including rights to mineral resources" (p.37). Thus, he maintains that the people of the delta should be entitled to equally sharing the ownership of oil with the Nigerian government.

The major problem is the gross mismanagement of such resources to an extent that African heads of state can stack millions or billions of dollars in foreign accounts while the average citizen struggles for such basic needs as food, housing, and clothing, and have no running water or electricity. The late Mobutu Sese Seko of Zaire (now the Democratic Republic of Congo) owned villas in the French Riviera, while Zaire nationals are some of the most impoverished people of the world. A civil war that was started to depose Sese Seko is still raging years after his death, with many lives lost, and many more people displaced. A small but symbolic effort has been made recently to recoup looted property from the son of a West African president. Cars and mansions worth hundreds of millions of dollars have been confiscated by Western government authorities. This would have more substantial impact if applied to all African leaders and their cronies.

George is alarmed by the level of corruption in Nigeria and suggests prosecuting corrupt officials as a means of reducing or eliminating corruption, lamenting that "...corruption in Nigeria has reached epidemic levels."

Prosecuting and imprisoning corrupt government officials would be a sound idea if we could identify "who will bell the cat." Doing so would require independent, efficient, and functioning judicial and police systems which are not themselves permeated with rampant corruption and bribery. Otherwise such well-intended anticorruption efforts may well be misused by powerful politicians and government officials just to target and eliminate their rivals and opponents.

The result of such swindling and misuse of resources is that Africans who get a chance to live and work elsewhere seize those opportunities, thereby contributing to the brain drain. Mr. Chibanda, Ken, and Dr. Omari are such examples. The experiences of Dr. Omari in Kenya are a fitting illustration of this disturbing trend. Not only did the government force him out of his lecturing position at the university; they also tried to arrest him, compelling him to flee the country. Hence, we can understand Ken's complaints and observation that educated and successful people are a resource that should not be feared or targeted. Dr. Omari was only an imaginary threat to his government. The government and the people would have benefited more by treating him and his colleagues as a resource and as an ally and not as an enemy. The change they were pushing for, if implemented, would have benefited the whole country.

Lack of economic development carries in its wake poverty and the inability to offer adequate remuneration for professionals. As a result, these professionals are encouraged to work elsewhere when they get the opportunity to do so. Ken expresses this quite effectively when asked if returning African professionals can help develop the continent. "… people cannot return on empty stomachs… the bottom-line is that remuneration is poor and not commensurate with training and experience…."

There is lingering concern among Africans in the diaspora, as they have come to be known, that they may return to Africa and not be compensated adequately to support their families and reward their years of toiling. And the fear is not unfounded, based on reports by their colleagues who have gone back, then returned to the United States after failing to survive in their home countries, as exemplified by the experiences of Dr. Uche and Laura. The same notion is expressed by Dr. Omari when he describes his fellow professor who was determined to stay and brave the tough situation but could not make ends meet, and, in the process, lost his family.

Therefore, to curb the brain drain, African governments need to do everything possible to reform their systems of government so that corruption is blotted out. This would be the most effective springboard for economic development. In turn, governments would create systems that work and can offer competitive terms to professionals abroad and locally. This view is supported by Werlin (2000), who did a comparative study of economic progress between Ghana and South Korea. He asserts that economic activity is greatly impacted by the political system. He concludes that the capacity of a government to champion economic progress is more influenced by cultural and political factors than by fiscal ones. He notes that while South Korea and Ghana equally suffered corruption, South Korea has superior governmental machinery, which enabled it to over-achieve economic expectations. Ghana, on the other hand, has a weaker political system and has underachieved. "In Ghana, corruption takes the form of a political illness, rather than merely a political problem, and until this political illness can be addressed, any hope of significant economic progress in Ghana is unlikely, regardless of the policies the government may be persuaded to undertake" (p. 463).

Likewise, Dugger (2004) reports that Malawian nurses "who make about US$1,900 a year, said that if their pay were doubled or tripled, they would be more likely to stay," but they did not trust the government to keep its promise, which it had failed to keep before. Malawi's Ministry of Health has recognized the problem and pledges to double the nurses' pay. Britain and other developed nations who poach nurses from Malawi and developing countries should reimburse such poor countries their investment in training their health care workers.

Poor working conditions also drive African professionals out of their home countries to the West. Dr. Uche, Mr. Chibanda, Dr. Malekha, and Laura are examples of those who experienced hostile or unfavorable work conditions in their countries. And those conditions at least partially contributed to their coming to and subsequently staying in the United States. As a pathologist in Nigeria, Dr. Uche was most frustrated with the unfavorable working conditions that led to a collapse of the system. Misappropriation of funds made it impossible to get basic supplies, such as gloves and water, needed to perform autopsy on dead bodies. Freezing facilities were overwhelmed, and bodies were decomposing.

He laments, "The conditions were totally unbearable!... I did what was in the best interest of the family." He subsequently went back to Africa but returned to the United States "to get a breath of fresh air" as life in Nigeria became "impossible" due to excessively poor working conditions resulting from mismanagement of resources.

Mr. Chibanda was disillusioned by the poor work conditions in his native country of Malawi that arose from circumstances different from those experienced by Dr. Uche. Mr. Chibanda felt discriminated against in Malawi because of employers' practice of paying expatriates higher wages and offering them better terms of service than those offered to locals.

Dr. Malekha's painful and stressful experiences working at the private university in Southern Africa after returning from the United States ironically suggest that he was being victimized without having violated any code of conduct set forth by the employing university. Such a hostile work environment is sometimes a result of poor communication between administrators and their employees. Accordingly, training opportunities for both parties would help by providing ongoing, professional development sessions that include communication and conflict resolution skills necessary for greater workplace harmony, efficiency and productivity.

One other cause of friction and poor productivity in the workplace is mismatched training and employment. Before appointing individuals to any position, especially leadership positions, they should be provided with training relevant to their new position, that will help them serve effectively. The political method of voting for institutional leaders may produce the most popular but not the most competent leaders. In addition, such a method causes undue stress and tension between workers jockeying for church leadership and other position. African churches and colleges need to devise methods of selecting institutional leaders based on character, training, and experience, as is opposed to popularity or tribal identity.

Celebrated Seventh-day Adventist pastor and recording and performing artist Wintley Phipps, addresses this vice quite candidly. In a sermon entitled "Experiencing God's Love" at a retreat for pastors, Phipps recounts how he was confronted by a prominent fellow pastor who vowed to have him removed from a leadership position in favor of a more preferred candidate. "I have seen personally the nasty face of church politics... When the politics start, people who are scared to lose their jobs also lose the courage to stand for what is right," he declares, lamenting the "bathroom friends" whose "courage never leaves the toilet" (Phipps, 2012). These friends will tell him how badly he was treated that morning but would say so only when they meet in the restroom during breaktime. For fear of losing their jobs, they would never speak up against evil in the course of the meeting sessions. These pastors at the top leadership of the church have betrayed their high calling to lead members to experience God's love and instead have focused on their quest for power. The church needs to address this issue and adapt new and less traumatic methods of choosing leaders; methods that exclude campaigning and political jockeying for position.

Laura tried to return home twice, but each time she found a system that was impenetrable and deeply rooted in its corrupt ways. As she states, "...The system is 'take your turn.' It doesn't matter what you have; you start at the bottom of the salary scale... so, it is difficult! Nobody is going home."

The inflexibility of the Nigerian system and Nigerian leaders' unwillingness to accept new ideas and change is a major contributor to the brain drain. Nigerians who have studied abroad and acquired new skills ought to be given a chance to apply those skills at home and thereby possibly change the system from one that does not work to one that works. Indeed, Mabuti's friend, who graduated with a Ph.D. in engineering from a top British university was equally frustrated when his supervisor derided his age and inexperience. Such practices only cause African states to continue to languish in obsolete techniques with little room for modernization and improvement. For Africa to develop and realize its full potential, such repressive attitudes must be discarded and replaced by more progressive and positive ones.

Such unnecessary conflict between individuals who are educated in the West and those who are trained at home is preventable. The already existing frustration due to inadequate infrastructure and lower standard of living is compounded by such conflict, making it hard for people to return and stay. Many useful ideas are rejected and discarded due to their sources rather than their merit.

Inadequate medical care in one's home country is another reason some African professionals live and work in the United States. This is primarily applicable to Mr. Chibanda, Joy, and Dr. Malekha. The lack of adequate health care causes brain drain, which in turn leads to poorer health care. Mr. Chibanda decries the poor health system in Malawi and states that if one has no money to go to South Africa, one is doomed to die of certain medical conditions that could be managed or cured with better health facilities. He also maintains that Malawian nurses have left the country in large numbers to seek better opportunities in England and elsewhere and "…there are only 356 nurses left in Malawi; the whole country has only 356 nurses left!"

Against the backdrop of this health-care workers' shortage is the AIDS epidemic, which has impacted victims who are personally known to Mr. Chibanda. According to Wines and LaFraniere (2004) of the *New York Times*, the epidemic has robbed Africa of many of its most valuable workers. "The sick are dying, sometimes alone, because they are too many, and the caretakers are too few."

Dugger (2004) describes the pathetic situation at Lilongwe's Bottom Hospital: "The sewage system at Bottom Hospital has never worked properly. The maternity ward often smells like [a] toilet. Blood, sweat, and amniotic fluid have seeped through torn vinyl covers into the thin mattresses, adding to the stale odor." Coupled with inadequate supplies, poor sanitation, and poor pay, a number of the few nurses left are making plans to go to England, where their predecessors say there is better pay and the work is easy—"like child's play compared to what we did in Malawi." Few nurses are left to cover the labor ward, so they must work extra shifts, at an hourly rate of 20 cents. Their colleagues in England make US$21 an hour for overtime and can send substantial money home to support their families.

Have these nurses and professionals failed their country or has their country failed them? If African leaders do not realize that they are there to serve the people, and not for the people to serve them, professionals who get an opportunity to leave will continue to do so. The trend of embezzling funds meant for hospital equipment and improvement must be reversed. Leaders enriching themselves while workers are poorly paid will only increase the brain drain. Funds from the IMF or World Bank or taxes, should be channeled to their intended development purposes and not into the pockets of individuals.

A British doctor, Anthony Harris, who has lived in Malawi for several years, has advised the developed countries to "train your own unemployed people." Under increasing criticism for its nurse-poaching practices, Britain adopted laws in 2001 aimed at limiting government recruitment of nurses and health-care workers from developing countries. While this is a good gesture, it is not enough; it is like covering a wound that has dirt and germs inside. The solution must come from the grassroots—from the Malawian government, and certainly all African governments and peoples, who must create

Consequently

health-care systems that work, that adequately remunerates professionals, and that will not push them out of the country in search of greener pastures. As it is now, the African countries and their corrupt leaders are at the basis for failing the professionals and causing their flight.

According to the *New York Times* editorial board, creating emigration restrictions without solving the problems in Africa would be the worst idea and would only discourage African students from pursuing medical professions.

> African doctors and nurses understand how much they are needed at home, and many would resist relocation if the conditions under which they work were more bearable. The obvious long term solution to the medical brain drain is for wealthier countries to reimburse Africa's health and educational systems for the cost of poaching their professionals, and to greatly increase the financing and technical help for Africa's health systems—in their entirety, not just the clinics that deal with AIDS (Editorial, August 13, 2004.)

Although quite a sound idea, this would work best with the concerted effort of the African governments and peoples to reform so that whatever funds the wealthier nations may give to help education and health-care systems will be channeled to those purposes. Kingman (2001) supports this view, suggesting that efforts should focus on long-term solutions that address the real problem of worldwide shortage of nurses. But concern about the health of a country's populace must be balanced with acknowledging the rights of individual nurses to migrate.

Similarly, Ouaked (2002) recommends long-term solutions based on economic growth to enable developing countries to retain their skilled workforce. Expanding educational opportunities and services would enhance such development since education improves skills, which in turn promotes faster development. Lack of education, on the other hand, retards development. He further suggests that migrants themselves can help promote economic progress by remitting money home, returning at least temporarily to share their skills, and through diaspora networks.

According to subjects George, Tammy, and Pastor Foster, violence and crime in their respective countries is a major reason they are staying and working in the United States. George gives a harrowing account of how people were sexually assaulted while traveling by bus in Nigeria. He also fears he would easily be targeted by the poor, who will know he is possibly returning with US dollars. Tammy recounts how her father was mugged and robbed at gunpoint., She also remembers several neighbors who were attacked at night while she still lived in Uganda.

This violence is a product of two conditions: one is the poverty of a large majority of the population, which has resulted from failed governments. Many African societies thus have a few very rich and many desperately poor sectors of the population. Some of the poor have resorted to robbery with violence, others to burglary and theft. The other condition is an extension of corruption in the government. The police systems not only have failed to protect the people, but they repeatedly have been accused of aiding and abetting in the robberies by leasing their weapons to thugs or by personally getting involved. This drives professionals away. To curb the brain drain, corruption must be eliminated, and the police systems straightened and rid of bandits.

Pastor Foster left South Africa partly due to fear of anticipated violence by a black population that had been oppressed for centuries and was expected to violently avenge themselves against the minority white population. Instead, the Truth and Reconciliation Commission led to the absence of vengeance-based violence. The violence that erupted was more poverty-based than revenge-oriented. There is probably more fear of violence than there is violence itself. As Dr. Poindexter states, what causes white fear in South Africa today is "...the lawlessness situation, a fear that there's no future for their kids..."

White South Africans now need to realize that they are Africans, whether they rule or not, and be part and parcel of the development efforts there. As Dr. Poindexter advises white South Africans "...not to leave but to be engaged..."

This would definitely be a beneficial move. But the South African government and people as a whole need to do more to curb violence and crime, whether aimed at whites or anyone else. Economic development and investment will not readily take off in a hostile environment where people do not feel secure enough to do business or make investments that would create jobs and raise incomes. Indeed, many African nations must deal with the crime situation, as Dr. Poindexter points out that "that's breaking down in the rest of Africa, too!"

Violence might be a spillover from apartheid, but poverty is still the main reason behind the violence and crime in most of Africa. It is hard to imagine that rich black South Africans would be committing violent crimes. Exceptions may occur, but poverty and great disparity in incomes and opportunities are dominant causes. With economic expansion and job creation, crime and violence can be reduced. Just as Tammy states, "I think a big part of it is unemployment. I don't think anybody says to themselves, 'I wanna go steal.'... Desperation drives people to commit crime." Crime rates in African countries can be significantly reduced by deliberate efforts to improve the economies and create jobs.

CONCLUSION

M
ost Africans are discontented with living in America. However, this option is "the lesser evil" between the stark realities of both lives. Members of a predominantly African church in Seattle recently went to console the family of a fellow member who had lost his 94-year-old father back in Tanzania. He tearfully recounted how his father had considered him a friend and was distraught when he left for America. On his last visit home, Dad had asked him to relocate back to Tanzania and stay with him, in his perceived last days of life. Considering all the financial responsibilities working in the United States had enabled him to take care of his dad and extended family (paying Dad's medical bills, tuition for relatives, to mention but a few), the said individual told his father, "I cannot help you if I stay here." So he painfully returned to Seattle after the visit, which turned out to be the last time he would see his father alive. His wife also narrated how close she had been to "the old man," stating, "When I was leaving home for America, my father-in-law cried tears."

Evidently, for most Africans in America, the choice is between being a Joseph or a Moses. Some have chosen to be Moses and have gotten out of Pharaoh's house to go and suffer with the people: they have returned home. A significant number, however, have gone the Joseph way—making friends with Pharaoh and using the resources of Egypt to help the family back home. Brain drain can be a blessing in disguise to sending countries. Professionals abroad send much money home, which provide much-needed financial support for their families and foreign exchange for their countries.

Conclusion

Some African countries, such as Tanzania, have recognized their "citizens in the diaspora" as a viable constituency, and even offered them representation in parliament. Some of these citizens have started investment projects at home using their financial resources and acquired entrepreneurial skills to boost development in their home countries. "In Chinese Taipei, for example, half of all the companies emerging from that economy's largest science park—Hsinchu—were started by returnees from the United States" (Cervantes et al, 2002). It is also estimated that returning students started most Internet-based ventures in China and India.

Similar practices could benefit African countries in the long run. Again, some governments have made baby steps in this area; Kenyans in diaspora recently met with top government officials, who invited them to invest at home. It remains to be seen whether African governments will reform their economies and government policies and practices to encourage and attract investment by potential returnees and other investors, and to realistically enable such investments to thrive. Will the church, too, look inward and create an environment that allows African graduates returning home from advanced studies to serve and make meaningful contributions in a safe environment?

With their exposure to, and experiences in systems that work, returning African professionals can help reform their societies' systems and make them work, too. These individuals can help put in place checks-and-balances systems that have helped the Western societies curb corruption and promote democracy despite the universally corrupt human nature. We could "make a brain train out of the brain drain," a train loaded with ideas and expertise that will transform Africa into an economic, cultural, and spiritual giant.

Such is already happening. Patrick Awuah quit his multimillion-dollar program manager job with Microsoft and returned to Ghana where he established a state-of-the art university. His aim, like Dr. Omari's, is to develop moral and ethical leadership among Ghanaian youths, which will hopefully steer the country towards progress. Students are required to take an oath of integrity and ethical conduct upon entering Ashesi University. Two Nigerian healthcare professionals recently returned to join the faculty at a thriving parochial University. They have reportedly revolutionized nursing practices not only at the university but also are impacting the whole country. "Their university now dictates what goes on in nursing in Nigeria," declares one subject jubilantly. Asked if the two did not meet any resistance from the establishment, he responds, "They did at first, but just ignored them."

Views of Patrick Awuah's Ashesi University in Ghana. Moral leadership and ethics are deliberately taught in order to forge a moral future for the country. Photos by Gabriel Nsiah 2015.

IMPLICATIONS

Many factors contribute to brain drain from Africa. Lack of adequate educational facilities, poverty, poor governance, rapid population growth, and wars are some of the "push factors," as Gordon refers to them. It will take a joint effort between the international community and African states and peoples to create circumstances that stimulate development and economic growth in order to reduce brain drain. As long as disparity between the rich and the poor countries continues to exist and grow larger, the brain drain will persist.

Rich nations need to reconsider their greed for more—the greed that has led to an increase in sweatshops around the world, shops that are located mainly in emerging economies and that supply the wealthy nations with cheap labor and finished products. As globalization is increasingly promoted, corporations from the wealthy nations need to look beyond wealth and profit making and put ethics first.

Evidently most Africans living in the United States would rather live in their home countries if it were not for the wretched conditions in those countries that affect their lives politically, educationally, and economically. Living in the United States is a last resort, a desperate escape from "an impossible situation" or from possible torture at the hands of an oppressive regime. In light of the issues raised by the study subjects as the main reasons influencing them to live and work in the United States as opposed to their respective African countries, the following recommendations are offered as a possible remedy to the socioeconomic factors that lead to the ongoing brain drain:

1. Expand and increase funding for higher education to meet the high demand.

2. Sponsor Africans studying abroad and bond them to serve in their home country for a mutually agreed-upon duration. Self-sponsored Africans students studying in America endure a great deal of financial hardship. When they complete their studies, they desire to work and make up for the years of "toiling." Sponsoring them would reduce the suffering and stress, while the bonding would ensure that the sponsoring government or church organization gets rewarded for its investment. The sponsored student would then be under legal and moral obligation to return and serve or to reimburse the sponsor.

3. Western governments that entice and recruit African professionals to work in their economies have a legal and moral obligation to refund those African countries the cost of training such professionals, as suggested by the *New York Times*.

4. To overcome ethnic-based conflicts and infighting, African institutions and governments may consider rotating the presidency regionally so that every province, county, or state has a fair chance of participating in their country's leadership. Minority groups will thus not feel permanently dominated and marginalized by others.

5. African governments need to take urgent reform measures to combat the corruption, nepotism, and the mismanagement of resources that have led to poverty and desperation-driven crime. Adapting new strategies for economic development is imperative to improving living conditions in African countries. Such strategies would include equitable distribution of development funds and

ensuring such funds are used for intended and approved purposes.

6. Leaders should understand that it is honorable to concede defeat in an election, much like Jonathan of Nigeria did in 2015 and not subject their citizens to unnecessarily manufactured crisis such as Kenya experienced in 2008 and subsequent elections.

Africa is the second largest continent after Asia. It is enormously rich in its diverse natural and human resources; yet poverty and underdevelopment still endure. All parties involved need to make deliberate efforts to reverse this trend. Such efforts would involve properly managing Africa's resources with skill, dedication, and integrity. Africans at home and abroad possess enough skill and ability to do this. Whether these professionals return home or remain abroad, they can still be a valuable economic and human resource to their countries. Given the right attitudes, policies, and international cooperation, says an unidentified Indian official, many countries "could see the 'brain drain' transformed into a 'brain bank.'"

EPILOGUE

A few years have passed since I began my study of Africans who live and work in the United States; and, as playwright Robert Bolt would say, "a lot of water has *flown* under the bridge."[11] Many of the subjects in the study are still "stuck here" as they were at the beginning of the study. A few of them have moved on, either professionally or socially.

Tammy had expressed a desire to open her own dental practice "so I can have others work for me as I have been working for them." She has done just that and is now able to take a vacation with pay, unlike in the past when she was employed by someone else. She acknowledges that this resulted in about "triple the amount of work I did before! But I don't mind it because I'm working for myself. Much of it is just paperwork—the charting that I have to do by myself. It is just that it's new to me; but once I get used to it, it will be OK." She smiles with satisfaction as she asserts, "I love it! I love it! It's quite different because now I can treat some patients I was not allowed to see before... I can now take time off anytime to go see my grandma."

Dr. Omari, too, has opened his own practice and is still a very busy man, though in a different way now. He bought a lovely house with a swimming pool, in a respectable neighborhood. Dr. Omari still manages to be involved in the political process and occasionally gives lectures on the virtues of moral leadership.

---

[11] Robert Bolt: author of "A Man for All Seasons."

Asked if he is still working on moral leadership initiatives, Dr. Omari responds excitedly, "Yes, I am! And many people are coming on board. Many people are interested. They have realized that we have educated people in power, we have educated people in leadership, but we still see no difference. It is still just the same corruption and underdevelopment that we had before. So, obviously it is the morality that is lacking in our leaders."

He states that he is now in the process of writing the curriculum for moral leadership and hopes to advance to the next step, which is to select young people with potential for leadership who will then be trained as the new generation of African leaders. "Right now, there is no method of evaluating the leaders; they are not accountable to the people. With the new curriculum, the people will have a tool for evaluating their leaders and the means to replace them if the leaders do not live up to the people's expectations," he argues.

Ken has had one of the most dramatic turns of events—akin to the legendary "series of unfortunate events,"[12] except that his story is nonfictional. Ken invested heavily in real estate near the peak of the housing boom early 2,000s that turned into a bubble. The bubble burst and he lost everything. "I had two houses—a four bedroom which we lived in and a five-bedroom nearby, which we rented out—and a twelve-plex in the suburbs," he states wistfully.

"I sold the twelve-plex and the five-bedroom house, and we broke even—barely paid the banks. But we lost our house. I just couldn't find a buyer; the market was bad." He had resigned from his psychiatric job and opened a gas service station, which also went under. "The economy hit everyone hard; I'm not the only one," Ken muses sadly. "We were changing oil for US$19.95, and people would just go buy oil and take it to a Mexican who would change it

---

[12] *Lemony Snicket's A Series of Unfortunate Events.*

for US$10," he states with a chuckle. "We were working and barely paying rent. I sold the business and paid the banks."

Ken then moved his family to the Midwest, where he and his wife separated. He still feels as strongly about *going home* as he did three years before, if not more so. "Man, I want to go home! I have been in this country for too long and I just want to go home. When I was coming here and the airplane took off and I looked at the lights of the city down below, I felt like a mother whose child has been plucked from her bosom, and I cried tears," he reflects somberly. "I have worked here; I have owned property; I have done business. I don't crave money anymore. Money doesn't mean anything! If I was in Kenya now, I would be going around and preaching in schools and churches like we did before. That's what matters." Asked if his business failures and family problems have contributed to this strong desire to return home, Ken quips, "Of course, of course!"

Ken does not have money to return home but does not want "to be a burden on society anymore," and so he does not want to ask his fellow Africans for help with airfare. "I will start walking to the east, and maybe someone will help me; or I'll keep walking," he says—almost delusional. A few friends have asked Ken to reconsider his decision to return home or at least to obtain a return ticket in case things do not work out in his favor; but he would have none of it.

"I don't want a return ticket!" Ken retorts angrily. "You haven't lost your job; you haven't lost your house; you haven't lost your family; you have not been homeless!" he continues, now choking with bitterness. "Those people who returned home and then returned here had high hopes. I do not have any hopes, any high hopes of making lots of money; I am just going home where I cannot be homeless. I never imagined I could be homeless! If the teaching job does not work out, I will be happy to build my small hut and live in it, sing from my hymnals, and read my Bible. I enjoy singing hymns in vernacular."

A few weeks later, Ken's friends donated enough money for his one-way ticket home; and he returned, passport or no passport—

his American dream having turned into an anticlimactic nightmare. Originally, Ken came to the United States via Canada because he could not obtain a Ugandan or Rwandan passport. Now he is in a mad rush to return *home*, where he had no sense of belonging. His situation is best summed up in the adage that the grass is always greener on the other pasture.

During the recent real estate boom, George bought a brand-new larger home, moved his family into it, and rented out the old one. He states that his tenant "is struggling; he's struggling to make the payments. They have missed a few months. I'll be forced to have him evicted," he states with his familiar, wide grin. He still commutes to his engineering job, almost 70 miles away.

Most of the other subjects are still doing the same things they were doing before. However, Pastor Foster has now joined the pastoral staff of a large church, where he serves as chief administrator. His daughter serves as chaplain of a nearby Christian college. Thus, he has realized his American dream of finding a pastoral career opportunity for his daughter, which was his main push factor from South Africa.

Dr. Nxumalo retired from his medical practice and sold the clinic he had worked so hard to establish. He now shuttles up and down San Francisco and Pretoria, living in his American home in the summer when the South African winter is too cold, while spending the remainder of the year in South Africa. This is a compromise: to live in both worlds, retire at home as he wanted to, and be able to visit with children and grandchildren. The doctor has bought a large piece of property near Pretoria, formerly owned by a white family, and spends most of his time gardening and ministering to his community, especially destitute children for whom he has taken responsibility.

Dr. Nxumalo recounts how his nephew's house was broken into and burglarized by thugs. He believes this was politically motivated robbery that targeted his nephew because he got in the way of a powerful and corrupt politician. His optimistic view of

South Africa has waned somewhat, and he states somberly, "If you're coming to visit me as you said, come quickly before things change."

"How come? What is changing?"

"Well, this is Africa and it is not ours. Anything can happen and things can change quickly." (This echoes Ken and his fateful prediction that war will break out anywhere, anytime.) Mandela, the lawyer, left power for Mbekki, the economist, who was replaced by Zuma, the populist who has been charged with corruption. Many observers are no longer comfortable with the way things are going politically, and with the uncertainty it signals for the future of South Africa. Dr. Nxumalo is now not an exception.

I must confess that, like Tammy and the others, I am still "in a limbo," still "stuck here"—*e kind akuru gi asumbi*[13], as the *Luo* saying goes. I took my family back to Kenya for a visit in December 2007. The joy of being among family and friends was overwhelming. The children were particularly happy to meet their cousins, uncles, and aunties, and most of all to visit with both Grandmas. Our daughter, then in sixth grade, was determined to stay with Grandma in Kogelo village and not return to the United States. But when we started to seriously consider the matter, she said we would have to physically relocate her elegant new school from the United States to the village so she could have the benefit of both worlds. She did not see herself surviving in the raggedy primary school that Daddy had attended, with little to no facilities. On the other hand, she loved the freedom of Grandma's big yard, her dogs, kittens, and chickens, and spending time with Grandma. "You mean I can go all the way over there, and I don't have to come back in thirty minutes!" she would ask in excited disbelief.

---

[13]Luo saying that means one is facing difficult choices, like between a rock and a hard place.

That effectively summarizes the dilemma of many Africans who work and live in the United States. While the United States offers quality educational, career, and other opportunities, Africans sacrifice much of their invaluable strong family, social, and cultural ties in order to benefit from these opportunities. (Ken and his wife would almost certainly still be together if they had stayed in Uganda, close to both his family and hers.)

The freedom of Grandma's large compound (above) versus the educational opportunities in a California elementary school (below). Photo by the author. July 2017

In Nairobi, we had to adjust quickly to the crowded nature of the city. Traffic jams made it difficult to get to places in good time. Going to the bank alone was an all-morning activity, much like Dr. Uche's trip to the post office. To go from one side of town to another and rent a car took a whole afternoon. Used cars imported from Japan and elsewhere have enabled more people to own cars but conversely flooded the streets of Nairobi and other cities with traffic, making driving in and out of the city dreadful. Road construction and maintenance has improved somewhat with 'by-pass' roads here and there, but not at a rate that can cope with the influx of vehicles.

The children were bewildered by *matatu*[14] and other drivers who defied all traffic rules and often drove on pavements and sidewalks in attempts to beat other traffic. At one point, we observed a *matatu* approach a group of pedestrians on what used to be the sidewalk, now illegally converted to a *matatu* raceway. The *matatu* driver honked loudly, and the pedestrians fled as it passed right on the now dusty sidewalk, covering the weary pedestrians in a hail of dust as the conductor, or *manamba*, hung on the door frame, his legs kicking excitedly in the air.

Matatu passengers are timidly resigned to their sorry state, caring only to get where they want to go as soon as they can, under the loud, dusty, and bumpy circumstances. The pedestrians, likewise, have passively surrendered all their rights, including the rights to safety on the former walkways. A *matatu* will drive through the bumps and potholes at the same speed it was going on the road. As a result, they have virtually no shock absorbers or struts, and a vehicle will jump up and down as it drives on and off road with no legal consequences. Traffic police are mostly overwhelmed or grossly outnumbered, or just purely bribed to inaction. The passengers sit silently with neither power nor will to complain. Unless some

---

[14]*Matatu* is a type of taxi that is used communally. It is the most common public means of transport in Kenya (probably now overtaken by the ubiquitous motor bike or *piki piki*.)

passengers and/or pedestrians step up and successfully sue *matatu* operators, the dangerously reckless trend is likely to continue. Yet the legal system is also paralyzed by delaying tactics. Court cases often take decades to resolve.

Above: Passengers hardly have any breathing room in an overloaded *matatu,* filled with traders and sacks of their merchandise. Stock photo.

Below: Nairobi National Park entrance. Photo by Marvin Opiyo, July 2017.

Some parts of Nairobi are quite clean and pleasant. The segment of Airport Road from Jomo Kenyatta International Airport to Mombasa Road is a particularly well-maintained part of Nairobi. Similarly, the area around the animal orphanage in Karen is kept very clean, with signs that are actually obeyed. One sign reads: "Warthogs and Children Have Right of Way" And motorists do obey the signs. Runda Estate—with its multimillion-shilling homes, modern shopping malls, and other social amenities—is strikingly beautiful. Yet less than a kilometer behind Runda, Githogoro slum thrives, a dangerous time-bomb.

One common factor is that these nice areas cater predominantly for foreign nationals living in Nairobi, like members of the diplomatic corps, or the numerous tourists who visit the country annually, bringing much needed boost to the economy. Yet other areas are incredibly dirty and run-down, with roads, streets, houses, and public facilities in wanton disrepair. Such neighborhoods, with old houses hardly painted or maintained and heaps of uncollected garbage, give an especially depressing feeling in some parts of Nairobi.

One such stinking illegal garbage dump had a big sign next to it that read "No Dumping." The dumping continued daily anyway, with no arrests or citations. Since garbage is not picked up, burning is the most common alternative; and the garbage pile is on fire almost every day. An acrid smell is produced from a mixture of everything: paper, plastic, paint, bones, and you name it, all going up in eternal Sodom and Gomorrah-like smoke. Yet the government faithfully collects taxes from Nairobi residents and other citizens; taxes that should pay for consistent garbage collection and adequate disposal in all parts of the city. Where does the money go?

Above: Determined to keep his furniture store premises clean at the end of the day, this Nairobi businessman sweeps, wraps trash in a large bag, then sets it on fire due to lack of trash collection services. Photo by the author (July 2017.) Posters of politicians seeking reelection are everywhere, with the same promises to improve services.

Below: Mechanics in Parklands burn trash to keep their premises clean. Incredible acrid smell! Photo by the author: July 2017.

Someone observed that one could find anything in Nairobi provided one had the money. The supermarkets have all sorts of goods and services, but they cater mostly to the rich or upper middle class. Yet most Nairobi residents are poor, in some cases desperately so, and struggle to survive daily. Income disparity between the rich and the poor is alarming, which explains the high crime rate mentioned by Tammy.

When someone was asked why he was relocating from Nairobi to Canada, leaving a lucrative job with a company car and driver, he responded, "I do not know anybody in Nairobi—friend, relative, or workmate—who has not been robbed or mugged." In his own case, the thieves sprayed some chemical that made the family sleep deeply, and then they warmed up the food in the kitchen and ate it before literally emptying the house. The family woke up in the morning, wondering for a long time if they were in a never-ending nightmare.

Kenyans and other African citizens, however, are increasingly demanding change and holding their elected leaders more accountable, especially enabled by social media. With these demands have come noticeable efforts to change. Increased attempts are being made to eradicate or at least reduce corruption, as can be seen in the photo below.

Kenyatta National Hospital in Nairobi has declared war on corruption. But does it mean corruption is condoned in other parts of the country? Photo by Victoria O.

Epilogue

Our visit to Kenya coincided with the infamous presidential and parliamentary elections of December 2007. The mood in the country was one of excitement and anticipation. It was just incredibly pleasing to see multiparty politics run so smoothly in the country, something one could not have dreamed of just a few years earlier. Throughout the city, all parties had life-size posters and banners promoting their candidates. After a few days in Nairobi, we rented a car to drive upcountry to Kogelo in South-Western Kenya and visit with my mother. On the way west, we encountered truckloads of various party supporters going to political rallies. All were excitedly but peacefully chanting party.

Then suddenly on election eve, everything changed. We were going to visit our friends who lived by the sugar factory near Awendo, about twelve miles away from home. As we approached the junction of the main road from Kisii to Migori, we noticed a large crowd gathered around a bonfire in the middle of the road. They immediately menacingly surrounded our car. Sensing danger, I flashed their party's thumbs up signal, while another car approached from the Kisii direction, honking relentlessly at the crowd on the road. The angered crowd left our car and surrounded the car with the 'offending' driver. We drove on to our friends' home and didn't drive back home until late in the night when we got word that the crowds had dispersed.

Later we learned that the largely unemployed mob were suspicious of plans to rig the elections in favor of the incumbent. The people had formed their own vigilante militia, who searched all vehicles for anyone who might cause disturbances and intimidations in opposition strongholds, thus resulting in low voter turnouts. One had to provide identification and/or speak the local language to prove one's innocence. That was a close call for us because we had left our IDs and passports in Nairobi, and my children spoke very little of the language. Later we learned that two people had been badly beaten at that same junction based on suspicion that they were part of the presidential plot to rig elections. They were rescued by police, but one later died of the injuries sustained from the beatings.

Election Day had been tense, but relatively peaceful. I drove to the nearby polling station and found men and women of all ages who had come to vote. Elderly women in their 80s had walked for miles to exercise their voting rights. 89-year-old World War II veteran, Jotham Ombuor (now deceased), had walked nearly two miles to vote. No major incidents occurred, and reports from around the country indicated that voting was conducted smoothly. However, several days later, an agent of the opposition ODM party testified that an aide with whom he had been riding was shot and killed while sitting right next to him.

Trouble began the following day when election results started to come in and were broadcast live on both radio and television. It appeared to many observers that the opposition leader had a convincing lead over the sitting president. Things took a dramatic turn vote counting was apparently compromised the president was suddenly now leading. Disillusioned voters, especially in opposition stronghold areas, went berserk—looting and burning shops, stoning vehicles, and setting up illegal roadblocks. At one point, the bridge over Kuja River was blocked by protesters who twisted the guardrail from one side of the road to the other and then welded it tightly thereon. At another point at Rongo Market, huge underground petroleum tanks were used to block the Kisii-Migori road. Other roadblocks were made of rocks and tree logs, and most had bonfires in the middle of the highways.

My second close call took place while driving to the trading center, about three miles from home, with my nephew to charge the car battery we were using to recharge cell phones, radios, and other appliances. (More than 40 years after independence, Kogelo and surrounding villages still had no electricity or running water.) We found a telephone pole lying across the road, got out and removed it, and then drove on. As we approached the market center, we noticed a raging bonfire in the middle of the road ahead.

Voters queue to cast their votes in the fateful 2007 Kenyan presidential and parliamentary elections. Perceived rigging of votes triggered unprecedented violence across the country. Photo by the author.

A *Good Samaritan,* waved us to a stop and said gently but firmly, "My friend, turn around and go back! Those people are going to smash your car for no reason." I thanked him and turned back. "Those people" were chanting war cries. My nephew insisted on walking to get the battery, so I hid the car in the thicket by the roadside and waited. A little while later, he came back with some sugar and milk but no battery; it needed to be charged overnight. On our way back, we found the log lying across the road as before. We made room enough for us to pass and left. Later I was told that we would have been in serious trouble if the people who had set the log across the road had seen us removing it.

When the time came for us to return to the United States, there was no way to drive back to Nairobi. Both my wife and I needed to resume work after Christmas break, and the children to return to school; but there we were, stranded deep in the countryside, about 350 kilometers from Nairobi and the airport. The roadblocks were now more widespread, making it impossible to drive even to the nearby church.

One time I got out of the car and spoke with every one of the protesters who had installed a roadblock near the church. I told them that I sympathized with their political cause of demanding fair election results, but that in blocking the road, they were just punishing themselves and their own people—including their mothers and wives who were unable to go sell or buy any food from the markets.

They smiled and let me pass, claiming that they had only blocked the road after a prominent government minister had passed there the previous night. I told them that the minister had the right to go anywhere he wanted to go, even if we disagreed with his political views. Some of them wanted money for "keeping the peace" but I ignored them.

I began to realize that the post-election violence was more of a class war rather than a political one. How come the roadblocks were only for motorists, even ones who spoke the same language, or shared the same political sentiments as those blocking the road? Why did they ask motorists for money but not pedestrians? It was *them* and *us*, and if you had enough to own a vehicle, you were one of *them*. The wide gap between the rich and the poor in Kenya is a dangerous time bomb that can be set off by any shaky social or political issue, like a perceived stolen election. It is a pressure cooker, and the stolen election just blew off the precarious lid.

After several days of being blockaded in the village, our supplies dwindled. First, we ran out of cooking gas. Then we could not go shop for food, soap, gasoline, and the like. The rental car was overdue for return to the company, but there was still no way to drive back to Nairobi. Our neighbor's son and his wife's 200 kilometers drive home from Kisumu took three days. They paid several thousand shillings in tips to the militias and at times had to be escorted by police.

Epilogue

Finally reports came that the General Service Unit (GSU) had cleared the roadblocks and people could travel to Nairobi. But revenge killings of members of the tribes where the opposition party had been strong were also reported, and the road to Nairobi was still treacherous. In addition, several days of road blockades had depleted petrol supply. In Oyugis town—about 100 kilometers away—we found exorbitantly priced petrol. We returned to Nairobi where tensions were running high between different ethnic groups because of stolen elections and the looting and killings that had ensued. Protesters tried to demonstrate against the government, which in turn cracked down harshly on them. With more reports of killings, revenge killings followed. The situation was chaotic and tense. More than 1,000 people reportedly lost their lives, and thousands more were displaced.

I looked at young Kikuyu children walking along the road with their mother in Kiambu. They worked tirelessly, picking up bottles and cans to recycle. They looked innocent to me, just following their mother and doing whatever they could to survive. They were children, like my own, and it did not matter that Kibaki, a Kikuyu, was in power. Their need for survival was the same as that of the children I had seen working in the fields in Kogelo or selling bananas and oranges in Awendo and Kisii. Kenyan children—whether they be Kikuyu, Luo, Luhya, or other—have the same needs for food, clothing, shelter, and quality educational and employment opportunities. That's what we demand from our leaders, of whatever tribe or ethnicity, to provide.

We finally rescheduled our missed flight to the United States. Before this, whenever we called home, someone would inevitably ask, "When are you coming back?" Now, even family members who had been urging us to return home to Kenya were anxious to see us return to the United States, lest we be caught up in more deadly violence that they feared would follow the planned protests. "When are you coming back" was replaced by "When are you going back?"

Back in the United States, our close Kikuyu friends would not call us or take our calls. Only much later when I went looking for them and found them in their church did I realize that they cut off ties with us because they believed we had gone home to Kenya as part of a larger Luo scheme to grab power from Kikuyus. They had listened to all sorts of political propaganda and read fake news on social media that said in part that Luos had returned home in anticipation of a Raila Odinga victory and had been promised rent-free housing. We supposedly had gone home to participate in this. "It is all over the Internet!" said my friend, fuming with rage. I was astounded and heartbroken that evil propaganda could thus poison decades of friendship and a shared Christian faith.

If the situation in Kenya was bad, the one in Zimbabwe is even worse. Rosa and her family may be indefinitely "stuck here." For years, Mugabe 'won' one presidential election after another. Reports abounded of his soldiers, police, and party militia intimidating, torturing, and killing opposition leaders and their supporters. He has since been overthrown by his own generals and subsequently died while seeking treatment abroad. But his successors have not done any better in terms of rigging elections and running down the already devastated economy.

This is the norm in many African countries: hold an election every four or five years, present fake or controversial election results, and brutalize, jail, or kill citizens who protest these results. Why then do African leaders call for elections, which are costly, time-wasting, and deadly, if the results have been predetermined?

Following is an excerpt of a report by a Kenyan journalist, Charles Nyende, who covered a soccer World Cup qualifying match between Kenya and Zimbabwe in an article he ironically entitled, "The pain of being a billionaire for a week."[15] "The moment you enter Harare International Airport, you sense something is just not

---

[15]*The Daily Nation*, Nairobi July 1, 2008

right. The airport is small and modern, glass and carpet. But it is eerily empty with little activity in the duty-free shops, the corridors and the lounges... You feel some sort of sadness or fear, or both... The army, the police and ruling party militias were on the rampage against opposition supporters, with nearly a hundred having been killed and tens of thousands wounded," Nyende (2008) recollects sadly.

Ethnic strife is rampant in Zimbabwe, much like it is in Nigeria, Kenya, and other African countries. In Kenya now it is showing its ugly head in the Adventist Church, threatening the century-old unity among the members. In Zimbabwe, the minority Ndebele feel oppressed by the majority Shona—just like the Delta People of Nigeria feel oppressed by the northerners, whom they blame for benefitting from the oil revenues although oil is produced at the delta.

A UK-based Ndebele man lamented how *Matabeleland* in Zimbabwe produces lots of resources yet lags in infrastructure and economic development because all the revenue is remitted by the central government to the capital Harare and benefits their rival *Mashonaland* instead.

If these ethnic tensions, political oppression and violence, and economic disparities continue, the brain drain from Africa to the more stable Western countries will persist. It is up to us as Africans, both at home and in the diaspora, to make the necessary effort and sacrifices to bring about meaningful and positive change and reverse the shameful trends that have plagued the beloved continent.

The five-week experience my family and I had in Kenya summarizes the subjects' major experiences and reasons for leaving their different African countries to remain in the United Sates—namely, political instability, violence, and lack of educational and career opportunities.

These conditions can be changed in Africa if the people at home and in diaspora, their leaders, and civil servants decide that they want to put self-interest aside and build the continent to its full potential. And that potential is infinite.

DEFINITION OF TERMS

The following terms are defined to reflect their usage herein:

Receiving country—a country outside Africa where an African immigrant lives and/or works.

Returnees—African professionals who have returned home from studying or working abroad.

Sending country—country from which an immigrant originates.

H1B visa—a type of visa issued by the US Immigration and Naturalization Services (Now under the Department of Homeland Security) that enables non- American born workers to stay and work legally in the US.

Brain drain—a term now widely used to refer to loss of skilled manpower by developing nations to developed ones.

Migrants—individuals who relocate from one country to another in search of work, education, or safety.

Conference—an administrative hierarchy in the Seventh-day Adventist Church that is made up of several "districts," which are in turn made up of several churches.

Union—an administrative hierarchy in the Seventh-day Adventist Church that is made up of several conferences.

Green card—the permanent residency visa that allows a foreign born person to legally reside and work in the US.

Definition of Terms

Tape inaudible = A word or part of a phrase missed. Subject spoke softly or noise interfered, and the recorded words could not be heard clearly enough for transcription.

ACKNOWLEDGEMENTS

I am grateful to Dr. Audrey Howard for her tireless efforts in providing outstanding structural support and making sound suggestions for improvement, while constantly encouraging me to have it published. Thanks to Dr. Clyde Cassimy for critically reading through the document and insisting it must be "published now!" I appreciate the subjects for sharing their incredible stories and experiences. Finally, I thank my wife and children for bearing with me during the challenging writing process.

I gave much thought to the title of the book and changed it several times before settling for "Stuck Here," because it is the most accurate reflection of how most of the subjects feel. It really is a direct quotation of at least three of the subjects who initially came to the US for something like further education, but then found themselves *stuck here* in an inexorable labyrinth of social, economic, and political issues.

All subjects' names and geographical locations are fictitious by mutual agreement, except for Dr. Omari, Dr. Omobokun, Mr. Mbajah, and Mr. Mabuti, who opted to use their real names.

BIBLIOGRAPHY

Achebe, C. (1975). *No longer at ease*. Heinemann Educational Books, Nairobi.

Aka, P. C. (2001). Education, economic development, and return to democratic politics in Nigeria. [Electronic Version] *Journal Third World Studies* 18, (1) 21-38.

Anonymous (1998). White South Africa on the wing. [Electronic Version] *The Economist*, 347, (8071) 43-4.

Armah, A. K. (1992). *The beautiful ones are not yet born*. Heinemann, Nairobi.

Brandi, M. C. (2001). Skilled immigrants in Rome. *International Migration* 39, (4) 101 – 131.

Brown, E. & Kirkpatrick, D. (2002). The reverse brain drain. [Electronic Version] *Fortune* 146, (9) 39-40.

Carrington, W. & Detragiache, E. (1999). How extensive is the brain drain? [Electronic Version] *Finance and Development*, 36, (2) 46-49.

Cervantes, M. and Guellec, D. (2002). The brain drain: old myths, new realities. [Electronic Version] *The OECD Observer* 40-42.

Creswell, J. (1998). *Qualitative inquiry and research design: Choosing among five traditions*. Thousand Oaks: Sage.

Christian Century (1997). [Electronic Version] *The African missionaries to U. S.* 718-720. New York Author.

Crush, J. (2002). The global raiders: nationalism, globalization, and the South African brain drain. *Journal of International Affairs* 56, (1) 147- 167.

Bibliography

Docquier, F. & Rapoport, H. (2012). Globalization, Brain Drain, and Development. *Journal of Economic Literature,* 5o (3) 681-730.

Dugger, C. W. (2004). An Exodus of African nurses puts infants and the ill in peril. *The New York Times,* [Premium Archive.]

Dunkin, S. (2002). Young space scientists - does the UK offer a future? [Electronic Version] *New Statesman* 131, (XXI ISSN) 364-7431.

Editorial Desk (2004). Africa's health-care brain drain. [Electronic Version] *The New York Times.*

Egbejuele, E. (2019). Nigeria must tackle its doctor brain drain. *The African Report.* www.theafricanreport.com/12252/nigeria-must-tackle-its-doctor-braindrain/ (Accessed June 10, 2019.)

Ejobowah, J. B. (2000). Who owns the oil? The politics of ethnicity in the Niger delta of Nigeria. [Electronic Version] *Africa Today,* 47, (1) 28 - 47.

Gordon, A. (1998). The new Diaspora-African immigration to the United States. [Electronic Version] *Journal of Third World Studies* 15, (1) 79-103.

Hale, B. (2003). The turning tales of Africa's brain drain. *BBC News Online business report.*

[http://news.bbc.co.uk/1/hi/business/2844277.stm] Last visited 5/22/05 2: 59 PM.

Iravani, M. (2011). Brain Drain Problem: A Review. *International Journal of Business and Social Science* 2, (15) 284-289.

Johnson, N. (2008). Analysis and Assessment of the "Brain Drain" Phenomenon and its Effects on Caribbean Countries. *Florida Atlantic Comparative Studies Journal,* 11, (2008-2009.)

Kerr, R. (2001). The brain drain: Why New Zealanders are voting with their feet. [Electronic Version] *Science,* 10326634, (17) 2.

Khadria, B. (2001). Shifting paradigms of globalization: The twenty-first century transition towards generics in skilled migration from India. *International Migration,* 39, (5) 45 – 90.

Kigotho, W. (1997). The lost tribe of East African dons. [Electronic Version] *The Times Higher Education Supplement* 13, (01) 13.

Kigotho, W. (2003). Zimbabwe shuts its doors as lecturers strike for pay raise. [Electronic Version] *The Times Higher Education Supplement,* 1580, 11.

Kigotho, W. (April 2003). Swedish pull aid to Africans after corruption allegations. [Electronic Version] *The Times Higher Education Supplement* 1584, 11.

Kingma, M. (2001). Nursing Migration: global treasure hunt or disaster-in-the-making? *Nursing Inquiry*, 8, (4) 205 – 212.

Kondro, W. (2002). New research chairs mean brain gain for universities. [Electronic Version] *Science*, 00368075, (298) 1 – 2.

LaFraniere, S. (2004). Zimbabwe's court clears opposition leader of treason. [Electronic Version] *The New York Times.*

Lawler, A. (2003). Iraq's shattered universities. [Electronic Version] *Science*, 00368075, (300) 1-3.

Leiman, L. (2004). Should the brain drain be plugged? *Texas International Law Journal*, 39, (675) 675 – 695.

Mahroum, S. (2001). Europe and the immigration of highly skilled labour. *International Migration*, 39, (5) 28 – 43.

Nevin, T. (2003). SA Attempts to halt medical brain-drain. [Electronic Version] *African Business,* 287 34-5.

Nica, E. (2013). The Causal Impact of Brain Drain Migration on Economic Development. Contemporary Readings in Law and Social Justice, January 1, 2013.

Nyikuli, P. K. (1999). Unlocking Africa's potential: Some factors affecting economic development and investment in Sub-Saharan Africa. [Electronic Version] *Law and Policy in International Business* 4, 623-36.

Odunsi, B. A. (1996). An analysis of brain-drain and its impact on manpower development in Nigeria. [Electronic Version] *Journal of Third World Studies* 13, 193-214.

Ogbu, J. (1998). Voluntary and involuntary minorities: a cultural-ecological theory of school performance with some implications for education. [Electronic Version] *Anthropology & Education Quarterly*, 29, (2) 155-188.

Ojo, O., Ugochukwu & Obina (2011). Understanding the escalation of brain drain in Nigeria from poor leadership point of view. *Mediterranean Journal of Social Sciences* 2, (3) 434-453.

Ortega, F & Perri, G. (2013). The effects of income and immigration policies on international migration. *Migration Studies*, 1, (1) 47-74.

Ouaked, S. (2002) Transatlantic roundtable on high-skilled migration and sending countries issues. *International Migration*, 40, (4) 154 – 166.

Patel, D. (2002). The round-trip brain drain. [Electronic Version] *HR Magazine* 47, (7) 1047-3149.

Pillay, A. L. & Kramers, A. L. (2003). South African clinical psychology, employment (in)equity and the "brain drain." *South African Journal of Psychology*, 33, (1) 52–60.

Poggioli, Sylvia: Eritrean Priest's Mission Takes on New Urgency Amid Migrant Crisis: NPR: http://www.npr.org/2015/11/25/457415567/eritrean-priests-mission-takes-on-new-urgency-amid-migrant-crisis . Accessed November 28, 2015.

Ragin, C. C. (1987). *The Comparative Method: Moving beyond qualitative and quantitative strategies.* Berkeley: University of California Press.

Raji, A., Akowe, J. et al (2018). The effects of brain drain on the economic development of developing countries: evidence from selected African countries. *Journal of health and social issues*, 7 (2) 66-77.

Schifrin, N. (2016). In Nigeria, A Culture of Bribery Turns Deadly: NPR:

http://www.npr.org/2016/01/03/461818452/in-nigeria-a-culture-of-bribery-turns-deadly. Accessed January 4, 2016.

South African Union of the Seventh-day Adventist Church (1998). Statement of confession to the Truth and Reconciliation Commission. July 22, 2004, from http://web.uct.ac.za/depts/ricsa/commiss/trc/sad.htm

Sheppard, R. (2001). The magnetic north. [Electronic Version] *Maclean*, 114, (27) 50-56.

Srivastava, B. (2018). Economic Impact of Brain Drain on Developed and Developing Countries. *William Paterson University*, 1-11.

Stake, R. (1995). *The Art of Case Study Research.* Thousand Oaks, CA: Sage.

Stone, R. (2003). Fears grow of nuclear brain drain to Iran. [Electronic Version] *Science*, 00368075, (299) 5612.

Tascu, M., Noftsinger, J., et al. (2002). The problem of post-communist education: The Romanian example. [Electronic Version] *The Journal of Social, Political, and Economic Studies* 27, (2) 203-26.

Tullio, R. (1998). South Africa: A continent's star. [Electronic Version] *Transportation and Distribution* 39, (8) 117-21.

Ushkalov, I. G. & Malakha, I. A. (2000). The "brain drain" as a global phenomenon and its characteristics in Russia. [Electronic Version] *Russian Education and Society* 42, (12) 18-34.

Vietti, F. (2013). Understanding International Migration from a Human Security Perspective. *Journal of Migration and Human Security*, 1 (1) 17-31.

Warner, Gregory: Pope Prepares to Visit Africa Amid Burundi Crisis: NPR http://www.npr.org/2015/11/24/457277909/pope-prepares-to-visit-africa-amid-burundi-crisis Accessed December 23, 2015.

Werlin, H. (2000). Politics versus economics: A comparison of Ghana and South Korea. [Electronic Version] *The Journal of Social, Political, and Economic Studies*, 25, (4) 439 - 464.

Bibliography

Wines, M. & LaFraniere, S. (2004). Hut by Hut, AIDS Steals Life in a Southern Africa Town. [Electronic Version] *The New York Times*, (11) 28, pp. 1-4.

World Bank Study (2003) [Electronic Version] p. 337. New York: Author.

ABOUT THE AUTHOR

Photo by Rehema Ochieng

Marvin Opiyo is an educator with vast experience in teaching and lecturing in California, Kenya, and Canada. He was born in Kogelo Location in what was then South Nyanza, Kenya, and attended Maseno National School, then graduated with a Bachelor's degree in Education from Kenyatta University, Nairobi. Later he earned Master's and Doctorate degrees in Education from La Sierra University, Riverside.

Dr. Opiyo is co-founder and the inaugural chairman of the Kenyan American Association of Inland Empire (KAA). His passion for the education and welfare of immigrants inspired him to research the lives of Africans in America, which culminated in the writing of this book.

Currently Dr. Opiyo teaches high school in Menifee, and lives in Riverside, California, with his wife Lillian and three college-age children; Nicholas, Geno, and Rehema.